# SIGNAL 2023

The Eighth International Conference on Advances in Signal, Image and Video Processing

March 13th - 17th, 2023

Barcelona, Spain

**SIGNAL 2023 Editors**

Constantin Paleologu, Polytechnic University of Bucharest, Romania

Pavel Loskot, ZJU-UIUC Institute, China

**Printed from e-media with permission by:**

Curran Associates, Inc.
57 Morehouse Lane
Red Hook, NY 12571

**Some format issues inherent in the e-media version may also appear in this print version.**



International Academy, Research, and Industry Association (IARIA)
412 Derby Way
Wilmington, DE 19810

Phone: (408) 893-6407
Fax: (408) 527-6351

petre@iaria.org

**Additional copies of this publication are available from:**

Curran Associates, Inc.
57 Morehouse Lane
Red Hook, NY 12571 USA
Phone: 845-758-0400
Fax: 845-758-2633
Email: curran@proceedings.com
Web: www.proceedings.com

## Table of Contents


Informational Analysis of MODIS Satellite Evapotranspiration Data of Vegetation Cover: a Method to Reveal the Presence of Plant Diseases 1
*Luciano Telesca, Rosa Lasaponara, Farid Faridani, Nicodemo Abate, and Michele Lovallo*

Stress Detection Based on Wearable Physiological Sensors Laboratory and Real Life Pilot Scenario Application 7
*Vasileios-Rafail Xefteris, Athina Tsanousa, Spyridon Symeonidis, Sotiris Diplaris, Francesco Zaffanela, Martina Monego, Maria Pacelli, Stefanos Vrochidis, and Ioannis Kompatsiaris*

Fruiting Mother-Shoot Counting System Based On Segmented Images 13
*RuoQi Zhao, Megumi Wakao, Naoki Morita, and Kenta Morita*

Requirements for Piano Lesson Support System 18
*Naoki Morita, Chiharu Nakanishi, Chiaki Sawada, Kenta Morita, and Kazue Kawai*

Development of a Score Click Playback System 21
*Motoya Wakiyama, Megumi Wakao, Naoki Morita, Kenta Morita, Chiharu Nakanishi, Chiaki Sawada, and Kazue Kawai*

Compression via Partial Pseudo-Randomization of Convolutional Neural Networks Under High Memory Constraints 24
*Florent Crozet, Stephane Mancini, and Marina Nicolas*

Improvement of SSVEP Detection Accuracy via Additive Averaging of Binaural Peripheral Electrodes 31
*Taichi Haba, Gaochao Cui, Fumiya Kinoshita, and Hideaki Touyama*

RCT-Net: TDNN based Speaker Verification with 2D Res2Nets on Frame Level Feature Extractor 37
*Razieh Khamsehashari, Fengying Miao, Tim Polzehl, and Sebastian Moller*

Supervised Spatial Divide-and-Conquer Applied to Fish Counting 43
*Gianna Arencibia-Castellanos, Alejandro Gonzalez-Fernandez, Maria Castillo-Moral, Ruben Fraile, Juana M. Gutierrez-Arriola, and Fernando Pescador*

In-video Searching for Melody in Piano Lesson Videos 48
*Tatsuya Oshiro, Megumi Wakao, Naoki Morita, Kazue Kawai, Chiharu Nakanishi, Chiaki Sawada, and Kenta Morita*

SL(2,R) Multi-scale Contour Registration Based on Riemannian Calculation 51
*Khaoula Sakrani, Sinda Elghoul, and Faouzi Ghorbe*

Comparison of Different Speech Features for Connected Number Recognition of Indian Vernacular Languages 56
*Mayurakshi Mukherji, Shreyas Kulkarni, Vivek Kumar, Senthil Raja G, Thiruvengadam Samon, Kingshuk Banerjee, and Yuichi Nonaka*

On Machine Integers and Arithmetic 63
*Pavel Loskot*

A Refined ERR-based Method for Nonlinear System Identification. Application to Epilepsy. 67
*Marc Greige, Ahmad Karfoul, Isabelle Merlet, and Regine Le Bouquin Jeannes*

Divergence-Based Regularization for End-to-End Sensing Matrix Optimization in Compressive Sampling Systems 72
*Roman Jacome, Henry Arguello, Alejandra Hernandez-Rojas, and Paul Goyes*

# SIGNAL 2023

# Foreword

The Eighteenth International Conference on Advances in Signal, Image and Video Processing (SIGNAL 2023), held between March 13 – 17, 2023, continued the inaugural event considering the challenges mentioned above. Having these motivations in mind, the goal of this conference was to bring together researchers and industry and form a forum for fruitful discussions, networking, and ideas.

Signal, video and image processing constitutes the basis of communications systems. With the proliferation of portable/implantable devices, embedded signal processing became widely used, despite that most of the common users are not aware of this issue. New signal, image and video processing algorithms and methods, in the context of a growing-wide range of domains (communications, medicine, finance, education, etc.) have been proposed, developed and deployed. Moreover, since the implementation platforms experience an exponential growth in terms of their performance, many signal processing techniques are reconsidered and adapted in the framework of new applications. Having these motivations in mind, the goal of this conference was to bring together researchers and industry and form a forum for fruitful discussions, networking, and ideas.

We take here the opportunity to warmly thank all the members of the SIGNAL 2023 Technical Program Committee, as well as the numerous reviewers. The creation of such a high quality conference program would not have been possible without their involvement. We also kindly thank all the authors who dedicated much of their time and efforts to contribute to SIGNAL 2023. We truly believe that, thanks to all these efforts, the final conference program consisted of top quality contributions.

Also, this event could not have been a reality without the support of many individuals, organizations, and sponsors. We are grateful to the members of the SIGNAL 2023 organizing committee for their help in handling the logistics and for their work to make this professional meeting a success.

We hope that SIGNAL 2023 was a successful international forum for the exchange of ideas and results between academia and industry and for the promotion of progress in the field of signal processing.

We are convinced that the participants found the event useful and communications very open. We also hope that Barcelona provided a pleasant environment during the conference and everyone saved some time for exploring this beautiful city

**SIGNAL 2023 Chairs:**

**SIGNAL 2023 Steering Committee**

Wilfried Uhring, Université de Strasbourg, France
Jérôme Gilles, San Diego State University, USA
Constantin Paleologu, Polytechnic University of Bucharest, Romania
Sergey Y. Yurish, Excelera, S. L. | IFSA, Spain
Pavel Loskot, ZJU-UIUC Institute, China

**SIGNAL 2023 Publicity Chairs**

Sandra Viciano Tudela, Universitat Politecnica de Valencia, Spain
José Miguel Jiménez, Universitat Politecnica de Valencia, Spain

# SIGNAL 2023

## Committee

**SIGNAL 2023 Steering Committee**
Wilfried Uhring, Université de Strasbourg, France
Jérôme Gilles, San Diego State University, USA
Constantin Paleologu, Polytechnic University of Bucharest, Romania
Sergey Y. Yurish, Excelera, S. L. | IFSA, Spain
Pavel Loskot, ZJU-UIUC Institute, China

**SIGNAL 2023 Publicity Chairs**
Sandra Viciano Tudela, Universitat Politecnica de Valencia, Spain
José Miguel Jiménez, Universitat Politecnica de Valencia, Spain

**SIGNAL 2023 Technical Program Committee**

Waleed H. Abdulla, The University of Auckland, New Zealand
Ahmed Al Hilli, Technical College of Najaf | Al-furat Al-Awsat Technical University, Iraq
Kiril Alexiev, Institute for Information and Communication Technologies -Bulgarian Academy of Sciences, Bulgaria
Djamila Aouada, SnT | University of Luxembourg, Luxembourg
Nadia Baaziz, Université du Québec en Outaouais, Canada
Junaid Baber, University of Balochistan, Pakistan
Vesh Raj Sharma Banjade, Intel Coporation, USA
Joan Bas, CTTC, Spain
Wassim Ben Chikha, Tunisia Polytechnic School, Tunisia
Amel Benazza-Benyahia, SUP'COM | COSIM lab. | University of Carthage, Tunisia
Anirban Bhowmick, Vellore Institute of Technology | Bhopal University, India
Larbi Boubchir, LIASD - University of Paris 8, France
Moez Bouchouicha, LIS - Laboratoire d'Informatique et Systèmes | Toulon University, France
Salah Bourennane, Ecole Centrale de Marseille, France
Geraldo Braz, Federal University of Maranhão, Brazil
Paula María Castro Castro, University of A Coruña, Spain
Aniruddha Chandra, National Institute of Technology (NIT), Durgapur, India
M. Girish Chandra, TCS Research & Innovation, India
Zhuyun Chen, South China University of Technology,Guangzhou, China
Doru Florin Chiper, Technical University Gheorghe Asachi of Iasi, Romania
João Dallyson Sousa de Almeida, Federal University of Maranhão, São Luís, Brazil
Natasja M. S. de Groot, Erasmus Medical Center | Technical University Delft, Netherlands
Laura-Maria Dogariu, University Politehnica of Bucharest, Romania
António Dourado, University of Coimbra, Portugal
Konstantinos Drossos, Tampere University, Finland
Hannes Fassold, JOANNEUM RESEARCH – DIGITAL, Graz, Austria
Laurent Fesquet, TIMA / Grenoble Institute of Technology, France
Sid Ahmed Fezza, National Institute of Telecommunications and ICT, Oran, Algeria

Óscar Fresnedo Arias, University of A Coruña, Spain
Faouzi Ghorbel, National School of Computer Science in Tunis | CRISTAL Laboratory, Tunisia
Mohammed Amine Ghrissi, Ministry of transport Algerian Civil Aviation authorities, Algeria
Gopika Gopan K, International Institute of Information Technology, Bangalore, India
Malka N. Halgamuge, University of Melbourne, Australia
Paul Irofti, University of Bucharest, Romania
Nobutaka Ito, Khon Kaen University, Thailand
Yuji Iwahori, Chubu University, Japan
Suresh K., Govt. Engineering College, Wayanad, India
Ahmad Karfoul, Université de Rennes 1, France
Ali Kariminezhad, Ruhr-Universität Bochum, Germany
Sokratis K. Katsikas, Center for Cyber & Information Security | Norwegian University of Science & Technology (NTNU), Norway
Csaba Kertész, University of Tampere / Neuroeventlabs Oy, Finland
Ted Kok, Canaan Semiconductor Ltd., Hong Kong
Chih-Lung Lin, Hwa-Hsia University of Technology, Taiwan
Pavel Loskot, ZJU-UIUC Institute, China
Lisandro Lovisolo, State University of Rio de Janeiro (UERJ), Brazil
Francois Malgouyres, Institut de Mathématiques de Toulouse | Université Paul Sabatier - ANITI, France
Depu Meng, University of Michigan, Ann Arbor, USA
Sudipta Mukhopadhyay, Indian Institute of Technology, Kharagpur, India
Abdelkrim Nemra, Ecole Militaire Polytechnique, Algiers, Algeria
Wesley Nunes Gonçalves, Federal University of Mato Grosso do Sul, Brazil
Constantin Paleologu, University Politehnica of Bucharest, Romania
Rodrigo Pereira Ramos, Federal University of São Francisco Valley (UNIVASF), Brazil
Jean-Christophe Pesquet, CentraleSupelec - Inria - University Paris-Saclay, France
Zsolt Alfred Polgar, Technical University of Cluj Napoca, Romania
Diogo Pratas, University of Aveiro, Portugal
J. K. Rai, Amity University Uttar Pradesh, Noida, India
Grzegorz Redlarski, Gdansk University of Technology, Poland
Aurobinda Routray, Indian Institute of Technology, Kharagpur, India
Diego P. Ruiz, University of Granada, Spain
Antonio-José Sánchez-Salmerón, Universitat Politècnica de València, Spain
Luiz Satoru Ochi, Instituto de Computação - UFF, Rio de Janeiro, Brazil
Lotfi Senhadji, Université de Rennes 1, France
Akbar Sheikh-Akbari, Leeds Beckett University, UK
Carlas Smith, TU Delft, Netherlands
Silvia F. Storti, University of Verona, Italy
Abdulhamit Subasi, Effat University - College of Engineering, Jeddah, Saudi Arabia
Simron Thapa, Louisiana State University, USA
Laszlo Toth, University of Szeged, Hungary
Carlos M. Travieso-González, University of Las Palmas de Gran Canaria, Spain
Rajesh Kumar Tripathy, BITS Pilani, Hyderabad, India
Filippo Vella, National Research Council of Italy, Italy
Tengfei Wang, The Hong Kong University of Science and Technology (HKUST), Hong Kong
Yi-Chiao Wu, Nagoya University, Japan
Nelson Yalta, Hitachi R&D, Japan
Ching-Nung Yang, National Dong Hwa University, Taiwan

Nicolas H. Younan, Mississippi State University, USA
Rafal Zdunek, Wroclaw University of Science and Technology, Poland
Shuanghui Zhang, National University of Defense Technology, Changsha, China
Siwei Zhang, German Aerospace Center (DLR), Germany
Guanlong Zhao, Google, USA

**Copyright Information**

# Informational Analysis of MODIS Satellite Evapotranspiration Data of Vegetation Cover: a Method to Reveal the Presence of Plant Diseases

Luciano Telesca, Rosa Lasaponara
Institute of Methodologies for Environmental Analysis, National Research Council
C.da S.Loja, 85050 Tito (PZ), Italy
email:luciano.telesca@imaa.cnr.it; email:rosa.lasaponara@imaa.cnr.it

Farid Faridani
Department of European and Mediterranean Cultures, Environment, and Cultural Heritage, University of Basilicata
85100 Potenza, Italy, email:farid.faridani@unibas.it

Nicodemo Abate
Institute of Heritage Science, National Research Council, C.da S. Loja, 85050 Tito Scalo, Italy
email:abate.nicodemo@gmail.com

Michele Lovallo
ARPAB, 85100 Potenza, Italy, email:michele.lovallo@arpab.it

*Abstract*—**The main goal of this paper is the evaluation of the potential of Fisher-Shannon statistical method applied to MODIS evapotranspiration satellite time series to explore the inner time dynamics of vegetation cover. In particular, we focused on two types of vegetation areas, peri-urban parks and olive orchards. For the first, we selected five sites in Italy, one of which (Castel Volturno) is affected by *Toumeyella Parvicornis*, a parasite that has been adversely impacting the Pinus trees of that area in the recent years. For the second, we selected seven sites in Southern Italy, four of which are affected by *Xylella Fastidiosa*, considered one of the most dangerous phytopathogenic bacteria in the world. For all the investigated sites, to remove the trend and seasonal variability, we firstly applied the Singular Spectrum Analysis (SSA); then, we analysed the de-trended series by means of the Fisher-Shannon statistical method, which combines the Shannon Entropy Power (SEP) and the Fisher Information Measure (FIM). In the Fisher-Shannon Information Plane (FSIP), the infected vegetated areas appear well characterized by the lowest FIM and the highest SEP. These preliminary results seem to envisage the usefulness of the Fisher-Shannon method as a reliable statistical tool to be included in an operational system for early diagnosis of status of deterioration of vegetation.**

***Keywords-Fisher-Shannon method; singular spectrum analysis; MODIS; vegetation.***

## I. INTRODUCTION

With the worsening of climate change and the increasing of global trade, plant diseases have been accelerating in outbreaking and spreading out. Invasive pests and alien plant bacteria are considered one of the major threats worldwide, because they can induce serious plant diseases with devastating impacts on both natural ecosystems and agriculture production with huge environmental (loss of biodiversity) and economic damage. For instance, *Xylella Fastidiosa*, considered one of the most dangerous plant bacteria in the world, causes a number of devasting diseases of significant economic importance in many crops as, but not only, grapevine, Citrus, Olive trees etc. As an example, in the EU only considering the impact on olive trees, it has been estimated that this bacterium has the potential of causing an annual production loss of 5.5 billion euros, affecting 70% of the EU production value of older olive trees. Thus, detecting, quantifying and identifying plant diseases is extremely crucial for assessing tempestive measures to contrast them [1].

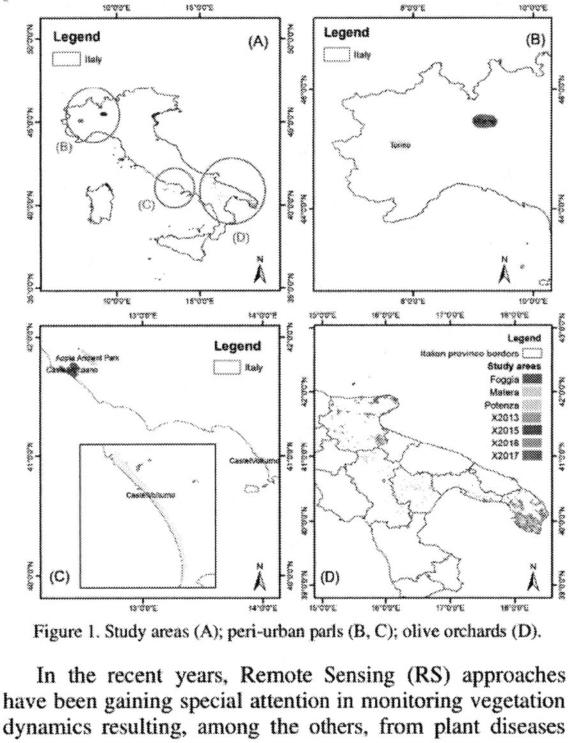


Figure 1. Study areas (A); peri-urban parls (B, C); olive orchards (D).

In the recent years, Remote Sensing (RS) approaches have been gaining special attention in monitoring vegetation dynamics resulting, among the others, from plant diseases

[2]. Several RS applications in phytopathology have been focused on the development of methodologies based on multi-temporal and multi-spectral satellite data for monitoring land-cover changes. Statistical approaches, such as principal component analysis [3] and curve fitting methods [4], are well known for detecting vegetation changes of land surface.

In this paper, we present a statistical approach, namely the Fisher-Shannon (FS) method, to capture evidence of the presence of plant diseases. The FS method relies on the informational content of a time series and, in our case, is used to analyse the time dynamics of MODIS Evapotranspiration (ET) satellite data of different vegetation covers, affected by *Toumeyella Parvicornis* and by *Xylella Fastidiosa*.

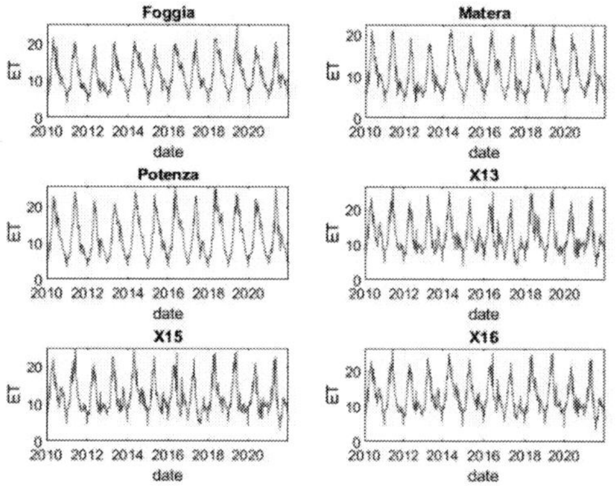


Figure 2. An example of evapotranspiration data.

The MODIS ET product is based on the logic of the Penman-Monteith equation, which includes inputs of daily meteorological reanalysis data along with satellite information. It is expected that ET will suitably characterize and capture the impact of plant infected by *Toumeyella Parvicornis* and by *Xylella Fastidiosa*, since one of the recognizable effects is that the plant dries up and dies.

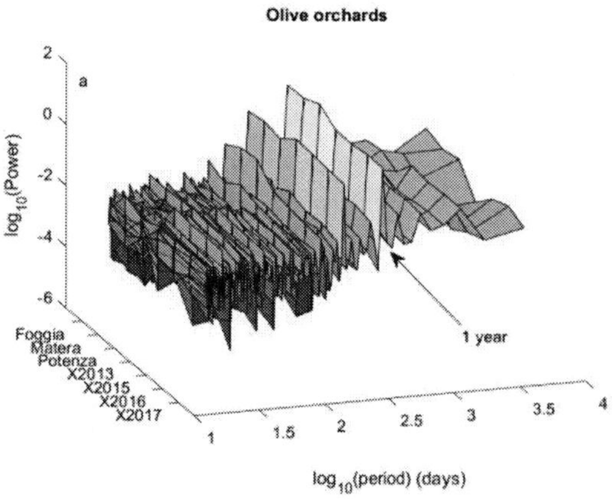


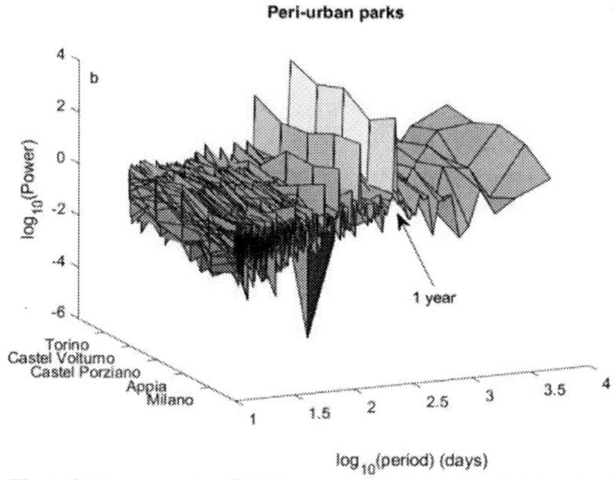


Figure 3. Power spectra of ET time *series* of olive orchards (a) and peri-urban parks (b).

## II. Data and Methods

For the purpose of this study, five peri-urban parks in Italy were selected, Milano, Torino, Appia, Castel Porziano and Castel Volturno, the last one attacked by the *Toumeyella Parvicornis* since 2015. Furthermore, seven olive orchard areas were selected, Foggia, Potenza, Matera, X2013, X2015, X2016 and X2017, the last four located in Southern Apulia and infected by *Xylella Fastidiosa* in different periods from 2013 to 2017 (Figure 1). For each site, one MODIS-based ET time series was obtained by averaging the ET values of all the 500m resolution pixels covering each investigated site. The sampling time of the MODIS ET satellite data is 8 days. Some examples of the analysed MODIS ET time series are shown in Figure 2.

The statistical approach used in investigating the data is composed by two steps: the singular spectrum analysis and the Fisher-Shannon method, described in the following subsections.

### A. *Singular Spectrum Analysis*

The decomposition of a time series into independent components can be performed by using several techniques, among which the Singular Spectrum Analysis (SSA) [5] represents an efficient and well-known tool based on phase-lagged copies of the series.

The independent components obtained by means of the SSA can be easily recognizable as slowly changing trend, oscillatory components and structureless noise [6].

Let us consider a time series $y_i$ ($i$ =1, .., $N$) and a lag $M$, then the Toeplitz lagged correlation matrix can be constructed:

$$c_{ij} = \frac{1}{N-|i-j|}\sum_{k=1}^{N-|i-j|} y_k y_{k+|i-j|}, 1 \leq i,j \leq M \qquad (1)$$

Sorting its eigenvalues $\lambda_k$ in decreasing order, the corresponding eigenvectors $E_{k,j}$ where $j$ and $k$ vary from 1 to $M$, are used to calculate the $k$-th principal component $i$

$$a_{ik} = \sum_{j=1}^{M} y_{i+j} E_{jk} \quad (2)$$

for $0 \le i \le N-M$, and the $k$-th reconstructed component of the time series:

$$R_k = \frac{1}{M} \sum_{j=1}^{M} a_{i-j,k} E_{jk} \quad (3)$$

for $M \le i \le N-M+1$. Since the eigenvalue $\lambda_k$ represents the fraction of the total variance of the original series explained in $k$-th reconstructed component $R_k$, the decreasing order of the eigenvalues also reflects the decreasing order of the reconstructed components by the fraction of the total variance of the series [7]. SSA requires that the lag $M$ is properly selected, on the base of a trade-off between the quantity of information extracted (large $M$) and the degree of statistical confidence in that information (large ratio $N/M$). Khan and Poskitt [8] calculated the maximum $M = (\log N)^c$, $1.5 \le c \le 2.5$.

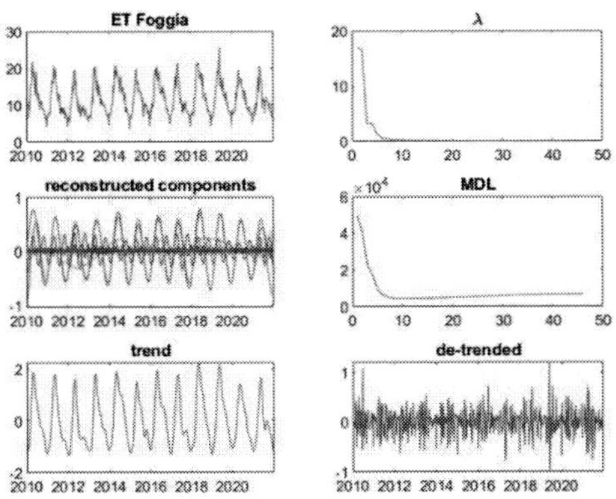


Figure 4. Application of SSA to Foggia MODIS ET data.

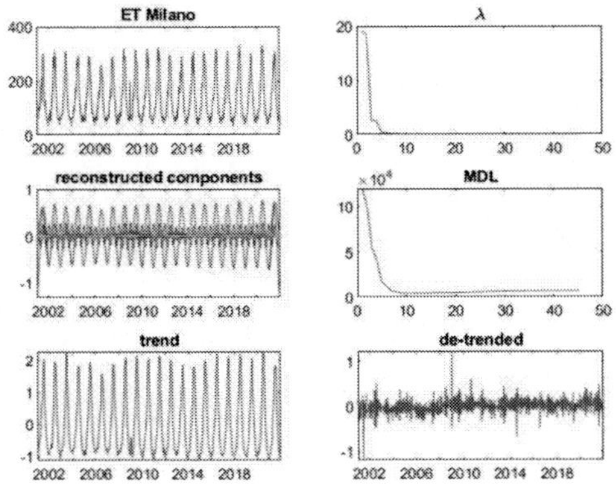


Figure 5. Application of SSA to Milano MODIS ET data.

The minimum description length (MDL) criterion [9]

$$MDL(k) = -\log \left( \frac{\prod_{i=k+1}^{p} \lambda_i^{\frac{1}{p-k}}}{\frac{1}{p-k} \sum_{i=k+1}^{p} \lambda_i} \right)^{(p-k)N} + \frac{1}{2} k (2p-k) \log N \quad (4)$$

is used to separate the series into two parts that we can define as trend and detrended series; $\lambda_k$ are the eigenvalues, $p$ is the number of eigenvalues, identical to $M$, and $N$ is the length of the original series. The separation occurs at the value of $k \in \{0, 1, 2, \ldots, p-1\}$ for which the MDL is minimized.

*B. Fisher-Shannon method*

The informational properties of a time series can be analysed by the Fisher Information Measure (FIM) and the Shannon entropy (SE) that quantify respectively the local and global smoothness of the distribution of a series. The FIM and SE can be utilized for characterizing the complexity of non-stationary time series described in terms of order and organization [10]. The FIM measures the order and organization of the series, and the SE its uncertainty or disorder [11]. The FIM and SE are defined by the following formulae:

$$\text{FIM} = \int_{-\infty}^{+\infty} \left( \frac{\partial}{\partial x} f(x) \right)^2 \frac{dx}{f(x)}, \quad (5)$$

$$\text{SE} = -\int_{-\infty}^{+\infty} f_X(x) \log f_X(x) dx, \quad (6)$$

where $f(x)$ is the distribution of the series $x$. Instead of SE, it is generally used the Shannon entropy power (SEP) $N_X$

$$N_X = \frac{1}{2\pi e} e^{2SE}, \quad (7)$$

that is defined positive. FIM and $N_X$ are not independent of each other due to the isoperimetric inequality $\text{FIM} \cdot N_X \ge D$ [12], where $D$ is the dimension of the space (1 for time series).

FIM and $N_X$ depend on $f(x)$, whose accurate estimation is crucial to obtain reliable values of informational quantities. For calculating FIM and $N_X$ we applied the kernel-based approach that is better than discrete-based approach in estimating the probability density function [13]. Thus applying the kernel density estimator method for $f(x)$ [14], [15] as shown in the following formula:

$$\hat{f}_M(x) = \frac{1}{Mb} \sum_{i=1}^{M} K\left( \frac{x - x_i}{b} \right), \quad (8)$$

where $M$ and $b$ denote the length of the series and the bandwidth respectively, while $K(u)$ is the kernel that is a continuous, symmetric and non-negative function satisfying the two following constrains:

$$K(u) \ge 0 \quad \text{and} \quad \int_{-\infty}^{+\infty} K(u) du = 1, \quad (9)$$

$f(x)$ is estimated by means of an optimized integrated procedure using the algorithms of Troudi et al. [16] and Raykar and Duraiswami [17] with the Gaussian kernel:

$$\hat{f}_M(x) = \frac{1}{M\sqrt{2\pi b^2}} \sum_{i=1}^{M} e^{-\frac{(x-x_i)^2}{2b^2}} \quad (10)$$

Due to the isoperimetric inequality, the Fisher-Shannon information plane (FSIP), which has the $N_X$ as x-axis and FIM as y-axis, represents a very useful tool to investigate the complexity of time dynamics of signals [18]. For scalar signals, the curve FIM·$N_X$=1 separates the FSIP into two parts, and each signal can be represented by a point located only in the space FIM·$N_X$>1.

## III. RESULTS

The SSA requires that the phase lag $M$ is selected to capture the main periodicities of the series. Thus, we firstly calculated the power spectrum of each ET time series (Figure 2) and identified the annual cycle as the main periodicity.

Thus, to detect at least the annual cycle, $M$ was set as 46, consistently with the sampling time of the data, which is 8 days. As an example, Figure 4 and Figure 5 show the application of the SSA to the ET time series of two sites. After normalized the series, the SSA eigenvalue spectrum $\lambda$ was obtained along with the reconstructed components; each eigenvalue represents the contribution of the corresponding component to the total variance of the original series. The behaviour of the reconstructed components varies from oscillatory trend with amplitude modulation to seemingly noisy. Applying the MDL criterion the signal is separated into a trend and a de-trended series; the value of $k_{min}$ corresponding to the minimum MDL represents the number of the first reconstructed components to sum up for obtaining the trend. For the series Foggia, for instance, $k_{min}$=9; thus, the trend is obtained summing up the first 9 reconstructed components and the de-trended series by subtracting the trend from the original normalized series. Table I and Table II show the SSA parameters (phase lag $M$ and $k_{min}$) used for each time series.

The trend is featured by an oscillatory behaviour and represents the seasonal cycles of meteo-climatic origin. The de-trended series, although apparently noisy, represents the inner time dynamics of the series that might not be influenced by external driving mechanisms. Thus, since our aim is the characterization of the time dynamics of inner vegetation by using the Fisher-Shannon method, for each site we analysed the de-trended series. Figure 6 and Figure 7 show the FSIP of de-trended MODIS ET time series of the peri-urban parks and the olive orchard areas, respectively. The FSIP indicates that among the peri-urban parks Castel Volturno that is effectively attacked by the *Toumeyella Parvicornis* is characterized by the lowest FIM and the highest SEP. Among the olive orchards, the four sites X2013, X2015, X2016 and X2017 that were infected by *Xylella Fastidiosa* occupy the bottom-right part of the FSIP, indicating a higher level of disorder and lower level of organization of the vegetation index, similarly to Castel Volturno.

TABLE I. SSA PARAMETERS USED FOR PERI-URBAN PARKS

| Peri-urban parks | | |
|---|---|---|
| ***Site*** | ***M*** | ***$k_{min}$*** |
| Torino | 46 | 7 |
| Castel Volturno | 46 | 5 |
| Castel Porziano | 46 | 7 |
| Appia | 46 | 11 |
| Milano | 46 | 12 |

TABLE II. SSA PARAMETERS USED FOR OLIVE ORCAHRDS

| Olive orchards | | |
|---|---|---|
| ***Site*** | ***M*** | ***$k_{min}$*** |
| Foggia | 46 | 9 |
| Matera | 46 | 8 |
| Potenza | 46 | 8 |
| X2013 | 46 | 7 |
| X2015 | 46 | 7 |
| X2016 | 46 | 6 |
| X2017 | 46 | 6 |

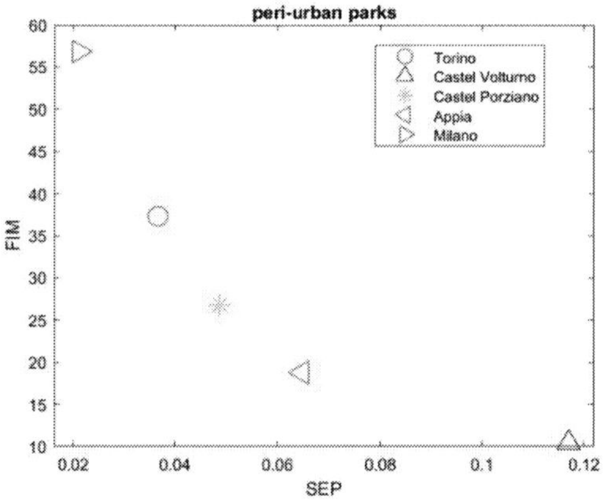


Figure 6. Fisher-Shannon Information Plane for the de-trended MODIS ET data of peri-urban parks.

## IV. DISCUSSION

The fatality rate for both *Toumeyella Parvicornis* (affecting pines) and *Xylella* Fastidiosa (affecting olive orchads) is as high as 100%, and their early detection is the critical issue to eradicate the disease and stop tree mortality. Therefore, the main question is how to quickly find the infected trees?

From the operational point of view, the existing solutions are only based on in situ analysis and visual inspection, and, therefore, are not suitable to identify early signals of plant diseases not visible at a naked eye.

Earth Observation (EO) technologies provide, instead, imaging beyond the visible and therefore much more information than those obtained solely from the ground. Moreover, EO undoubtly offer cost-effective tools for monitoring wide areas at both local and global scale.

Nevertheless, previous studies based on satellite EO or drone surveys did not utilize analyses of long term time series that enabled the identification of early signals of degradation. Moreover, the use of evapotranspiration time series as proxy indicator of plant conditions also improved the early detection capability (and facilitate the forecasting of pest outbreak) that is the critical issue to eradicate destructive disease and pest infestations, as those from both for *Xylella* and *Toumeyella Parvicornis*.

There is a strong requirement for reliable operational tools for multiscale, multi-sensor, multi-temporal monitoring of biophysical parameters relating to the state of vegetation to assess and monitor land degradation and capture early signs of both degradation productivity declines and related temporal dynamics that often precede tree mortality years to decades before death. In more details, the following tasks would be useful to implement: i) setting up of EO-based metrics/indicators suitable for an early diagnosis of vegetation deterioration trends to improve ability to forecast tree disease and mortality from local up global scale; ii) effective satellite-based near real time monitoring of forest disease and pest damage for the development of prevention and control strategies.

## V. Conclusions

The vegetation of several study areas from the North to the Southern part of Italy was analysed. The study areas were peri-urban parks and olive orchards. The peri-urban parks were selected as key in improving environmental quality, being rich in biodiversity and allowing urban areas to be more sustainable, helping to combat climate change and make cities more comfortable. The olive orchards were selected as extremely important for the economy of Southern Italy; in fact, Apulia (were some of the investigated sites are located) accounts for about 40% of Italy's olive oil production.

Thus, for each site we focused on the SSA de-trended series since this represents the inner time dynamics of the vegetation.

Our findings point out to the following results: (i) the trend of each series is characterized by an oscillatory behaviour that might be linked with the meteo-climatic cycles, (ii) the de-trended series, although apparently noisy, might be not influenced by external driving mechanisms; (iii) among the investigated peri-urban parks, Castel Volturno, and among the olive orchards, X2013, X2015, X2016 and X2017 are characterized by the lowest FIM and the highest SEP; (iv) Castel Volturno, X2013, X2015, X2016 and X2017 share similar phytopathogenic conditions, which is induced by *Toumeyella Parvicornis* for Castel Volturno and *Xylella Fastidiosa* for the remaining four sites; (v) a plant disease seems to be well revealed by analysing the informational properties of MODIS ET time series.

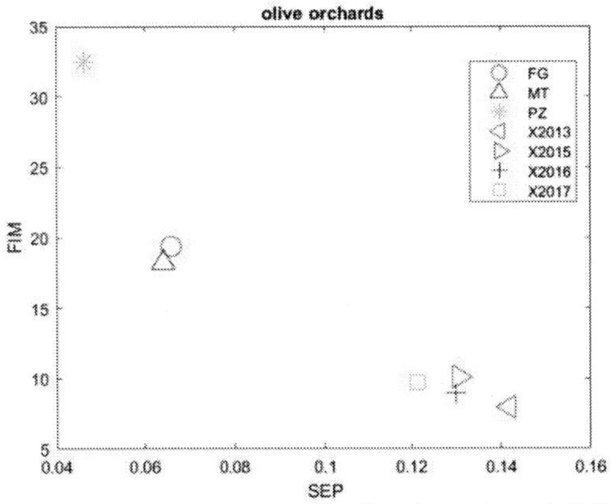


Figure 7. Fisher-Shannon Information Plane for the de-trended MODIS ET data of olive orchards.

Our results could contribute to the definition of methodologies able to diagnose the deterioration and operational tools for the monitoring of biophysical parameters of the status of vegetation.

## Acknowledgment

This work was supported by the project COELUM funded by CNR.

## References

[1] N. Zhang, et al. "A review of advanced technologies and development for hyperspectral-based plant disease detection in the past three decades," Remote Sens., vol. 12, 3188, 2020.

[2] D. S. Reddy, and P. R. C. Prasad, "Prediction of vegetation dynamics using NDVI time series data and LSTM. Model," Earth Syst. Environ., vol. 4, 409–419, 2018.

[3] M. Hall-Beyer, "Comparison of single-year and multiyear ndvi time series principal components in cold temperate biomes," IEEE Trans. Geosci. Remote Sens., vol. 41, 2568–2574, 2003.

[4] G. L. Galford, J. F. Mustard, J. Melillo, A. Gendrin, and C. E. P. Cerri, "Wavelet analysis of MODIS time series to detect expansion and intensification of row-crop agriculture in Brazil.," Remote Sens. Environ., vol. 112, 576–587, 2008.

[5] R.Vautard, and M. Ghil, "Singular spectrum analysis in nonlinear dynamics, with applications to paleoclimatic time series," Phys. D, vol. 35, 395–424, 1989.

[6] H. Hassani, "Singular Spectrum Analysis: Methodology and Comparison," J. Data Sci., vol. 5, 239–257, 2007.

[7] D. Schoellhamer, "Singular spectrum analysis for time series with missing data, " Geophys. Res. Lett., vol. 28, 3187–3190, 2001.

[8] M. Khan, and D. S. Poskitt, D.S. "Description Length Based Signal Detection in singular Spectrum Analysis," Monash Econometrics and Business Statistics Working Papers 13/10;

Monash University, Department of Econometrics and Business Statistics: Melbourne, Australia, 2010.

[9] M. Wax, and T. Kailath, "Detection of signals by information theoretic criteria," IEEE Trans. Acoust. Speech Signal Process., vol. 33, 387–392, 1985.

[10] R. A. Fisher, "Theory of Statistical Estimation," Math. Proc. Camb. Philos. Soc., vol. 22, 700–725, 1925.

[11] C. E. Shannon, "A Mathematical Theory of Communication," Bell Syst. Tech. J., vol. 27, 379–423, 1948.

[12] K. D. Sen, J. Antolín, and J. C. Angulo, "Fisher-Shannon Analysis of Ionization Processes and Isoelectronic Series," Phys. Rev. A, vol. 76, 032502, 2007.

[13] L. Telesca, and M. Lovallo, "On the performance of Fisher Information Measure and Shannon entropy estimators," Physica A, vol. 484, 569–576, 2017.

[14] A. Janicki, and A. Weron, Simulation and Chaotic Behavior of Alpha-Stable Stochastic Processes," Chapman & Hall/CRC Pure and Applied Mathematics; CRC Press: Boca Raton, FL, USA, 1993.

[15] L. Devroye, "A Course in Density Estimation; Progress in Probability," Birkhäuser Boston Inc.: Cambridge, MA, USA, 1987.

[16] M. Troudi, A. M. Alimi, and S. Saoudi, "Analytical Plug-In Method for Kernel Density Estimator Applied to Genetic Neutrality Study," EURASIP J. Adv. Signal Process., vol. 2008, 739082, 2008.

[17] V. C. Raykar, and R. Duraiswami, "Fast optimal bandwidth selection for kernel density estimation," in Proceedings of the 2006 SIAM International Conference on Data Mining; Proceedings; Society for Industrial and Applied Mathematics: Philadelphia, PA, USA, 2006.

[18] C. Vignat, and J.-F. Bercher, "Analysis of Signals in the Fisher–Shannon Information Plane," Phys. Lett. A, vol. 312, 27–33, 2003.

# Stress Detection Based on Wearable Physiological Sensors: Laboratory and Real-Life Pilot Scenario Application

Vasileios-Rafail Xefteris*, Athina Tsanousa*, Spyridon Symeonidis*, Sotiris Diplaris*, Francesco Zaffanela†, Martina Monego†, Maria Pacelli‡, Stefanos Vrochidis*, and Ioannis Kompatsiaris*
* Information Technologies Institute - CERTH, Thessaloniki, Greece
Email: {vxefteris, atsan, spyridons, diplaris, stefanos, ikom}@iti.gr
† Autorita di Bacino Distrettuale delle Alpi Orientali, Venice, Italy
Email: {francesco.zaffanella, martina.monego}@distrettoalpiorientali.it
‡ Smartex, Prato, Italy
Email: m.pacelli@smartex.it

***Abstract*—Stress as a mental/physiological reaction of a person in a challenging situation of high discomfort can affect his/her ability to focus and perform fast and accurate decisions. Thus, stress can be a key factor in cases of emergency, when first responders need to be fast and accurate. Continuous monitoring of the stress levels of the first responders can be crucial in cases of disaster management situations. Wearable devices and physiological sensors provide real-time monitoring of physiological signals, which can be helpful for real-time stress monitoring. This work describes the stress detection module of the xR4DRAMA project and the results of its application during a disaster management pilot scenario. For this cause, a wearable smart vest equipped with an electrocardiograph (ECG) sensor, respiration (RSP) sensor, and an Inertial Measurement Unit (IMU) with an accelerometer, gyroscope, magnetometer, and quaternion sensors has been used. An initial data collection was performed to train the stress detection module, and the trained model was deployed for real-time stress detection of first responders in the pilot scenario. The training performed includes a massive feature extraction from the different modalities, and the test of four machine learning algorithms and six fusion and three feature selection techniques. The results of the continuous valued stress levels detection indicate that the best performing combination is the eXtreme Gradient Boosting (XGB) algorithm with the use of a Genetic Algorithm (GA) feature selection technique, achieving a Mean Square Error (MSE) of 0.0567. Results from the pilot show that the stress level detection module can operate in real-time in real life conditions, offering reasonable results regarding the detected stress levels.**

***Index Terms*—Stress level detection, wearable sensors, smart vest, multimodal fusion**

## I. Introduction

Stress is among the most important problems in our society. It can be defined as the reaction of a person when being subject to high discomfort and challenging situations. As stated by World Health Organisation "Work-related stress is the response people may have when presented with work demands and pressures that are not matched to their knowledge and abilities and which challenge their ability to cope" [1]. Stress can impact the mental clarity of a person decreasing his ability of precise and fast decisions. High levels of stress might also influence person's performance, even in actions they are trained to perform. Thus, stress can be considered one of the most vital aspects of disaster management situations.

Apart from the effects of stress on first responders performance, their exposure to highly stressful events for long periods can result in serious health problems. Mental health issues, such as Post-Traumatic Stress Disorder (PTSD) and major depressive disorder [2], or other physical health problems, such as sleep disturbances and musculoskeletal problems [3], are some of the most common health problems induced by chronic stress. Therefore, monitoring the stress levels of first responders during emergencies is of crucial importance. Simulating a disaster management scenario with first responders or volunteers assists in collecting physiological data and build models for prediction of stress. Protocols that induce stress might be adopted or the exact scenario can be reproduced, such as in [4].

With the development of the Internet of Things (IoT), smart devices are equipped with many sensors able to monitor physiological signals and human body motion attributes. Since stress is a mental/physiological reaction the monitoring of physiological signals can be considered useful in the task of stress detection. Also, in many cases, abnormal human body movements along with certain physiological signal attributes can be beneficial for stress detection applications. The IoT advances with the deployment of multiple sensors in wearable devices and the high computational power of smart devices and computers can lead to real-time stress detection capabilities.

In the current work, an application of an experimental design for stress level detection of first responders is described. The stress level detection module exploits data from a wearable smart vest equipped with sensors, designed for this application, and predicts the levels of stress as a continuous value, which is not the case in most stress detection applications, where only a categorical variable of two or three classes is typically predicted. The stress detection module was trained using data collected through an initial data collection, where subjects underwent various challenges that induce different levels of stress, and they reported their stress level after each challenge. The trained stress detection module was deployed for real-time stress level detection during the pilot scenario, where subjects had to perform certain tasks simulating a real flood scenario. These tasks include going to certain areas on the field and sending incident reports. Since there was no flood simulation or any other stressor to induce high levels of stress, the pilot scenario mainly tested the ability of the stress detection module to perform real-time stress level monitoring in real life conditions. The current work is an application of stress detection in a general framework of eXtended Reality (XR) technologies for disaster management, as part of the xR4DRAMA project [5], which is a solution that makes use of XR in disasters, or media production scenarios. The pilot scenario is part of the first pilot of the project regarding the disaster management pilot use case, where the need for real-time stress level monitoring using wearable physiological sensors is present.

The rest of the paper is organized as follows; in Section 2 state-of-the-art methods for stress detection are presented. In Section 3 the methods used for the data collection and analysis are described followed by the results of the experiments in Section 4 and the conclusion of our work in Section 5.

## II. RELATED WORK

The most common stress detection methods based on physiological signals include a feature extraction step that attempt to describe the various affective states. The extracted features are used to train a state-of-the-art machine learning classifier which eventually learns to detect the stress levels of the subjects. A more recent approach attempts to omit the feature extraction step by utilizing a Deep Neural Network (DNN), which can do the representation learning of the different affective states directly from the physiological signals.

Physiological sensors can be exploited separately or in combination for the task of stress detection. Electrocardiography sensors (ECG) are amongst the best performing ones in predicting stress and are often utilized individually. In [6] machine learning algorithms were applied on features extracted from ECG signals to detect stress in drivers. ECG signals were used in [7] in a simulated stress scenario and their performance was compared to electromyogram (EMG) signals. Galvanic Skin Response (GSR) sensors are often combined with ECG signals and other physiological sensors to detect stress. Early fusion was used in [8] to combine features extracted from GSR, Electroencephalogram (EEG) sensor and Photoplethysmogram (PPG), in order to improve the individual performance for monitoring stress.

Schmidt et al. [9] created a benchmark for their publicly available dataset for stress detection using a large number of well-known features (extracted from physiological and motion signals) and common machine learning methods (Decision Tree (DT), Random Forest (RF), AdaBoost (AB), Linear Discriminant Analysis (LDA) and k-nearest neighbor (kNN)). The authors validated their methods on a three-class problem (neutral, stress, amusement) achieving 80.34 % accuracy with the AB classifier, and on a two-class problem (stress, no stress) achieving 93.12 % accuracy with the LDA classifier.

Rusell Li et al. [10] proposed a novel Deep Learning (DL) based method for stress detection, which was trained and evaluated on the same dataset as [9]. This work attempts to address the limitation of the handcrafted features that traditional machine learning methods rely upon and their potential decrease in accuracy due to the misidentification of features. The authors designed a novel 1D Convolutional Neural Network (CNN) and a Multi-Layer Perceptron (MLP) that take as input the raw physiological signals and do not require hand-crafted features but instead extract features from raw data through the layers of the neural networks. The authors validated their classifiers on both the three and two-class problems of [9] achieving 97.48 % for the three-class and 99.14 % for the two-class problem.

Sriramprakash et al. [11] proposed a method for detecting stress during working conditions based on feature extraction and machine learning. The authors trained and validated their data on the SWELL-KW dataset [12]. They utilized a set of 17 statistical features derived from ECG and GSR signals and evaluated which of them are the most dominant to increase accuracies. They trained a kNN classifier and a Support Vector Machine (SVM) classifier. The SVM classifier trained on the dominant selected features achieved the highest classification accuracy of 92.75 % for the stress vs no-stress classification task. Another work based on feature extraction and SVM was reported by Yuan Shi et al. [13]. The authors proposed a set of 26 handcrafted features derived from ECG, GSR, skin conductance, temperature and respiration. They reported an 80 % recall over the binary classification of stress vs no stress problem.

Feng-Tso, et al. [14] extracted statistical features from ECG, GSR, and accelerometer and trained a DT, Bayesian Network (BN), and SVM classifier for stress detection inference combined with physical activities (sitting, standing, and walking). The best classification accuracy (92.4%) was obtained by using the DT classifier with the all-feature combination.

Keshan et al. [15] proposed an ECG-based feature extraction scheme for driver stress detection. They trained and evaluated their data on [16]. They utilized a set of 14 statistical features derived from ECG signals and found that stress levels can be successfully detected from ECG signals alone; with a random tree classifier allowing for the identification of the three classes of stress, low, medium, and high, with 88.24% accuracy, and Naïve Bayes for two stress levels, low and high, with 100% accuracy.

In the work of Nath et al. [17] the authors extracted statistical features from GSR and PPG sensors for stress detection of healthy elders. They utilized the Trier Social Stress Test to induce stress in the subjects and a fingertip sensor to monitor physiological signals. The extracted features were fed into a feature selection algorithm to remove redundant information before utilizing a machine learning algorithm for the final stress detection. They tested kNN, RF, and SVM classifiers along with a deep learning Long Short-Term Memory (LSTM) based classifier and found out that the LSTM classifier performs the best, achieving 0.87 macro F1-score, 0.95 micro F1-score, and 0.81 AUC.

In all of the previous works, the data were derived from publicly available datasets. Even though this makes the comparison of the different methods easier, since all methods are based on the same data, this might influence the performance of the models when deployed in a real-life scenario, where the sensors will be different. Also, all of the aforementioned methods are classification methods, with two or three classes. Our work goes beyond predicting only binary (stress, no stress) or categorical (low, medium, high) variables by using regression models to produce continuous values of stress levels.

## III. METHODS

In this Section, the main methods of our work are described.

### A. Smart vest and sensors

The physiological data were acquired using a sensing platform based on textile sensors fully integrated into a smart vest and a data logger that can record and process data on board and transmit them via Bluetooth 2.1.

Furthermore, an Inertial Measurement Unit (IMU) system is integrated into the data logger, including accelerometer, gyroscope, magnetometer and quaternion sensors with the aim of monitoring the movements of the trunk. The Fig. 1 shows the wearable sensing platform in which its features are presented:

- two textile electrodes to acquire ECG signal
- one textile respiratory (RSP) movement sensor
- one jack connector to plug the garment into the electronic device
- a pocket to hold the electronic device during the activity

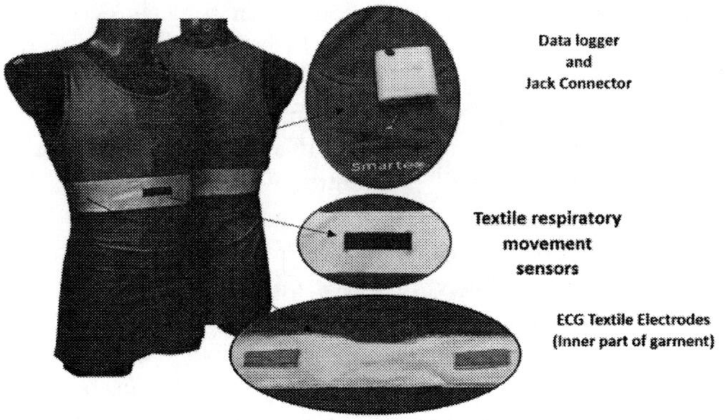


Fig. 1. Wearable sensing platform architecture.

### B. Data collection protocol

The data collection is divided into two different protocols; the training data collection and the pilot scenario. The training data collection protocol is an experimental design based on interchanges between stressful challenges and relaxing situations. The pilot scenario is designed to evaluate an overall disaster management use case using XR technologies, including the real-time stress detection module and all of the other features of the platform.

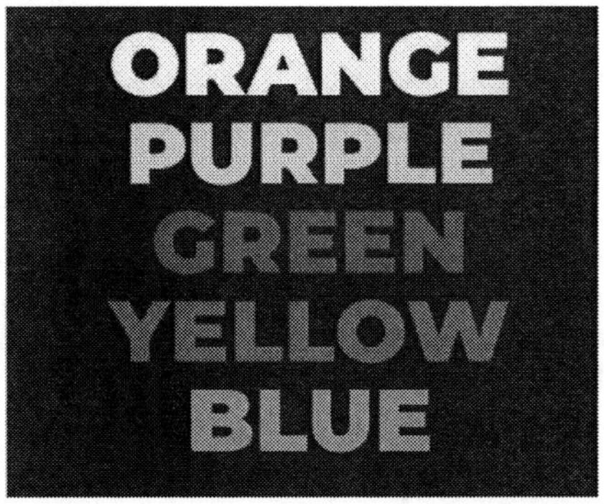


Fig. 2. The Stroop test

*1) Training data collection protocol:* The training data collection protocol has been designed to induce stress in the users followed by calmness. The basis of experimental design is based on known stressors for both psychological and physiological stress. The stressors selected, divided into the two aspects of stress they induce, are the following:

- Psychological:
  - The Stroop test. Is a commonly used task to induce stress [18], in which some slides with certain words of different color names are presented to each user. The words are written in different colors than those they describe (Fig. 2). The user is asked, in a short period of time, to describe the color in which each word is written.
  - The descending subtraction test. In this also commonly used task for inducing stress [19], the user is asked to begin counting backward from a certain number, subtracting each time another certain number. In the context of the training data collection experiment, the users were asked to begin with the number 1324, subtracting 17, until 17. If the users make a mistake, they must start over.
  - Explain a stressful situation in your life.
  - Explain how it has been the day. This is not a stressful challenge, but it is used to get low stress values as well.
  - Listen to relaxing music. This task was also used to get low stress values.
- Physiological:
  - Place a hand in cold water (2° C) for two minutes, make pause, and then place it again.
  - Ascend and descend four levels of stairs.
  - Tie and untie shoes after exercise.

These different challenges were combined in a different order each time, to induce various levels of stress, from calmness to high stress. The users were asked to report their stress levels as a number from 0 to 100 after each challenge. During the whole experiment, the users were wearing the smart vest to collect their physiological data.

*2) Pilot scenario:* The pilot scenario of the disaster management use case of the xR4DRAMA project was designed to evaluate the overall disaster management solution of the project. During the phases of the pilot, the roles of control room operators, first responders, and citizens were assigned to the participants. The storyline of the pilot scenario can be summarized in two different phases; the pre-emergency phase and the emergency phase.

The pre-emergency phase focuses on the forecasting of flood incidences. In more detail, the storyline starts with the reception of an official warning message by the municipality of Vicenza, dealing with the worsening of safety conditions along the Bacchiglione river. Since the stress detection module is not involved in this phase there is no need for further analyzing the design of the certain phase.

During the emergency phase, the first responders are asked to perform certain tasks from the control room. These tasks include sending incident reports to signal the authorities that there were flooding events in various areas of the city center. For the whole time of the emergency phase, the first responders were wearing the smart vest to monitor their stress levels in real time. There was no simulation of flood events during the experiment, thus the first responders did not experience any certain stressor that could induce high levels of stress.

### C. Data analysis

The data analysis is referring to extraction of features from the received data and the training of the different machine learning algorithms and the different fusion and feature selection techniques. The best performing method was selected to be implemented for the disaster management pilot scenario.

After receiving the data from the training data collection, we performed a data analysis involving preprocessing of the data and feature extraction. The preprocessing of the data involves only simple transformation of the data by multiplying them with certain weights. Feature extraction was applied to all the preprocessed data. The features were extracted using a 60-second window with 50% overlap. We used the data of all subjects that were monitored. In total 94 ECG, 28 RSP, and 192 IMU (16 per single-axis data) features were extracted for a total of 314 features. The ECG features include statistical and frequency features regarding the signal and the R-R (the physiological phenomenon of variation in the time interval between heartbeats) intervals, along with Heart Rate (HR) variability time and frequency domain statistical features. For the ECG features, we used the hrv-analysis [20] and the neurokit [21] toolboxes. The respiration features include statistical and frequency features of the signal, breathing rate, respiratory rate variability, and breath-to-breath intervals. The respiration features were also extracted using the neurokit toolbox [21]. The IMU features include simple statistical and frequency features from the IMU signals. These features are mean, median, standard deviation, variance, maximum value, minimum value, interquartile range, skewness, kurtosis, entropy, energy, and 5 dominant frequencies.

For the ground truth values, the self-reported stress levels of the users refer to the whole challenge they performed right before they were asked to report their stress. Thus, each of the 60-second time windows used for the feature extraction was assigned the stress value the user reported for the whole challenge that took place at the certain window. The ground truth values were integer values in the range of 0 to 100.

After extracting the features, the data were split into train and test with an 80/20 ratio. We applied four different ML algorithms; namely SVM, k-Nearest Neighbors (kNN), RF, and eXtreme Gradient Boosting trees (XGB) to perform regression of the stress level since the stress level is a continuous variable. The evaluation was performed using the Mean Squared Error (MSE) metric and 10-fold cross validation. Before computing the MSE we normalized the values of stress level to be in the range of 0 to 1. We tested each modality alone, all different combinations of modalities in early-level fusion (concatenation) and two late-level fusion methods: mean and median of the predicted stress level of each modality. We also tested the performance of three different feature selection algorithms, those being Recursive Feature Elimination (RFE), Principal Component Analysis (PCA), and Genetic Algorithm (GA).

## IV. RESULTS

In this Section, the main results of our work are presented. First, the training data collection's main results are presented, including the different early and late fusion and feature selection methods. Following are the results of the pilot scenario, including the real-time outcomes of the stress detection module during the disaster management pilot scenario.

### A. Training data collection

For the training data collection, seven subjects (4 female, age: 40±7.78) participated, each one performing a series of challenges as described above. The results from all the different fusion methods tested are presented in Table I. From the Table, it can be seen that the IMU modality performs better than the ECG and RSP modalities when used alone. Also, when combining only two of the three different modalities it can be seen that when the IMU modality is used, the results are better. Since IMU sensors are typically used for activity recognition, this might indicate that along all the users, the physiological stressors, which include more specific movements, might have a larger influence on the users' stress levels. The best performing method of all the different tested methods is the early fusion of all the modalities while using the XGB classifier, achieving an MSE score of 0.073.

Since the best performing fusion method was the early fusion of all the modalities, we tested the different feature selection methods on the concatenated feature set of all the different modalities. In Table II the results from the different feature selection methods are presented. All the different

TABLE I
MSE RESULTS OF THE DIFFERENT FUSION TECHNIQUES WITH ALL FOUR DIFFERENT REGRESSORS.

| | ECG | RSP | IMU | ECG + RSP | ECG + IMU | RSP + IMU | ECG + RSP + IMU | Late mean | Late median |
|---|---|---|---|---|---|---|---|---|---|
| **SVM** | 0.1709 | 0.1530 | 0.1305 | 0.1723 | 0.1306 | 0.1305 | 0.1305 | 0.1412 | 0.1363 |
| **kNN** | 0.1439 | 0.1553 | 0.1107 | 0.1285 | 0.1106 | 0.1106 | 0.1107 | 0.1170 | 0.1125 |
| **RF** | 0.1113 | 0.1280 | 0.0918 | 0.1073 | 0.0916 | 0.0871 | 0.0886 | 0.0984 | 0.1025 |
| **XGB** | 0.1237 | 0.1307 | 0.0844 | 0.1092 | 0.0835 | 0.0858 | 0.0730 | 0.0958 | 0.1006 |

feature selection algorithms improve the overall performance of the different classifiers, nevertheless the GA feature selection algorithm when again applied with the XGB regressor performs the best, achieving an MSE score of 0.0567. All the feature selection methods retained features from all modalities.

TABLE II
MSE RESULTS OF THE DIFFERENT FEATURE SELECTION TECHNIQUES WITH ALL FOUR DIFFERENT REGRESSORS.

| | RFE | PCA | GA |
|---|---|---|---|
| **SVM** | 0.1052 | 0.1201 | 0.1305 |
| **kNN** | 0.1023 | 0.1106 | 0.1106 |
| **RF** | 0.0790 | 0.1044 | 0.0742 |
| **XGB** | 0.0772 | 0.0953 | 0.0567 |

Since in all cases the XGB classifier achieves the best results, it is important to see how the feature selection method improves the overall performance of the stress detection module. In Fig. 3 we present concatenation and GA feature selection results along with the ground truth values in each subfigure respectively. From the figure, it can be seen that the use of GA feature selection improves the overall performance of the XGB regressor, by minimizing the error between the ground truth values and the predictions.

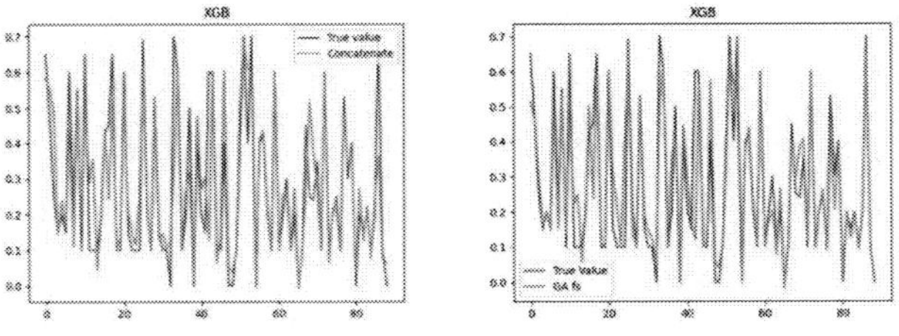


Fig. 3. Plot of the ground truth stress levels reported versus the predicted stress levels using the XGB regressor with and without the use of GA feature selection technique

*B. Disaster management pilot scenario*

For the pilot, we trained an XGB model using a GA feature selection, since it was the best performing method for stress detection. The model was deployed for real-time stress detection using the data from the smart vest. Four different subjects were participating, having the role of the first responder and performing tasks on the field, as described above. Each subject was wearing a smart vest during the whole experiment.

Data from the smart vest were streamed while the users were following the instruction given to them for the pilot scenario. The streamed data are packed in 5-second packages before being sent to the stress detection module. The streamed data were received from the stress detection module, which stacks them until a full minute of data is collected, and then the feature extraction, feature selection, and final stress detection process are taking place. Therefore a 1 min long time window with 5 seconds step is applied. The full procedure can be seen in Fig. 4, where the stack of the 5-second packages of data along with the main stress detection process including feature extraction, feature selection, and stress detection, are presented.

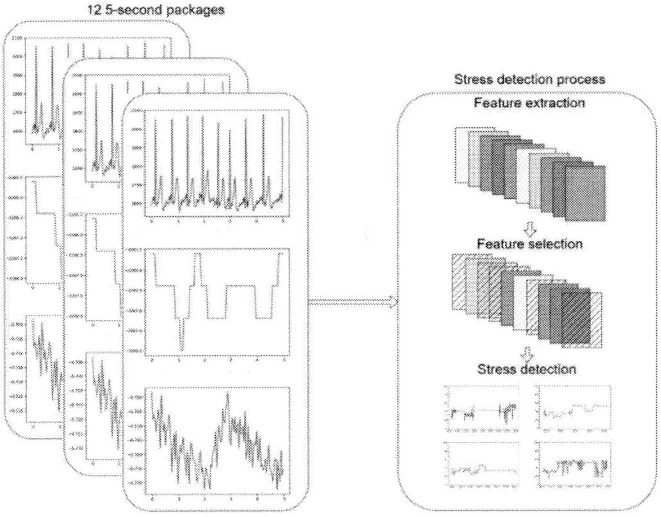


Fig. 4. Workflow of the stress detection module during the pilot.

The results from the pilot can be seen in Fig. 5. Each one of the four different subfigures presents the results of a different user. Knowing that the users during the pilot were performing simple tasks, their stress levels are reasonable to be in a range from 40 to 60. From the Figure, it can be seen that the stress levels are at a medium level indicating that users were calm, which is reasonable considering the tasks they were asked to perform.

## V. CONCLUSION

In this paper, we present a solution for real-time stress level detection based on sensors in the general context of XR technologies for disaster management. This work focuses on the training of the sensor-based stress level detection module from data gathered during a training data collection, and its implementation into a real-life disaster management pilot

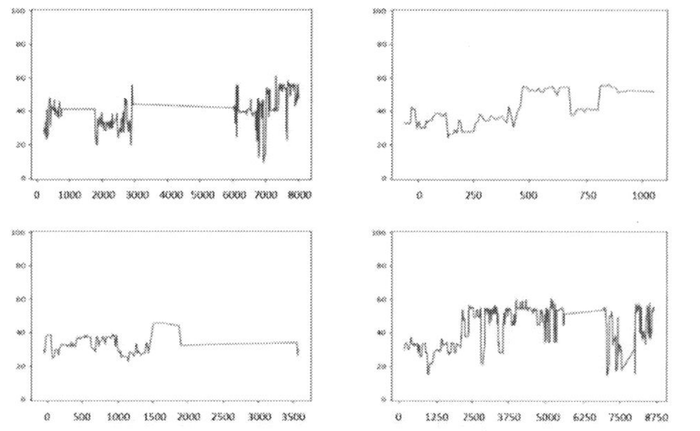


Fig. 5. Stress level results of the stress detection module (x-axis) from data from the pilot over time (y-axis) for each subject.

scenario. The sensor-based stress level detection module is based on data gathered from a smart vest developed for the current application consisting of an ECG sensor, an RSP sensor, and an IMU system with 3-axis accelerometer, gyroscope, magnetometer and quaternion sensors. Data gathered from these sensors are analyzed in order to extract features that are fed into a trained model for the final continuous-valued stress level detection. From the results of the evaluation study, where multiple fusion and feature selection methods were tested using four different machine learning algorithms, it was revealed that the best performing combination was the use of XGB regressor along with GA-based feature selection method, achieving 0.0567 MSE. We retrained the XGB model with the feature sub-set selected from the GA-based feature selection method, and deployed it into a real-world disaster management pilot scenario. Results from four subjects serving as first responders in this pilot scenario indicate that our model works reasonable even in real-life conditions and in real-time. Future work includes performing a second disaster management pilot scenario in the context of the xR4DRAMA project, where a more well defined protocol to induce stress will be implemented. Also in this pilot scenario, the sensor based stress level detection system will be tested alone and in combination with the predicted stress of an audio-based system, through the fusion module of the xR4DRAMA project.

## Acknowledgment

This work was supported by the xR4DRAMA project funded by the European Commission (H2020) under the grant number 952133.

## References

[1] W. H. Organization, "Occupational health: Stress at the workplace." https://www.who.int/news-room/questions-and-answers/item/ccupational-health-stress-at-the-workplace, 2020. [Online; accessed 4-November-2022].

[2] B. Kleim and M. Westphal, "Mental health in first responders: A review and recommendation for prevention and intervention strategies," *Traumatology*, vol. 17, no. 4, pp. 17–24, 2011.

[3] M. J. Friedman and B. S. McEwen, "Posttraumatic stress disorder, allostatic load, and medical illness.," *Trauma and health: Physical health consequences of exposure to extreme stress*, p. 157–188, 2004.

[4] J. Strahler and T. Ziegert, "Psychobiological stress response to a simulated school shooting in police officers," *Psychoneuroendocrinology*, vol. 51, pp. 80–91, 2015.

[5] S. Symeonidis, S. Diplaris, N. Heise, T. Pistola, A. Tsanousa, G. Tzanetis, E. Batziou, C. Stentoumis, I. Kalisperakis, S. Freitag, *et al.*, "xr4drama: Enhancing situation awareness using immersive (xr) technologies," in *2021 IEEE International Conference on Intelligent Reality (ICIR)*, pp. 1–8, IEEE, 2021.

[6] N. Keshan, P. Parimi, and I. Bichindaritz, "Machine learning for stress detection from ecg signals in automobile drivers," in *2015 IEEE International conference on big data (Big Data)*, pp. 2661–2669, IEEE, 2015.

[7] S. Pourmohammadi and A. Maleki, "Stress detection using ecg and emg signals: A comprehensive study," *Computer methods and programs in biomedicine*, vol. 193, p. 105482, 2020.

[8] D. Das, S. Datta, T. Bhattacharjee, A. D. Choudhury, and A. Pal, "Eliminating individual bias to improve stress detection from multimodal physiological data," in *2018 40th Annual International Conference of the IEEE Engineering in Medicine and Biology Society (EMBC)*, pp. 5753–5758, IEEE, 2018.

[9] P. Schmidt, A. Reiss, R. Duerichen, C. Marberger, and K. Van Laerhoven, "Introducing wesad, a multimodal dataset for wearable stress and affect detection," in *Proceedings of the 20th ACM international conference on multimodal interaction*, pp. 400–408, 2018.

[10] R. Li and Z. Liu, "Stress detection using deep neural networks," *BMC Medical Informatics and Decision Making*, vol. 20, no. 11, pp. 1–10, 2020.

[11] S. Sriramprakash, V. D. Prasanna, and O. R. Murthy, "Stress detection in working people," *Procedia computer science*, vol. 115, pp. 359–366, 2017.

[12] S. Koldijk, M. Sappelli, S. Verberne, M. A. Neerincx, and W. Kraaij, "The swell knowledge work dataset for stress and user modeling research," in *Proceedings of the 16th international conference on multimodal interaction*, pp. 291–298, 2014.

[13] Y. Shi, M. H. Nguyen, P. Blitz, B. French, S. Fisk, F. De la Torre, A. Smailagic, D. P. Siewiorek, M. al'Absi, E. Ertin, *et al.*, "Personalized stress detection from physiological measurements," in *International symposium on quality of life technology*, pp. 28–29, 2010.

[14] F.-T. Sun, C. Kuo, H.-T. Cheng, S. Buthpitiya, P. Collins, and M. Griss, "Activity-aware mental stress detection using physiological sensors," in *International conference on Mobile computing, applications, and services*, pp. 282–301, Springer, 2010.

[15] N. Keshan, P. Parimi, and I. Bichindaritz, "Machine learning for stress detection from ecg signals in automobile drivers," in *2015 IEEE International conference on big data (Big Data)*, pp. 2661–2669, IEEE, 2015.

[16] J. A. Healey and R. W. Picard, "Detecting stress during real-world driving tasks using physiological sensors," *IEEE Transactions on intelligent transportation systems*, vol. 6, no. 2, pp. 156–166, 2005.

[17] R. K. Nath, H. Thapliyal, and A. Caban-Holt, "Machine learning based stress monitoring in older adults using wearable sensors and cortisol as stress biomarker," *Journal of Signal Processing Systems*, vol. 94, no. 6, pp. 513–525, 2022.

[18] R. Nawaz, J. T. Ng, H. Nisar, and Y. V. Voon, "Can background music help to relieve stress? an eeg analysis," in *2019 IEEE International Conference on Signal and Image Processing Applications (ICSIPA)*, pp. 68–72, IEEE, 2019.

[19] M. Tanida, M. Katsuyama, and K. Sakatani, "Relation between mental stress-induced prefrontal cortex activity and skin conditions: a near-infrared spectroscopy study," *Brain research*, vol. 1184, pp. 210–216, 2007.

[20] R. Champseix, "hrv-analysis 1.0.4." https://pypi.org/project/hrv-analysis/, 2021. [Online; accessed 19-September-2022].

[21] D. Makowski, T. Pham, Z. J. Lau, J. C. Brammer, F. Lespinasse, H. Pham, C. Schölzel, and S. Chen, "Neurokit2: A python toolbox for neurophysiological signal processing," *Behavior research methods*, vol. 53, no. 4, pp. 1689–1696, 2021.

# Fruiting Mother-Shoot Counting System Based On Segmented Images

Zhao RuoQi, Megumi Wakao, Naoki Morita
School of Information and Telecommunication Engineering
Tokai University
Tokyo, Japan
E-mail: 0mjnm002@mail.u-tokai.ac.jp, 9bjt2103@cc.u-tokai.ac.jp, morita@tokai.ac.jp

Kenta Morita
Faculty of Medical Engineering
Suzuka University of Medical Science
Mie, Japan
E-mail: morita@suzuka-u.ac.jp

***Abstract*—To grow sweet grapes, it is important to be able to count the number of fruiting mother shoots accurately. In a previous study, segmentation of aerial photographs containing fruiting mother shoots and branches was conducted to count the number of fruiting mother shoots. However, counts were inaccurate for areas where fruiting mother shoots were incorrectly segmented into branches. In this study, a fan-shaped search method was proposed to correctly count shoots that could not be properly counted in that previous study. Experiments confirmed the effectiveness of the newly proposed method.**

***Keywords-Smart Agriculture; Artificial Intelligence; Image Processing.***

## I. INTRODUCTION

To grow sweet grapes, it is vital to be able to determine the number of fruiting mother shoots properly. Most vineyards in Japan have adopted shelf cultivation, and farmers can only see a small area when they are working in the vineyard. However, aerial photography has made it possible to check the branching over a wide area [1]. Figure 1 shows an example of such an aerial photograph. The red outlined areas in Figure 1 represent the fruiting mother shoots extending from the upper left branch, which is outlined in blue.

Ito et al. [2] marked branch in red, fruiting mother shoot in yellow, and the rest in gray to produce teacher data for training SegNet [3] network. Thus, a neural network system was developed to separate branches from fruiting mother shoots in aerial photographs. Finally, they try to determine the number of fruiting mother shoots by counting the yellow region in the image.

Figure 2 shows the analysis results from the same aerial photograph shown in Figure 1 using the method proposed by Ito et al. From Figure 2, we can instantly see that the upper left branch has seven fruiting mother shoots growing from it.

The branches and the fruiting mother shoots in the aerial images used for testing in the first study were in the best ideal condition, with the fruiting mother shoot not being obscured by the branch. As a result, the fruiting mother shoot in the aerial image is also depicted in the recognition image as a single fruiting mother shoot, without any division. Therefore, there is no error when counting the yellow areas in the recognition image to determine the number of fruiting mother shoots. However, not all of the branches in the aerial image are actually in the best possible condition with respect to the fruiting mother shoot. One fruiting mother shot is counted as more than one in the calculation of the number of fruiting mother shoots if the fruiting mother shoot breaks during the recognition process for a variety of reasons, which results in an error. Ito et al. and others have failed to offer a workable answer to this issue.

In order to lessen the inaccuracies that can occur while counting the number of fruiting mother shoots, the purpose of this research is to propose a method for correct the divided fruiting mother shoots. Specifically, the following methods are used. First, the system automatically selects the areas that need to be corrected and the areas that do not need to be corrected. Then, it considers only the areas that need to be corrected as one area. Finally, it counts the number of fruiting mother shoots.

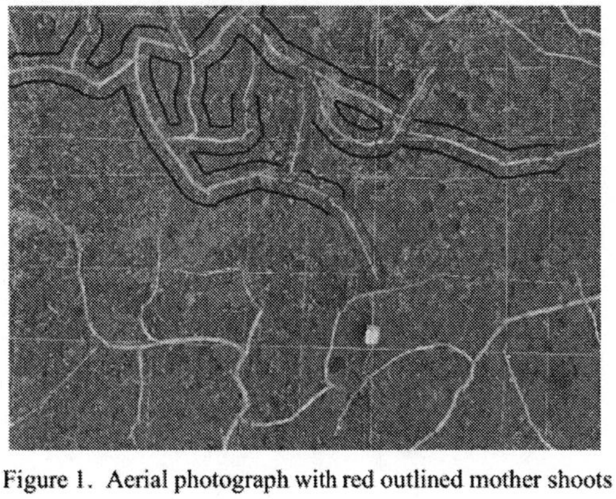

Figure 1. Aerial photograph with red outlined mother shoots

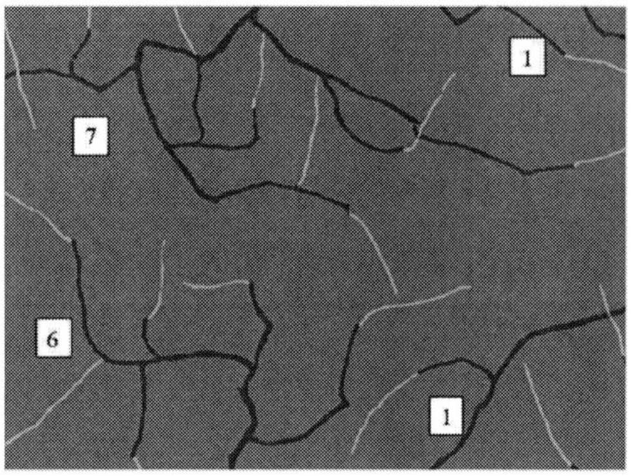


Figure 2. Segmentation analysis results

In Section 2, we will concentrate on the challenges in tackling this problem.

## II. Problem

In Section 1 we indicated that the output of SegNet occasionally contains incorrectly recognized areas. This error may cause the fruiting mother branch to divide, which could result in inaccurate count of its number.

Figure 3 shows another example of an aerial photograph, and Figure 4 shows a misidentification corresponding to the blue box in Figure 3. In the aerial photograph, there is only one fruiting mother shoot, but because it is partially misidentified as branch instead of a single fruiting mother shoot, there is a small division, and two fruiting mother shoots are counted. This problem, which was not addressed in the study by Ito et al., results in an incorrect final count when the number of fruiting mother shoots is aggregated.

The pixel range at the division in Figure 4 is 65px, and the area within this range is calculated to correct the figure. Figure 5 shows other errors generated when correcting Figure 4. The correction range can be adjusted, and the blue outline shown in the Figure 5 is the correction area formed when the correction range is 65px. If the area of the fruiting mother shoots in the correction area is corrected to one area, the number of fruiting mother shoots, which should be counted as two, will instead be counted as one. Therefore, the number of fruiting mother shoots cannot be calculated correctly only by adjusting this pixel range.

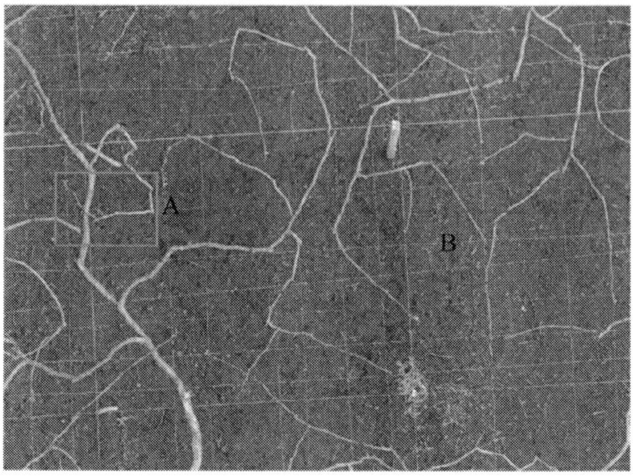


Figure 3. Aerial photography example

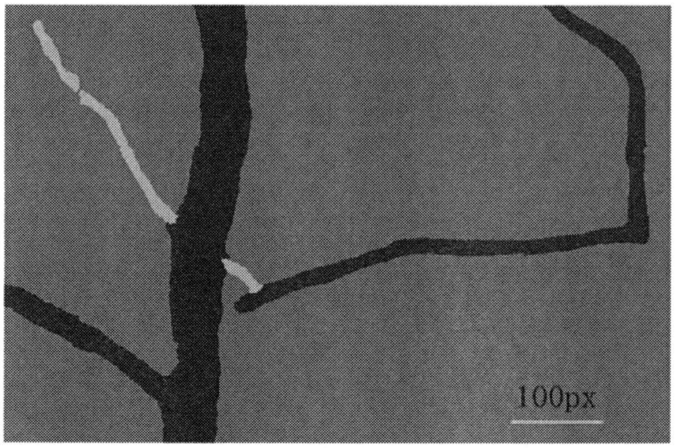


Figure 4. Divided single shoot counted as two

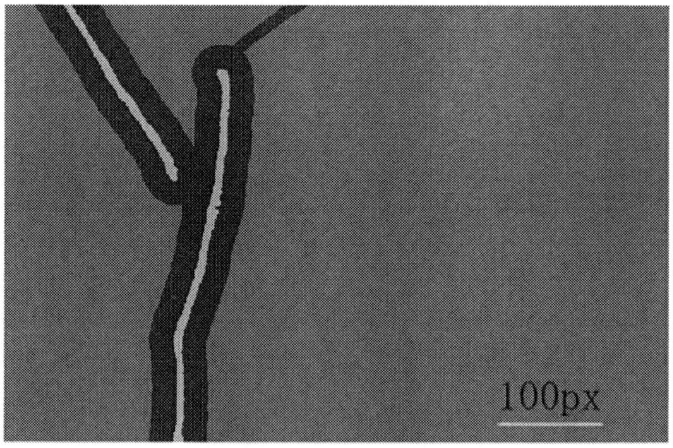


Figure 5. Falsely corrected shoot

In Section 3 we explain how we used a fan-shaped search to overcome this issue.

## III. Proposed Method

The unique approach we have suggested for correcting a divided fruiting mother shoot in a recognition image will be the main topic of this section. We reviewed the data and found that there is no relevant correction method for the recognition images of branches. As a result, we had to change how we were thinking to address this brand-new subject.

The fruiting mother shoots has characteristics of grow as straight as possible [4]. Therefore, if there are two close fruiting mother shoots in the recognition image, when they are connected start for end, the whole fruiting mother shoot tend to be straight, or slightly curved to a certain extent. In that case, we can judge that these two fruiting mother shoots belong to the same divided single shoot.

If we ignore the width of fruiting mother shoot and take it as a line, then the problem can be reduced to the correct of straight line. Studies on line correct, such as fingerprint correct [5][6] and object contour correct [7], all have examples to analyze the vector and curvature at both ends of the broken part of line. Both vector and curvature are correlated to angles and directions. Therefore, for the correct in our study, we thought it would be a good idea to introduce angles and directions.

If we use the fan-shaped area to control the distance and angle of search, at the same time simulate the extension line at both ends of fruiting mother shoot along the extension direction to fix the direction of fan-shaped area. For example, as shown in Figure 6 and Figure 7, a fan-shaped search area is made at both ends of each fruiting mother shoot, through which the parts that need to be corrected can be found. The part that requires to be corrected in Figure 6 is between points B and C. We stipulate that if two endpoints appear in each other's fan-shaped area, the area between these two points shall be judged as the part that needs to be corrected.

Points C and D exist in the fan shape formed by point B in Figure 5. Point B exists in the fan shape formed by point C. Therefore, since points B and C are within each other's fan shape, the divided part will be corrected by connecting points B and C. Points A and D in Figure 5, points E and F in Figure 6 do not meet the judgment criteria, so these points will not be connected. Figure 8 and Figure 9 show the correct results after judging Figure 4 and Figure 5, respectively.

The process involved in the fan-shaped search method is described below.

(1) Find the two endpoints of a fruiting mother shoot.

(2) Make an extension line for each endpoint.

(3) Plot a fan-shaped area at the specified angle and radius using the extension line as the base.

(4) Search for other endpoints within each fan-shaped region.

(5) When the two endpoints are within each other's fan shape, connect only the single endpoint closest to the search target.

Through the fan-shaped search area, the divided fruiting mother shoots can be screened and corrected correctly.

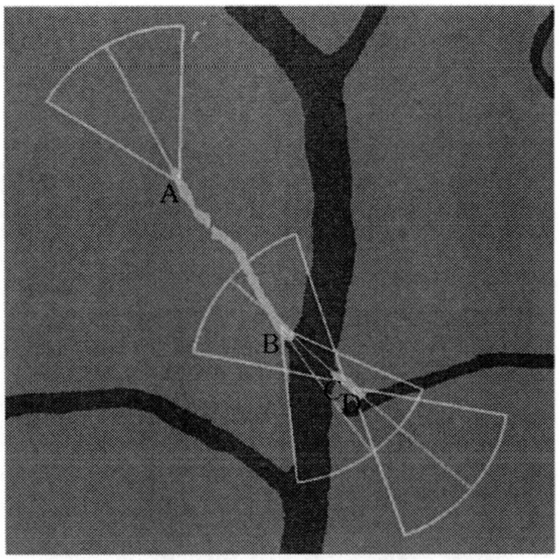


Figure 6. Fan-shaped area of A

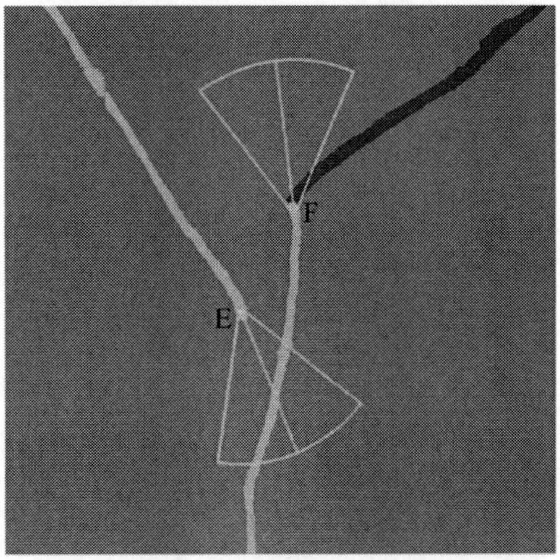


Figure 7. Fan-shaped area of B

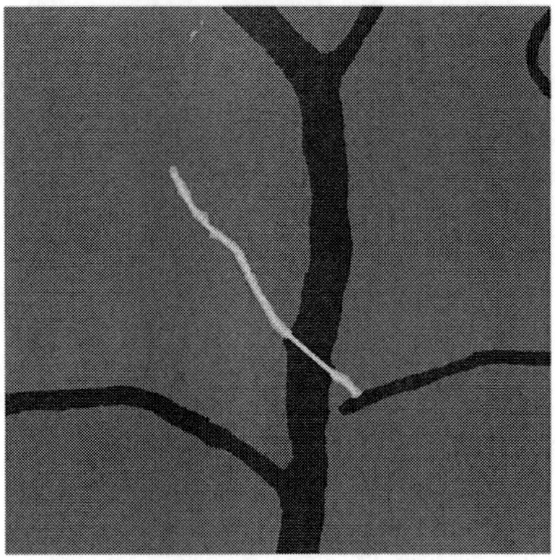

Figure 8. Correction result for A

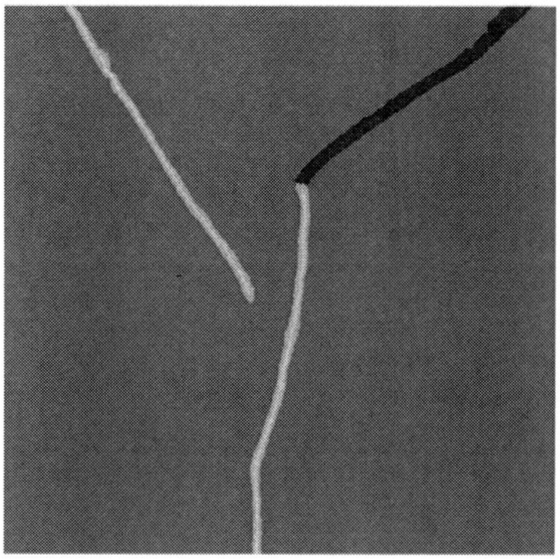

Figure 9. Correction result for B

We have created a comparative experiment for Section 4 to help further demonstrate the validity of the approach.

## IV. EXPERIMENT

In this section, to verify the effectiveness of the proposed method, we compared the number of fruiting mother shoots counted by the method that corrects only by pixel range, and that by our method.

The images used for comparison were 12 vineyard aerial photographs in which there are fruiting mother shoots divided by branches. The correct number of fruiting mother shoots in the 12 images is 285. There are 57 fruiting mother shoots that need to be corrected.

Any of the fruiting mother shoots in aerial photograph can be counted correctly in recognition image within the following two conditions:

1. There is no single shoot being counted as two or more due to divided problem.
2. There are no multiple fruiting mother shoots being counted as one because of the error correct with other fruiting mother shoots.

The fruiting mother shoots that are counted correctly should contain those that can be counted correctly without correct and that can be counted correctly after correct. But the fruiting mother shoots with error correct should be excluded. Therefore, the accuracy of fruiting mother shoots that are counted correctly can be expressed by formula (1).

$$\text{Accuracy} = \frac{228 + \text{Number of Corrected} - \text{Number of False Corrected}}{285} \quad (1)$$

In the 12 images, the minimum range that needs to be corrected is 62px, and the maximum range is 173px. The minimum fan-shaped angle that needs to be corrected is 14°, and the maximum is 52°. For this reason, in this study, the radius threshold is set every 50px from 50px to 200px, and the angle is set every 20° from 20° to 60° for comparison.

Table 1 summarizes the results using the method of correcting only by pixel range, and Table 2 gives the results using the proposed method. The numbers in the upper line of each row are the numbers of fruiting mother shoots that were successfully corrected. The numbers in parentheses are shoots that were corrected erroneously. The lower line in each row shows the accuracy.

TABLE I. RESULTS CORRECTING ONLY BY PIXEL RANGE

| 200px | 150px | 100px | 50px |
|---|---|---|---|
| 57(53)<br>81.4% | 55(18)<br>93.0% | 52(14)<br>93.3% | 0(0)<br>80.0% |

TABLE II. RESULTS USING PROPOSED METHOD

| | 200px | 150px | 100px | 50px |
|---|---|---|---|---|
| 60° | 57(2)<br>99.3% | 55(2)<br>98.6% | 52(0)<br>98.2% | 0(0)<br>80.0% |
| 40° | 55(2)<br>98.6% | 53(2)<br>97.9% | 50(0)<br>97.5% | 0(0)<br>80.0% |
| 20° | 49(2)<br>96.5% | 47(2)<br>95.8% | 44(0)<br>95.4% | 0(0)<br>80.0% |

For images in which the fruiting mother shoot is divided by branches, the method that corrects only by pixel range has a highest accuracy of 93.3% for a range of 100px. In the proposed method, when the radius is 200px and the angle is 60°, it a highest accuracy of 99.3% is achieved. This is a 6.0% improvement over the method using only the pixel range.

The experimental results demonstrate that, using the method that depends only on the pixel range, the accuracy decreases as the range increases because erroneous correction occurs. In the fan-shaped search method, the correction effect can be improved by extending the radius, and at the same time, erroneous corrections can be better avoided. Therefore, it is possible to improve the estimation accuracy of the number of fruiting mother shoots that are correctly counted.

## V. CONCLUSION

In this study, we proposed a fan-shaped search method that is effective for aerial photographs where a fruiting mother shoot is divided by branches, resulting in a more accurate count of the number of fruiting mother shoots. Not only can the pruning efficiency of fruiting mother shoots be improved by quickly and accurately mastering the number of fruiting mother shoots, but also it is possible to accurately predict grape yield.

All images in the experiments used to investigate the effectiveness of the fan-shaped search method were taken for only one part of a single farm. In the future, we would like to make a panoramic image from the partial images of vineyards and correct the number of fruiting mother shoots in entire vineyards for accurate aggregation.

The research breakthrough takes the grape-growing process one step further towards full automation.

## REFERENCES

[1] https://www.cupidfarm.co.jp/ [retrieved: February, 2023]

[2] Funa Ito, Duke Maeda, Naoki Nakamura, Kenta Morita, Naoki Morita,:"Shoot Counting System Based on SegNet",eKNOW 2020:The Twelfth International Conference on Information, Process, and Knowledge Management. [retrieved: February, 2023]

[3] V. Badrinarayanan, A. Kendall, R. Cipolla,:"SegNet :A Deep Convolutional Encoder- Decoder Architecture for Image Segmentation.", IEEE trans. on PAMI, vol. 39, pp. 2481-2495, 2017. [retrieved: February, 2023]

[4] https://www.pref.shimane.lg.jp/nogyogijutsu/gijutsu/budou-sisin/4_2.html [retrieved: February, 2023]

[5] L. C. Jian, U. Halici, I. Hayashi, S. B. Lee,:"Intelligent biometric techniques in fingerprint and face recognition[M]." Boca Raton: CRC Press, October 1999. [retrieved: February, 2023]

[6] CHEN Pei-hua, CHEN Xiao-guang,:"A new approach to healing the broken lines in the thinned fingerprint image.", CNKI: Vol. 25, No. 6, June 2004. [retrieved: February, 2023]

[7] ZHANG Gui-mei, LIU Pi-yu,:"Gestalt psychology and Euler spiral for contour completion.", CNKI: Vol. 30, No. 8, Aug. 2013. [retrieved: February, 2023]

# Requirements for Piano Lesson Support System

Developing "Piano Lesson Whole Visualization System"

Naoki Morita
School of Information Telecommunication Engineering
Tokai University
Tokyo, Japan
e-mail: morita@tokai.ac.jp

Chiharu Nakanishi, Chiaki Sawada
Kunitachi College of Music
Tokyo, Japan
e-mail: {nakanishi.chiharu, sawada.chiaki}@kunitachi.ac.jp

Kenta Morita
Faculty of Medical Engineering
Suzuka University of Medical Science
Mie, Japan
e-mail: morita@suzuka-u.ac.jp

Kazue Kawai
Miyagi University
Miyagi, Japan
e-mail: kawaik@myu.ac.jp

***Abstract*—The authors aim to pass on the tradition of classical music to the next generation by greatly reforming and evolving the traditional pedagogy of piano education using Information and Communication Technology. Specifically, we aim to shift the paradigm from conventional subjective performance learning that rely on sensitivity and memory of lessons to objective, independent and autonomous performance learning through the sharing of objective performance video data. This presentation is a part of research of the "Whole Visualization of Piano Lesson." This presentation reports on the necessary functions of the system and its implementation method, based on a questionnaire survey conducted to investigate current needs in preparation for the development of the "Piano Lesson Whole Visualization System."**

***Keywords- piano; support; system; visualization; connections.***

## I. INTRODUCTION

This report is part of a study being conducted at a music college in Japan to pass on the classical piano tradition to the next generation. The Ideas, Connections, and Extensions model (ICE model) [1] is a framework that describes phases of learning. In the ICE model for piano, there is the Ideas phase in which students play the score with rhythmic and percussive accuracy, the Connections phase in which the learning elements of Ideas are applied to music with expression, empathy, and technical connections, and the Extensions phase in which the music resonates with the audience. With regard to these ICE models, previous studies of piano lesson in Japan [2]-[18] have focused on the Ideas phase for beginners using electronic keyboards. In these studies, the goal is for students to be able to read music and hit the keyboard in a precise rhythm without mistakes. This study will focus on piano lessons during the Connections phase.

The purpose of this study is to summarize the requirements for a piano lesson support system in the Connections phase and how to achieve them. Specifically, we will analyze the problems in looking back at the lesson video archive. Then, we will examine what kind of support or functionality can be realized to make the most of the lessons, enhance students' awareness, and link this to their improvement in piano playing.

The rest of this paper is organized as follows. Section II describes the flow of piano lessons in the Connections phase. In Section III, we conduct a survey on looking back piano lesson videos, and in Section IV, we present two key points for looking back piano lesson videos necessary for the development of the "Piano Lesson Whole Visualization System" and Section V provides our conclusions.

## II. PIANO LESSON

In the Connections phase of the ICE model, expressiveness, empathy, and technical connections are important. The goal is for students to immerse themselves in the music and acquire the technical (physical) and sensory skills to perform a certain piece of music as they wish, even under pressure, in a practical exam, competition, or other performance.

The lessons leading up to a concert, competition, or other performance are given once a week for three to four months, as a standard practice.

### *A. Before the lesson begins: Preparation*

Student: A student (1) reads score, (2) researches the piece, (3) listens to recordings by performers for reference, etc., and practices and studies on his /her own to get the piece in shape for the day of the lesson.

### *B. Every Lesson (beginning)*

Student: The student performs through a piece of music.

Instructor: The instructor gives a critique (guide) of the student's performance. The instructor will discuss any musical or technical problems the student may have, and will give the student the necessary tasks to complete the performance. The instructor will share the image of the piece with the student by mentioning the background of the piece, episodes, traditional (common) performance techniques, etc.

Student: After listening to the instructor's critique (guide), the student understands the task at hand. The student writes down the assignment in the score (the student is encouraged to memorize the critique heard from the instructor, not during the lesson, and to make a summary note after the end of the lesson). The student should also communicate to the instructor any problems or questions that emerge from the independent practice, and exchange opinions.

### C. *During the lesson*

Instructor: The instructor asks the student to resume playing, stopping the performance at various points, and instructing the student to improve on the issues pointed out in B.

Student: The student immediately improves on the instructor's tasks based on the instructor's instructions. If the student cannot do so on the spot, the student shall make it an assignment until the next lesson.

### D. *Review at home*

Student: At home, the student should try to overcome the tasks given by an instructor, relying on the experience and memory of the lesson and the writing on the sheet music, and connect them to the next week.

## III. Questionnaire Survey

Between April and May 2022, a survey on video review of performances was conducted on Google Forms [19]-[21]. The subjects were 20 piano instructors and 24 students at a music college, with 10 and 9 questions, respectively.

There are four main things that can be said from the instructors' and students' questionnaires.

1. Not a few of the students record their lessons. However, students rarely review all of their previously recorded lesson videos. Students do not have the time or motivation to watch a long lesson recording from beginning to end.
2. Students are dissatisfied with the content of the videos when they watch them. e.g. "I can't see how I touch the keyboard." "I can't see my own face and tone."
3. Students were dissatisfied with the video viewing. e.g. "It takes too much time to find the video I want to watch from the video archive," "It is difficult to pinpoint the part I am interested in," "It is difficult to go back in time to watch."
4. Students and instructors are dissatisfied with the device itself and the application when handling the device. e.g. "It is complicated to connect," "I don't know how to operate the application."

## IV. Requirements For The System

Based on the analysis of the needs of the questionnaires, the following two things are required to the system.

(1) The system can instantly locate and view the part of the performance that the student wants to see.
(2) The system can instantly locate videos of certain parts of the lesson at different recording times.

The "Piano Lesson Whole Visualization System" which we are developing this time, can be used to connect a score and video will locate:

(1) a certain part of the lesson.
(2) a certain part of the lesson at a different time for comparison of previous performance and current one.

The connection between the score and the video is made by comparing and associating the scale recognized from the score and the pitch recognized from the video. This allows the user to click on a section of the target score to bring up the playback position of the video. Furthermore, the score and the video taken at that time are automatically associated with the calendar with the date and time of the practice. This makes it easy to select videos for comparing one's own previous and current performances, or for comparing one's own performance with an instructor's model performance. For students comparing previous and current performances will be a great opportunity to improve their piano.

## V. Conclusion

The purpose of this study is to summarize the requirements for a piano lesson support system in the Connections phase and how to achieve them. Specifically, we will analyze the problems in looking back at the lesson video archive. Then, we will examine what kind of support or functionality can be realized to make the most of the lessons, enhance students' awareness, and link this to their improvement in piano playing.

## Acknowledgment

This work was supported by the Japan Society for the Promotion of Science (JSPS) KAKENHI Grant Number 21K18528.

## References

[1] F. S. Young, and R. J. Wilson, *Assessment and learning: The ICE approach.* Winnipeg, MB: Portage and Main Press., 2000.

[2] C. Oshima, K. Nishimoto, and M. Suzuki, "A Piano Duo Performance Support System to Motivate Children's Practice at Home," IPSJ Journal, Vol. 46, No. 1, pp.157-171, 2005.

[3] K. Nakahira, M. Akabane and Y. Hukami, "Faculty Development for Playing and Singing Education with Blended Learning," Japan Society for Educational Technology, Vol.34, pp.45-48, 2010.

[4] Y. Yokoyama and K. Nishimoto, "A piano practice support system for preventing performance cessation caused by performance errors," IPSJ Interaction, pp.118-127, 2010.

[5] K. Yamada and K. T. Nakahira, "Development of Training Support System for Learners to Acquire Piano Rudimental Techniques," Proceedings of the 73th National Convention of IPSJ, Vol.2, pp.303-304, 2011.

[6] E. Nakamura, H. Takeda, R. Yamamoto, S. Sako, and S Sagayam Proceedings of the 81th National Convention of IPSJ, Vol.2, pp.337-338, 2019.a, "Score Following Handling Performances with Arbitrary Repeats and Skips and Automatic Accompaniment," IPSJ Journal, Vol. 54, No. 4, pp.1338-1349, 2013.

[7] Y. Takegawa, T. Terada, and M. Tsukamoto, "Design and Implementation of a Piano Learning Support System Considering Rhythm Learning," IPSJ Journal, Vol. 54, No. 4, pp.1383-1392, 2013.

[8] H. Kato, N. Emura and M. Miura, "Support system for practicing piano-scale performances," Acoustical Society of Japan, Vol.70, No.6, pp.273-276, 2014.

[9] F. Yuto, T. Yoshinari and Y. Hidekatsu, "Design and Implementation of a Piano Learning Support System Considering Motivation," IPSJ Interaction, pp.118-127, 2015.

[10] K. Yamada, K. Yamamoto and T. Noma, "A Piano Learning System with Visual Correspondence Between Musical Scale and Keyboard," IPSJ EC, pp.378-385, 2015.

[11] K. Ueda, Y. Takegawa, and K. Hirata, "Design and Implementation of a Piano Learning Support System Focusing on Visualization of Keying Information and Annotation," IPSJ Journal, Vol. 57, No. 12, pp.2617-2025, 2016.

[12] Y. Takegawa, K. Hirata, E. Tayanagi, and M. Tsubakimoto, "Evaluation Analysis of a Piano Learning Aupport System Fpcusing on the Learning Process," IPSJ Journal, Vol. 58, No. 5, pp.1093-1100, 2017.

[13] T. Ishigami and T. Hamamoto, "A Piano Practice Support System Visualizing Correspondence Between Music Scores and Key Positions," ITE Technical Report, Vol.41, No.14, pp.71-76, 2017.

[14] A. Shimada, H. Matsumura, Y. Morijiri and T. Kitahara, "A Prototype of Musical Score Display System for Piano Practice Support," Proceedings of the 79th National Convention of IPSJ, Vol.2, pp.105-106, 2017.

[15] N. Takaya, S. Nakahira and M. Kitajima, "Analysis of the relationships between the proficiency levels of piano playing and the changes in visual behaviors while reading score and performing piano," IPSJ SIG Technical Report, pp.1-7, 2017.

[16] T. Suzuki, K. Tanaka, R. Ogura and Y. Tsuji, "Practice of Beginners' Piano Skill Training Support Using 'Visualization System for Piano Performance (VSPP)'," IPSJ SIG Technical Report, Vol.2018-MUS-119 No.16, pp.1-6, 2018.

[17] M. Hori, C. M. Wilk and S. Sagayama, "Visualizing deviations form examplary performances for piano practice assistance (including retry detection)," Proceedings of the 81th National Convention of IPSJ, Vol.2, pp.337-338, 2019.

[18] R. Matsui, A. Hasegawa, Y. Takegawa, K. Hirata and Y. Yanagawa, "Design, Implementation and Assessment of a Support System to Find Bad Fingering Habits for Piano Teachers," IPSJ Journal, Vol. 61, No. 4, pp.789-797, 2020.

[19] Questionnaires for instructors. [Online]. Available from: https://forms.gle/PNBTPsgxQ1VoDDTJA 2023.02.01

[20] Questionnaires for students. [Online]. Available from: https://docs.google.com/forms/u/1/d/10p3-Azsv4wMQ22FymDGnGFmDdhvB-1sozlPjRsgVE_Y/edit 2023.02.01

[21] C. Nakanishi, C. Sawada, K.Kawai, K.Morita, and N. Morita, "An Analysis of Needs for Developing a Tool for Piano Learning," Proceedings of the 2022th National Convention of Society for Educational Technology, pp.35-36, 2022.

# Development of a Score Click Playback System

Motoya Wakiyama, Megumi Wakao, Naoki Morita
School of Information Telecommunication Engineering
Tokai University
Tokyo, Japan
e-mail: {9bjt2116@cc, 9bjt2103@cc, wv062303@tsc}.
u-tokai.ac.jp

Chiharu Nakanishi, Chiaki Sawada
Faculty of Music Studies
Kunitachi College of Music
Tokyo, Japan
e-mail: {nakanishi.chiharu, sawada.chiaki}@kunitachi.ac.jp

Kazue Kawai
Miyagi University
Miyagi, Japan
e-mail: kawaik@myu.ac.jp

Kenta Morita
Faculty of Medical Engineering
Suzuka University of Medical Science
Mie, Japan
e-mail: morita@suzuka-u.ac.jp

***Abstract*— In a piano lesson, the instructor returns feedback to the student for each set of measures using a score. In this case, we would like to use a video to facilitate the process of instantly returning feedback to the student. Specifying the playback start position for each section using the seek bar in the video is difficult. In the present study, we propose a method by which to connect a score and a video by analyzing the score and video and comparing sound changes. The effectiveness of the proposed method was verified using scores practiced by beginning piano students.**

***Keywords- Score Analysis; Video Analysis; Piano Lesson; Without Seek Bar***

## I. Introduction

Sound is important in playing music, and knowing how to perceive and perform music is important. In piano playing in particular, tone changes depending on how players use their arms, legs, and body. Therefore, it is important to feedback how to use their arms, legs, and body on video. In such cases, the performance may be feedbacked by means of a video.

Prior research has studied various ways to support piano lessons [1]-[6]. For example, improvement of remote assistance using neural networks and multiple angles [7] and bad habits developed when using multiple cameras [8]. It is possible to add more information and look back at the way the score was played when the video was recorded. However, it is not possible to instantly project the points that the instructor wants to point out.

In a piano lesson, the instructor returns a feedback to the student using a score. In that case, when using a video for feedback, it is necessary to playback the video from the beginning of each musical section. However, it is difficult to specify the playback position for each passage using the seek bar control.

The purpose of the present study is to support piano lessons using video so that instructors can smoothly return comments to their students. Specifically, we propose a system that enables playback from the corresponding starting point by clicking on a measure in the score. Although some piano lessons involve the repetition of the same section of music, the present study targets videos played through an entire piece of music.

The remainder of the present paper is organized as follows: Section II presents the development system. Section III describes the experiments conducted and presents the results and considerations, and Section IV provides our conclusions.

## II. Development System

The developed system consists of a user interface (UI) module, a score analysis module, and a video analysis module.

In this system, the UI module is first used to upload the score and the video. When a music score is uploaded, the music analysis module extracts the musical scale from the score. When a video is uploaded, the video analysis module extracts the musical scale from the video, and then combines this scale with the musical scale extracted from the score. The video can then be played back from the corresponding time by clicking on a measure in the music score display screen of the UI module. The following sections describe the UI module, score analysis module, and video analysis module.

### *A. User Interface Module*

The UI module provides a screen for uploading scores, a screen for uploading videos, and a screen for displaying scores and playing videos. Figure 1 shows the score display and video playback screens.

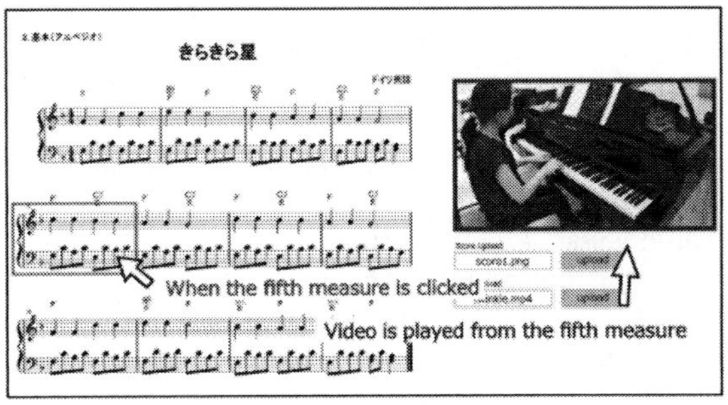


Figure 1. Displaying a score and playing a video.

This screen consists of the music notation screen on the left-hand side and the video screen on the right-hand side. In Figure 1, when the fifth measure is clicked, the video is played from the fifth measure.

### *B. Score Analysis Module*

The score analysis module creates a scale list from an uploaded score, recording measure numbers and scales for each clef. This module identifies clefs, staff, bars, sharp, natural, flat, and note head symbols in the score. This module then finds the relative coordinates of the notehead of each note relative to the staff and detects the scale for each note stem. Sharp and flat symbols are unified as sharps during identification. Figure 2 is a scale list consisting of measure numbers and scales generated when the score in Figure 3 is uploaded.

```
1,F4,F3
1,C4
...
1,C4
2,D5,F3
2,C3
2,D5,A#3
...
```

Figure 2. Scale list.

Figure 3. Scores to be analyzed.

In the present study, we used OpenCV library [9] to identify a number of symbols.

### *C. Video Analysis Module*

The video analysis module creates a time stamp list that records the start time of each measure from the uploaded video. The method for creating a time stamp list is as follows.

First, a constant-Q transformation is performed to generate a list of constant-Q values from the video. The constant-Q transform is a frequency analysis method that works well with pitch, chord, and melody analysis of musical signals [10].

Then, the scale list is read for each line, and the time of the beginning of the playing of each note stem is acquired from the list of constant-Q values. The acquisition condition is when the change in the constant-Q value exceeds a certain threshold value. After obtaining the start playing time of the first note, the time of the second note is searched. If the search process does not find the start playing time within a certain period of time, the next note is searched again. When the measure of the scale list to be searched changes, the measure number and the start time are recorded in the time stamp list. In the present study, we used Librosa library [11] to audio analysis.

## III. Experiments

We confirmed the effectiveness of the proposed system. We conducted an evaluation of the score analysis module and the video analysis module. In this experiment, we prepared performance videos of playing each of the 12 measures of the "Twinkle, Twinkle Little Star" score (the C melody score, the arpeggio score, and the open harmony score) [12]. The evaluation of the score analysis module compares whether the identified scale is correct for each note stem with the score. The evaluation of the video analysis module compares the start time of each measure with the video.

Table I shows the aggregate results of the scale identification for each stem. The C melody score consists of 42 stems of 42 notes. The arpeggio score consists of 94 stems of 140 notes. Finally, the open harmony score consists of 68 stems of 164 notes. Pattern matching with scores resulted in a 100% notehead recognition rate for each of the three score stems.

TABLE I. Results for Identification of Each Stem

| | C Melody | Arpeggio | Open harmony |
|---|---|---|---|
| Detected/Total(stem) | 42/42 | 94/94 | 68/68 |
| Detected/Total(notehead) | (42/42) | (140/140) | (164/164) |
| Stem identification rate | 100% | 100% | 100% |

Table II shows the aggregate results for the match rate on the start time for each measure. The threshold of the constant-Q value for judging the beginning of a note in this experiment was set to 1.00. For the C melody score and arpeggio score, the start time of the video matched for all 12 measures out of 12. However, for the open harmony score, the start times did not match.

TABLE II. Results for Match Rate on the Start Time

| | C Melody | Arpeggio | Open harmony |
|---|---|---|---|
| Detected/Total(measure) | 12/12 | 12/12 | 0/12 |
| Measure match rate | 100% | 100% | 0% |

As a reason, the starting time was either undetectable or could be detected but was actually delayed in each measure. We focused on the constant-Q value to find out why the start time of any measure did not match the open harmony score. Open harmony contains overtone components of certain tones. The beginning of the first measure of the open harmony score is F4, A3, and F2, and the constant-Q value of F2 was 0.078 when F4 was 1.119 and A3 was 1.281. The maximum constant-Q value of F2 was 0.224 and never exceeded 1.00.

Therefore, in the open harmony section, instead of detecting all notes, it was necessary to detect either note as having started playing as being in an overtone relation.

## IV. Conclusion

The purpose of the present study is to make it possible to playback videos from the starting point of each corresponding measure by clicking on the measure. When looking back at the video, it was difficult to specify the playback position for each measure using the seek bar because fine control was required. In the present study, we developed a system that relates the starting point of each measure and the score and the video by analyzing the score and video and comparing the tone changes between the score and the video. As a result of experiments to verify the effectiveness of the system, we confirmed that the proposed method is effective for the C melody score and arpeggio score. On the other hand, through speech analysis of open harmony score, we found that there were cases in which overtone-related notes could not be detected by the fixed-Q transformation.

In the future, we intend to update the proposed system to relate the rise time of a note even when the note is an overtone and to validate the effectiveness of the proposed system using target music at a music academy.

## ACKNOWLEDGMENT

The present study was supported by the Japan Society for the Promotion of Science (JSPS) through KAKENHI Grant Number 21K18528.

## REFERENCES

[1] Y. Takegawa, T. Terada, M. Tsukamoto, "Construction of a Piano Learning Support System considering Rhythm", IPSJ Interaction 2012, March 2012.

[2] Y. Fukuya, K. Takegawa, H. Yanagi , "Design and Implementation of a Piano Learning Support System Considering Motivation", IPSJ Interaction 2015, March 2015.

[3] T. Ishigami, T. Hamamoto, "A Piano Practice Support System Visualizing Correspondence Between Music Scores and Key Positions", ITE Technical Report Vol.41, No14, May 2017.

[4] T. Nagai, K. T. Nakahira, M. Kitajima, "Analysis of the relationships between the proficiency levels of piano playing and the changes in visual behaviors while reading score and performing piano", IPSJ SIG Technical Report, Vol.2017-CE-142 No.20, December 2017.

[5] T. Suzuki, K, Tanaka, R. Ogura, Y. Tsuji, "Practice of Beginners'Piano Skill Training Support Using "Visualization System for Piano performance (VSPP)" ",IPSJ SIG Technical Report, Vol.2018-MUS-119 No.16, Jun 2018.

[6] M. Hori, Christoph M. Wilk, S. Sagayama, "Visualizing deviations from exemplary performances for piano practice assistance (including retry detection)", The 81st National Convention of IPSJ IT-02, March 2019.

[7] R. Matsui, K. Takegawa, K. Hirata, "Design, Implementation and Assessment of a remote piano lesson support system that automatically generates optimal multi-view camera work.". [Online]. Available from: https://ipsj.ixsq.nii.ac.jp/ej/?action=repository_uri&item_id=177639&file_id=1&file_no=1 2023.01.30

[8] R. Matsui, K. Takegawa, K. Hirata, "Design, implementation and Assessment of a Support System to Find Bad Fingering Habits for Piano Teachers", 2020 Information Processing Society of Japan Vol.61 No.4 789-797, April 2020.

[9] Open_CV Library. [Online]. Available from: https://docs.opencv.org/4.7.0/index.html 2023.01.29

[10] Constant-Q Transform (CQT) Description. [Online]. Available from: https://www.wizard-notes.com/entry/music-analysis/constant-q-transform 2023.01.30

[11] Librosa Library. [Online]. Available from: https://librosa.org/doc/latest/index.html 2023.01.29

[12] Score of "Twinkle Twinkle". [Online]. Available from: https://atelier-music.com/sheetmusic/twinkle-twinkle-little-star 2023.01.30

# Compression via Partial Pseudo-Randomization of Convolutional Neural Networks Under High Memory Constraints

Florent Crozet
*STMicroelectronics*
Grenoble, France
email: florent.crozet@st.com

Stéphane Mancini
*Univ. Grenoble Alpes, CNRS, Grenoble INP, TIMA*
Grenoble, France
email: stephane.mancini@univ-grenoble-alpes.fr

Marina Nicolas
*STMicroelectronics*
Grenoble, France
email: marina.nicolas@st.com

***Abstract*—With the proliferation of convolutional neural network (CNN)-based computer vision solutions, computing inference on smart sensors has become a challenge. The inference of CNN is difficult to embed in such tiny devices due to the constraints on memory. To address this challenge, we propose a compression method able to reduce the number of weights to store in a structured way, so that the gain in the number of weights comes with a gain in the number of computations at inference. Our solution is based on the replacement of the convolutional filters by a linear combination of some stored filters and a set of seeds corresponding to pseudo-random generated filters. During the inference, pseudo-random number generators are used to compute the non-stored filters, thanks to the associated seeds. On the other side, the linear combination allows mutualizing partly the cost of convolutions. We show that further exchanging memory for a small logic cost to generate the pseudo random filters allows to decrease the number of weights significantly, on several state-of-the-art networks without sacrificing the accuracy. For example, applying this method to CNNs like ResNet50 leads to a compression factor of 2.5 for less than 5% accuracy drop. Furthermore, our method is compatible with compression methods targeting the precision of the weights to store, namely quantization. This gives room to further increase compression gain on specific implementation platforms.**

***Keywords*—*Convolutional Neural Network compression, pseudo-random number generators***

## I. Introduction

Computer vision applications widely use convolutional neural networks to achieve several vision tasks. The accuracy of Convolutional Neural Network (CNN) drives the development of these applications, but the memory usage is rarely taken into account leading to a difficult deployment on embedded devices.

To improve their performance, CNNs keep increasing the number of weights they use. With ResNet50 [1] and its 25M weights or ConvNeXt-XL [2] and its 350M weights, the goal is to get the best accuracy, but without taking into account any other constraint, such as memory usage. For an embedded device, the memory and the computational resources are the key factors impeding the deployment of state-of-the-art CNNs in IoT devices.

As well as occupying a significant part of circuit die surface, the memory also has a high energy consumption due to the memory accesses. The high number of weights to store to achieve a CNN inference leads to use a device with high memory capabilities. But smart sensors used for computer vision applications are rather tiny, with limited memory capability and power consumption.

To address the problem, different compression algorithms have been proposed. Most methods either reduce the memory requirement by reducing the precision of the weights [3] or by reducing the number of weights [4]. Several methods just compute what is possible to do and the accuracy loss, but do not speak about memory, like unstructured pruning where the goal is just to get a sparse CNN. Sparse neural network compression has the drawback that the decompression of the CNN produces a tensor requiring several operations with many zeros processing convolutions.

In this article, we propose a new compression method for CNNs where some weights are stored in the memory, while the others are generated from stored seeds in a pseudo-random process during the inference. Replacing memory access by on-the-fly generation with pseudo-random generators actually leads to a lower consumption. The identification of the weights to store and the weights to regenerate relies on a dimensionality reduction method, the Principal Component Analysis (PCA). The PCA allows the decomposition of each convolutional tensor in the CNN in a linear combination, with an ordering of vector importance. Most significant vectors are stored while the least significant are pseudo-randomly generated. This compression method comes not only with a memory gain, but also with a gain in hardware logic as the original convolution can be replaced by a double convolution solution.

The article starts with a brief overview of convolutional neural network compression methods and the usage of random weights in neural networks. Then, our compression method with the randomization is described in Section 3. The impact on inference is described in Section 4. The Section 5 discusses the performance obtained when our method is applied to several convolutional neural networks. Finally, the article ends with some perspectives to capitalize further on this new compression method for CNNs.

## II. Related work

Our work is at the intersection of the following two topics: the compression of CNN and the use of random weights in neural networks. CNN compression directly serves our goal as it reduces the memory use. On the second topic, most works focus on evaluating the impact of introducing random weights in CNN with no compression goal.

### A. CNN compression

CNN compression techniques are widely studied through two main approaches: the reduction of the precision of the weights, thanks to quantization, or the reduction of the number of the weights, thanks to pruning or dimensionality reduction. Both approaches aim at reducing the memory usage of CNN, and they can be combined to further increase the compression gain.

*a) Quantization:* This approach focuses on reducing the precision of the weights. As deep learning frameworks work with Floating point on 32 or even 64 bits, this precision of the weights can be reduced to be used on embedded devices. Quantization is a relatively mature topic in CNN compression, whether it is INT quantization [5] or Binary quantization [6]. Our work firstly focuses on reducing the number of parameters before considering quantization.

*b) Pruning:* This approach reduces the number of weights to store by removing less significant weights. The goal is to get a high sparsity percentage in the set of weights. Pruning techniques can be separated into two types: the unstructured pruning [7], that sets weights to zero, and the structured pruning [8], that sets filters to zero. The sparse matrices of weights are then stored, with efficient encoding techniques like Huffman coding [9], and decompressed on the embedded devices to do the inference. Despite high compression results, the pruning remains difficult to embed on tiny devices as the decompression stage requires high specific computational capability. So the memory gain does not come with a logic gain.

*c) Dimensionality reduction:* By finding a new representation of the weights in a lower dimensional space, this approach reduces the number of weights to store. This can be a linear decomposition, such as PCA [10], separable filters [11] or sparse decomposition [12]. Our approach will use the PCA as a part of the compression pipeline.

### B. Neural networks with random weights

The use of random number in convolutional neural networks is reported in two main topics: Extreme Learning Machine (ELM) [13] and random neural networks.

ELM algorithm proposes a learning method where the first layers of neural networks are randomly initialized and fixed, and the last layer is learned with a pseudo-inverse method. The algorithm is applied to neural networks [14] and CNNs [15] [16]. In CNNs, the random weights are introduced in the convolutional layers only. These layers representing the major proportion of the weights, so saving from memory will bring tinier memory. However, as mentioned in [17], the accuracy of the models are significantly degraded when the computer vision task becomes more complex. The use of random weights, for the ELM, is therefore restricted to simple vision tasks. In our application we cannot make assumption about the task complexity.

The neural networks with random weights present better results than ELM on similar tasks. The method differs in the training part, for example in [18] the neural networks is partially trained, after a random initialization of the weights, only some of them are trained. The challenge is to evaluate the proportion of the weights that need to be trained. Another approach described in [19] relies on searching a subnetwork inside an initially over-parameterized and randomly initialized CNN. Most other works focus on Neural Architecture Search (NAS), with the idea of finding the weights that must be trained.

However, these approaches are different from ours as we do not start with a from-scratch CNN. Our method capitalizes on the information present in the trained CNN. Despite this, the use of random weights for compression purpose becomes an interesting option as such pseudo-random weights can be generated from the seeds.

## III. Randomization method

To compress CNNs, our method replaces the filters' tensor of each convolutional layer with a set of principal filters, a set of coefficients and a set of seeds. This process allows saving memory as the seeds are used to generate pseudo-random filters at the inference. To compute these elements, the filters' tensor is processed in three steps. The first step decomposes the tensor in a linear combination made of the principal basis and a set of coordinates in this basis with a PCA and an energy threshold processes. Secondly, the pseudo-randomization step replaces a part of the vectors of the principal basis by pseudo-random vectors and their associated seeds. The pseudo-random vectors are chosen, so they do not degrade the accuracy of the CNN significantly. Lastly, the set of coordinates is retrained in order to recover accuracy.

### A. General Notations

Starting from a learned CNN, each convolutional layer can be described with the following notations:

- **T**: The tensor of the convolutional layer of dimensions $(kernel_h, kernel_w, c_{in}, c_{out})$.
- **W**: The matrix of the convolutional weights, where each column represents a flattened filter of dimensions $(kernel_h * kernel_w * c_{in})$. The matrix is composed of $c_{out}$ columns.

The method introduces the filter decomposition in several vector subspaces. In order to reduce the number of notations, each vector subspace is associated to its basis. To differentiate each basis, we use the following notations:

- $B_{PCA}$: The basis produced by the PCA step. $B_{PCA} = \{b_1, ..., b_{c_{out}}\}$, such that $rank(B_{PCA}) = c_{out}$. The $b_i$, with $i \in \{1, ..., c_{out}\}$, corresponds to the eigenvectors arranged in decreasing order of importance.

- $B_T$: The basis produced after the energy thresholding step. $B_T = \{b_1, ..., b_t\}$, such that $rank(B_T) = t$ with $t \leq c_{out}$.
- $B_E$: The basis of the $e$ first eigenvectors of $B_T$ that will be stored. So $B_E = \{b_1, ..., b_e\}$ with $e \leq t$.
- $B_R$: The basis of the pseudo-random vectors $\{r_1, ..., r_g\}$. Each $r_i$ is generated from the seed $s_i$, such that $Seeds = \{s_1, ..., s_g\}$.
- $B_S$:The basis composed of $B_E$ and $B_R$ corresponding to an approximation of the vector subspace $B_T$.

To represent the weights in the different bases defined previously, we use the following notations:

- $C_{PCA}$: The coordinates of the weights $W$ in $B_{PCA}$.
- $C_T$: The coordinates of the weights $W$ in $B_T$.
- $C_S$: The coordinates of the weights $W$ in $B_S$.
- $C_{SL}$: The new representation of the weights $W$ in $B_S$ once the retraining step is done.

The following methods will be used for the pseudocode of the algorithm:

- *ToMatrix(T)*: Method to transform the tensor T in the matrix W.
- *ZeroCenter(W)*: Method for zero-centering the matrix W.
- *PCA(M, $E_{threshold}$)*: Method to compute the PCA of the matrix W followed by pruning the eigenvector below the energy threshold $E_{threshold}$.
- *RandOrtho()*: Method to iteratively build the random basis $B_R$.

*B. Method overview*

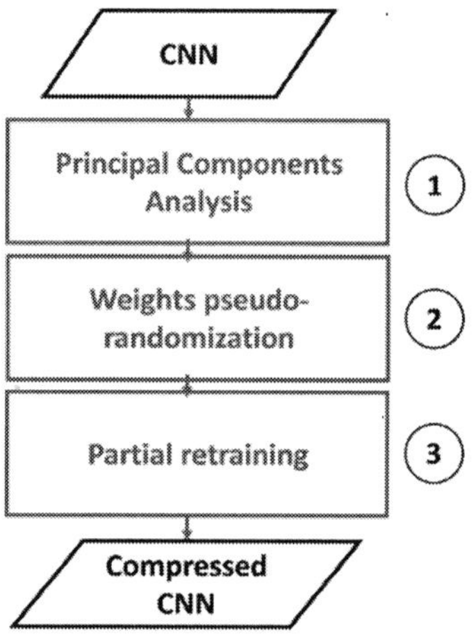


Figure 1. Compression method flow, the CNN passes through the three steps: PCA, pseudo-randomization of weights and partial retraining to be compressed.

The method, described in Figure 1, compresses each convolutional layer of a CNNs one after the other. The goal of the compression algorithm described in Algorithm 1 is to approximate the vector subspace $B_T$ by finding another vector subspace, $B_S$, defined by the concatenation of filters from $B_E$ and pseudo-random filters from $B_R$. By replacing eigenvectors of $B_T$ by pseudo-random vectors, we want to get a maximum overlap, such that:

**for** ConvLayer in Model **do**
  $T \leftarrow GetWeights(ConvLayer)$
  $W \leftarrow ToMatrix(T)$
  $W_c \leftarrow ZeroCenter(W)$
  $B_T, C_T \leftarrow PCA(W_c, E_{Threshold})$
  $B_E \leftarrow KeepFirstEigenvectors(B_T)$
  $B_R, Seeds \leftarrow RandOrtho()$
  $Model \leftarrow SetNewWeights(B_E, B_R, C_S)$
**end for**
$B_E, B_R, C_{SL} \leftarrow ReTrainCoef(B_E, B_R, C_S)$
**for** ConvLayer in Model **do**
  $Save(B_S, Seeds, C_{SL})$
**end for**

Figure 2. Algorithm for the replacement of eigenvectors by random filters.

$$B_R = \arg\max B_T \cap B_S \tag{1}$$

Starting from a trained CNN, a principal component analysis and an energy threshold are done in step ① to get an efficient representation of the weights, with the basis $B_T$. Then step ② replaces some filters in $B_T$ by pseudo-random filters in $B_R$ to further reduce the weights to store. The retraining step ③ corrects the coordinates $C_S$ to reduce the error. Finally, three elements are stored:

- A subset of PCA basis: $B_S$
- The $Seeds$ to generate the pseudo-random filters
- The new representation of the weights in $B_S$: $C_{SL}$

*C. PCA and energy threshold*

The first step performs the PCA linear decomposition and energy thresholding of $W$ to get a lower dimensionality representation of the weights. As in [10], the idea is to store the PCA linear decomposition of the weight matrix $W$ to save memory.

The linear decomposition is obtained by the principal component analysis:

$$W = C_{PCA} B_{PCA}^T + \mu \tag{2}$$

With $C_{PCA}$ being the coordinates of the weights $W$ in the basis $B_{PCA}$ and $\mu$ the means of $W$.

Once the eigenvectors are computed, we can lighten the linear combination by performing an energy thresholding step with a threshold $E_{threshold}$. Only the eigenvectors of energy below the threshold $E_{threshold}$ are kept, the others are pruned. The threshold is chosen according to the defined accuracy/performance trade-off. As the goal is to embed state-of-the-art CNNs, we will not keep a high energy threshold value, such as 99%, but use a lower one, such as 70%, to get a more aggressive memory reduction while preserving a good accuracy. $B_T$ is built with the kept eigenvectors, and we define an approximation of $W$, $\tilde{W}$, such that:

$$\tilde{W} = C_T.B_T^T + \mu \tag{3}$$

where $B_T$ a subset of the eigenvectors of $W$ and $C_T$ the coordinates of $W$ in $B_T$.

Memory is saved since the size of $C_T$ and $B_T$ are lower than the size of $W$.

### D. Pseudo-randomization of the basis $B_T$

The purpose of the second step is to replace some filters of $B_T$ with pseudo-random filters in order to further alleviate the storage of the CNN weights, as a part of the filters will be replaced by their corresponding seeds. To address this, pseudo-random filters are chosen in order to build a vector subspace close to the original one, as described in the next paragraphs. The approximated vector subspace $\tilde{W}$ is built by concatenating the selected pseudo-random vectors and $B_E$. The set of pseudo-random filters $B_R$ will be generated at each inference from the stored seeds.

As the CNN performance will depend on the number of randomized basis filters, there is a trade-off between the number of filters from $B_T$ and pseudo-random generated ones. An arbitrary number $e$ of $B_T$ filters are kept to build $B_E$. Additional to these filters, $g$ filters are randomly generated to build $B_R$. In order to ensure the generated filters span $B_T$, to preserve dimensionality and remove redundancy, the basis $B_S$ must verify the following rules:

$$B_T \cap B_S \neq \{0\} \tag{4}$$

and

$$rank(B_S) = e + g \tag{5}$$

$e$ and $g$ are set according to the wanted trade-off. In section 5, several values are tested to show the impact of these parameters on the accuracy of the CNN and the compression gain. We detail two ways of building $B_R$ in the following paragraphs.

*1) Basis-wise construction:* We want to minimize the distance between the vector subspaces $B_T$ and $B_S$. To do so, the adopted strategy consists of selecting the $r_i$, based on the Grassmann distance [20]:

$$\min_{B_R} GrassmannDistance(B_T, \{B_E, B_R\}) \tag{6}$$

By evaluating the distance between the two equidimensional vector subspaces $B_T$ and $B_S$, the set $B_R$ that lowers the distance will be chosen, and the seeds that generate the corresponding set of filters will be saved. The method gives us control only on the entire set $B_R$ and not on each filter.

*2) Filter-wise construction:* To improve the selection filter by filter, an iterative method is proposed. The idea is to find a random filter approximation for each eigenvector we want to replace. The selection is achieved through the criterion:

$$\min_{r_k} GrassmannDistance(\{B_E, b_i\}, \{B_E, r_k\}) \tag{7}$$

with $k \in \{1, ..., g\}$, and for $i \in \{e+1, ..., p\}$ eigenvectors replaced.

The selected pseudo-random filter $r_k$ is added in the basis $B_R$ and the associated seed is saved in $Seeds$. Iteratively, we construct $B_R$ and $Seeds$ in order to control each filter we add. The results presented in the Section 5 are based on the second approach.

Once the basis $B_S$ containing $B_E$ and $B_R$ is built, the new approximation of the weights $\tilde{W}$ in the vector subspace $B_S$ is computed:

$$\tilde{W} = C_S.B_S^T + \mu \tag{8}$$

The pseudo-randomization alleviates the needed storage for each convolutional layer as it replaces memory by on-the-fly generation at the inference.

### E. Retraining and storage

The final step deals with the retraining. The purpose of this step is to correct the new representation of the weights in the vector subspace $B_S$. Once the retraining is done, each convolutional layer has a compressed version that is stored.

As $B_E$ and $B_R$ computed during the previous steps define the directions of the vector subspace $B_S$, they stay fixed. We will only train the coefficients $C_S$ to correct the error of the representation and recover from the accuracy drop of the CNN. The retraining process returns $C_{SL}$ which are the coefficients corresponding to the learned representation.

Once the retraining has ended, for each convolutional layer, we store the following elements:

- the set of principal filters: $B_E$, representing a subset of the eigenvectors of $W$.
- The coefficients: $C_{SL}$ representing the new coordinates of the weights $W$ in the vector subspace $B_S$.
- The seeds: $Seeds$, used to generate the pseudo-random filters of $B_R$ at inference time.

## IV. Inference

The linear combination provided by the method also reduces the inference computational cost. The computation of each convolutional layer can be performed without recomputing $\tilde{W}$. In order to save computational cost, we use a two-stage convolution solution.

Indeed, the computation cost of W is heavy and can be avoided. The convolution can be performed as followed:

$$f_{out} = (C_{SL} * B_S) * f_{in} = C_{SL} * (B_S * f_{in}) \tag{9}$$

The input features maps $f_{in}$ will be computed with the principal filters and the generated pseudo-random filters in the first convolution to get intermediate features maps. And then, the second step will do a 1x1 convolution between the intermediate features maps and the coefficients to get the output features maps $f_{out}$.

By modifying slightly the architecture of the CNN as shown in Figure 3, the gain in memory comes with a computational saving.

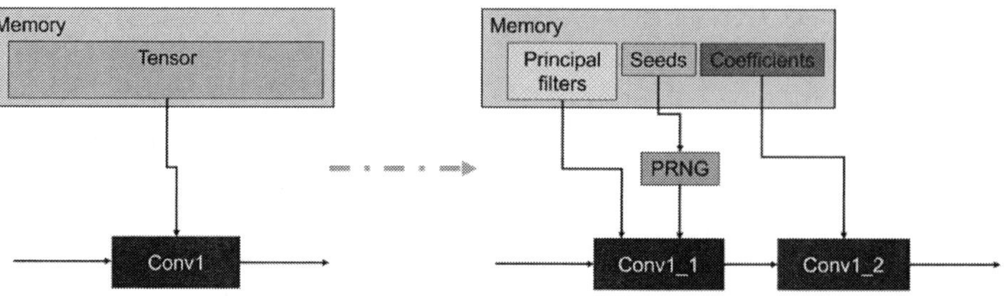


Figure 3. Architectural modification for the inference, the convolution operation is replaced by a two-convolutions solution to avoid computing the approximation of the weights.

## V. Results

We experiment of Cifar10 dataset with three state-of-the-art CNNs: VGG16, ResNet50 and MobileNetV2. We start the section defining the figures of merit and the parameters used to make the comparison between our method, one unstructured pruning method and a PCA compression. The results are presented in Figure 3 for the compression gain and in Figure 4 for the computational cost.

### A. Figures of merit

*1) Compression gain:* To represent the memory gain of our method, we compute the ratio between the number of weights in the baseline CNN ($\#W$) and the number of weights in the compressed version. We define the following figure of merit:

$$G_{Compression} = \frac{\#W}{\#F + \#S + \#C + \#O} \quad (10)$$

Where $\#F$ is the number of weights in the principal filters, $\#S$ is the number of seeds, $\#C$ is the number of coefficients and $\#O$ the number of the weights in fully-connected layers of the CNN.

*2) Computational cost:* To represent the computational cost, we compute the number of Multiply And Accumulate (MAC) operations. The number of MAC per convolution layer can be computed as followed:

$$k_{size}^2.c_{in}.h_{out}.w_{out}.c_{out} \quad (11)$$

where $k_{size}$ is the size of the convolutional kernel, $c_{in}$ the number of input channels, $h_{out}$ and $w_{out}$ the dimension of the output features maps and $c_{out}$ the number of output channels. For our method, the number of MAC per convolution can be computed as followed:

$$k_{size}^2.c_{in}.h_{out}.w_{out}.t + 1^2.t.h_{out}.w_{out}.c_{out} \quad (12)$$

with $t$ the number of filters in $B_S$.

*3) Number of principal filters kept e:* To introduce pseudo-random filters in the CNN, we firstly define $B_E$. This basis contains the $e$ kept eigenvectors. In order to define the parameter $e$ for each convolutional layer, we use the parameter $p$: the percentage of principal vectors.

$$e = \lfloor t.p \rfloor \quad (13)$$

The number of pseudo-random filters $g$ can also be defined with $e$:

$$g = t - e \quad (14)$$

We experiment with three different values of $p$: 0.75, 0.50 and 0.25.

### B. Compression methods used in the benchmark

As our method is focusing on the reduction of the number of weights in the CNN, we compare it to other compression methods.

The first one is an unstructured pruning approach based on the magnitude of the weights described in [21]. The pruning method uses the sparsity metric to measure the proportion of zero weights. In our experiments, the sparsity is set to 80% meaning that only 20% of the weights are non-zero values. We cannot express the compression gain from the sparsity metric as the sparse matrices have to be stored with an encoding technique. In our benchmark, compressed sparse column algorithm is used to allow counting the number of stored weights and compare pruning with our method.

The second approach is a dimensionality reduction based on PCA [10]. As our method is based also on this dimensionality reduction technique, the comparison is more straight forward. In the PCA approaches, two matrices are stored per layer, and the number of weights is easily countable. The comparison is done using the same energy threshold: 70%, so we directly compute the gain of replacing some basis filters by random ones.

### C. Neural networks experiments

*1) VGG16:* We start evaluating the performance of our method on VGG16. We use a modified version of TensorFlow VGG16, where we reduce the fully-connected layers and the last three convolutional layers to alleviate the training and keep only 7.7 millions weights in our test version. The neural network achieves 82.08% accuracy on Cifar10.

As shown on Figure 4, our method allows us to divide by 11 the number of stored weights to perform an inference with less than 7% error. It also allows tuning the compromise between loss and memory gain, depending on the hardware constraints. We get a low accuracy degradation with $p$=75% and $p$=50% where the error is below 5%. The proposed trade-offs drastically decrease the number of stored weights

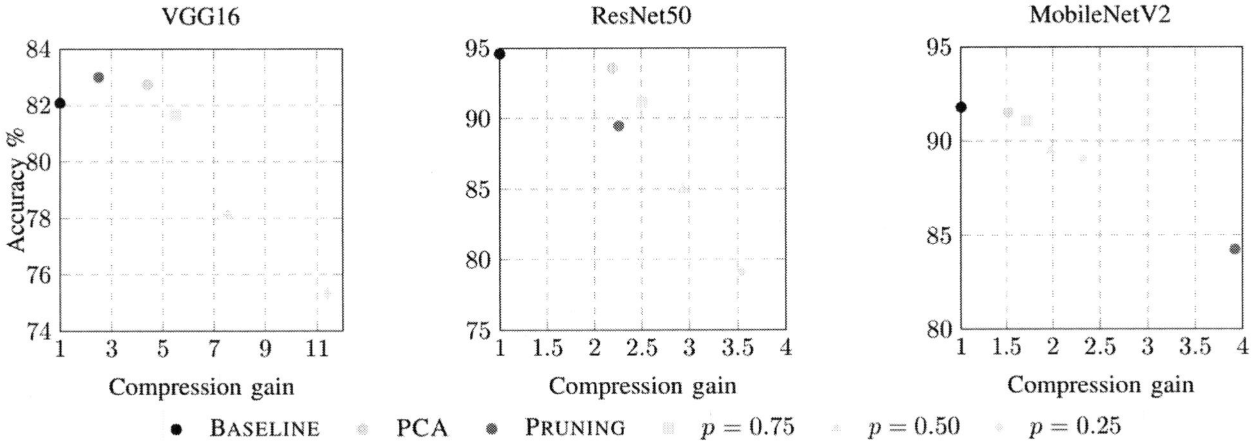


Figure 4. Compression gain/accuracy for VGG16, ResNet50 and MobileNetV2. We test our method with three different values for $p$: 0.75, 0.5 and 0.25. We compare the results to PCA compression and unstructured pruning with 80% sparsity.

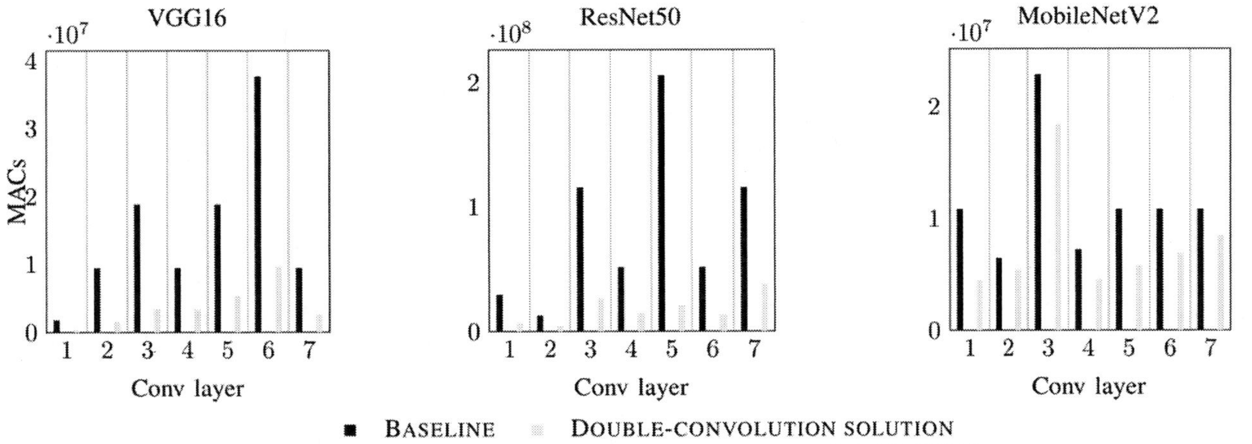


Figure 5. Computational cost for VGG16, ResNet50 and MobileNetV2. The computational cost is the same for each value of $p$ as the number of filters $t$ remains constant.

compared to original PCA and pruning with an acceptable accuracy loss. For each convolutional layer, the use of the double-convolution solution also reduces the computational cost to the same extent. For VGG16, the number of MAC is divided by 4. So, compared to the pruning method where the computational cost is similar to the baseline, without including the decompression cost, our method brings another advantage to the memory saving.

*2) ResNet50:* We then examine the performance of our compression algorithm on ResNet50. We use the TensorFlow ResNet50 version with two fully-connected layers. It contains 25M parameters and achieves 94.60% accuracy on Cifar10.

The use of our method allows us to divide by more than 3 the number of stored weights to perform an inference with 15% error. The accuracy loss is higher when $p$ decreases, but the compression gain is increased compared to PCA or Pruning. For $p$=75%, the loss degradation remains inferior to 5% with an improvement for the compression gain compared to PCA. For inference, the computational cost is divided by more than 3 with the double-convolution solution, as shown in Figure 5.

*3) MobileNetV2:* We finally examine the performance of our method on MobileNetV2. We use the TensorFlow MobileNetV2 version where we modify the output layer to get 10 neurons. It represents 2.2M weights and achieves 91.8% accuracy on Cifar10.

MobileNetV2 is already optimized for achieving embedded computer vision tasks with a particular architecture. We apply our method on the convolutional layers, except on the separable depthwise convolutions. With our method, we can still reduce the number of stored weights by more than 2 without degrading the accuracy. The retraining step becomes an important part of the method for this network, our method controls the learning rate to ensure the convergence of the retraining. Our method provides a powerful tool for the compression gain but also for the computational saving, the use of the double-convolution solution reduces the computational cost, by a factor of 1.5.

*4) Accuracy consideration:* On some cases, mainly for $p$=25%, the accuracy degradation is higher than 5%. For classification purpose this accuracy loss may be difficult to overpass, however, on other tasks it could still be acceptable. For example, in detection tasks where we would target a low number of false negative rather than high accuracy level.

## VI. Conclusion and Future Work

We have introduced a new compression method that reduces the number of weights to store, and with a slight CNN architecture modification, it also reduces the computational cost at inference. Our method introduces pseudo-random weights in CNN and generates them when an inference is performed. Through the experiments, the method has been validated successfully on several CNN architectures, always improving the compression gain. We can exchange memory cost for less expensive pseudo-random numbers generator logic on low cost integrated circuits, allowing the embedding of convolutional neural networks in constrained cases.

With our method, we address only one topic in the CNN compression: reducing the number of weights to store. Our next research will focus on improving our solution by reducing the precision of the stored weights, to further reduce memory use. Our method can be combined with integer quantization, both to further reduce the memory needed to achieve an embedded inference and to reduce the cost of the pseudo-random generation part.

## References

[1] R. Wightman, H. Touvron, and H. Jégou, "ResNet strikes back: An improved training procedure in timm", NeurIPS 2021 Workshop on ImageNet: Past, Present, and Future, 2021.

[2] Z. Liu et al., "A ConvNet for the 2020s", 2022 IEEE/CVF Conference on Computer Vision and Pattern Recognition (CVPR), New Orleans, LA, USA, 2022, pp. 11966-11976, doi: 10.1109/CVPR52688.2022.01167.

[3] B. Jacob, "Quantization and Training of Neural Networks for Efficient Integer-Arithmetic-Only Inference", 2018 IEEE/CVF Conference on Computer Vision and Pattern Recognition, Salt Lake City, UT, USA, 2018, pp. 2704-2713, doi: 10.1109/CVPR.2018.00286.

[4] I. Garg, P. Panda, and K. Roy, "A Low Effort Approach to Structured CNN Design Using PCA", in IEEE Access, vol. 8, pp. 1347-1360, 2020, doi: 10.1109/ACCESS.2019.2961960.

[5] Y. Yao, B. Dong, Y. Li, W. Yang, and H. Zhu, "Efficient Implementation of Convolutional Neural Networks with End to End Integer-Only Dataflow," 2019 IEEE International Conference on Multimedia and Expo (ICME), 2019, pp. 1780-1785, doi: 10.1109/ICME.2019.00306.

[6] W. Zhao, T. Ma, X. Gong, B. Zhang, and D. Doermann, "A Review of Recent Advances of Binary Neural Networks for Edge Computing," in IEEE Journal on Miniaturization for Air and Space Systems, vol. 2, no. 1, pp. 25-35, March 2021, doi: 10.1109/JMASS.2020.3034205.

[7] S. Han, J. Pool, J. Tran, and W. J. Dally, "Learning both Weights and Connections for Efficient Neural Networks",In Proceedings of the 28th International Conference on Neural Information Processing Systems - Volume 1 (NIPS'15). MIT Press, Cambridge, MA, USA, 1135–1143.

[8] S. Srinivas, and R. Venkatesh Babu, "Data-free parameter pruning for Deep Neural Networks", oRR abs/1507.06149 (2015): .

[9] S. Han, H. Mao, and W. J. Dally, "Deep Compression: Compressing Deep Neural Networks with Pruning, Trained Quantization and Huffman Coding", 4th International Conference on Learning Representations, ICLR 2016, San Juan, 2-4 May 2016.

[10] L. F. Brillet, S. Mancini, S. Cleyet-Merle and M. Nicolas, "Tunable CNN Compression Through Dimensionality Reduction," 2019 IEEE International Conference on Image Processing (ICIP), 2019, pp. 3851-3855, doi: 10.1109/ICIP.2019.8803585.

[11] R. Rigamonti, A. Sironi, V. Lepetit, and P. Fua, "Learning Separable Filters," 2013 IEEE Conference on Computer Vision and Pattern Recognition, 2013, pp. 2754-2761, doi: 10.1109/CVPR.2013.355.

[12] X. Yu, T. Liu, X. Wang and D. Tao, "On Compressing Deep Models by Low Rank and Sparse Decomposition," 2017 IEEE Conference on Computer Vision and Pattern Recognition (CVPR), 2017, pp. 67-76, doi: 10.1109/CVPR.2017.15.

[13] Guang-Bin Huang, Qin-Yu Zhu and Chee-Kheong Siew, "Extreme learning machine: a new learning scheme of feedforward neural networks," 2004 IEEE International Joint Conference on Neural Networks (IEEE Cat. No.04CH37541), 2004, pp. 985-990 vol.2, doi: 10.1109/IJCNN.2004.1380068.

[14] L. Kasun, H. Zhou, G. -B. Huang, and C. Vong, (2013). "Representational Learning with ELMs for Big Data", IEEE Intelligent Systems. 28, pp 31-34.

[15] G. -B. Huang, Z. Bai, L. L. C. Kasun and C. M. Vong, "Local Receptive Fields Based Extreme Learning Machine," in IEEE Computational Intelligence Magazine, vol. 10, no. 2, pp. 18-29, May 2015, doi: 10.1109/MCI.2015.2405316.

[16] S. Pang and X. Yang, (2016). Deep Convolutional Extreme Learning Machine and Its Application in Handwritten Digit Classification. Computational Intelligence and Neuroscience. 2016. 1-10. 10.1155/2016/3049632.

[17] C. Gallicchio and S. Scardapane, "Deep Randomized Neural Networks", in Recent Trends in Learning From Data. Studies in Computational Intelligence, vol 896. Springer, Cham. doi: 10.1007/978-3-030-43883-8_3.

[18] A. Rosenfeld and J. K. Tsotsos, "Intriguing Properties of Randomly Weighted Networks: Generalizing While Learning Next to Nothing", arXiv e-prints, 2018.

[19] V. Ramanujan et al., "What's Hidden in a Randomly Weighted Neural Network?", 2020 IEEE/CVF Conference on Computer Vision and Pattern Recognition (CVPR), Seattle, WA, USA, 2020, pp. 11890-11899, doi: 10.1109/CVPR42600.2020.01191.

[20] K. Ye and L.-H. Lim, "Schubert varieties and distances between subspaces of different dimensions", SIAM Journal on Matrix Analysis and Applications. 37, pp 1176-1197, 2014, 10.1137/15M1054201.

[21] M. Zhu and S. Gupta, "To prune, or not to prune: exploring the efficacy of pruning for model compression", CoRR abs/1710.01878 (2017): .

# Improvement of SSVEP Detection Accuracy via Additive Averaging of Binaural Peripheral Electrodes

Taichi Haba
*Department of Electronics and Information Engineering,*
*Graduate School of Engineering,*
*Toyama Prefectural University*
Imizu-City, Toyama Prefecture, Japan
ORCID: 0000-0003-4329-9682

Gaochao Cui
*Department of Electronics and Information Engineering,*
*Graduate School of Engineering,*
*Toyama Prefectural University*
Imizu-City, Toyama Prefecture, Japan
e-mail: cuigaochao@pu-toyama.ac.jp

Fumiya Kinoshita
*Department of Electronics and Information Engineering,*
*Graduate School of Engineering,*
*Toyama Prefectural University*
Imizu-City, Toyama Prefecture, Japan
e-mail: f.kinoshita@pu-toyama.ac.jp

Hideaki Touyama
*Department of Electronics and Information Engineering,*
*Graduate School of Engineering,*
*Toyama Prefectural University*
Imizu-City, Toyama Prefecture, Japan
e-mail: touyama@pu-toyama.ac.jp

***Abstract*—Recently, Brain–Computer Interfaces for healthy subjects have attracted considerable attention. Steady–State Visual Evoked Potential (SSVEP) has garnered particular attention because it can be used by anyone without training. However, SSVEP is mainly used for head measurements and is unsuitable for daily measurements. We attempted to measure SSVEP via the application of electrodes around the ears. The highest average macro F–value was 45.33±16.84 %, and the highest average Information Transfer Rate (ITR) was 13.86±13.21 bits/min with the L2+R2 method. A comparison between electrodes 1–3 and the head showed no significant difference, except in the occipital area, and the combination of right and left electrodes around the ear produced the same accuracy as that of the head.**

***Keywords—Steady–State Visual Evoked Potential (SSVEP); Canonical Correlation Analysis (CCA); ear EEG.***

## I. INTRODUCTION

Recently, several efforts have been made to apply brain information to engineering. One example of such an application is the Brain–Computer Interface (BCI), which is being actively pursued, particularly in the medical and welfare fields. This is because BCI can operate machines using only brain information without the use of limbs and can be used to replace some body functions. However, because devices for measuring brain information are now commercially available at a relatively low cost, research on BCI using healthy subjects has also attracted attention. Many studies using brain information from healthy subjects have reported using ElectroEncephaloGraphy (EEG), among other methods to collect brain information.

Steady–State Visual Evoked Potential (SSVEP) is a type of EEG that has attracted considerable attention for its applications. The frequency range of the SSVEP is wide, ranging from 1 to 100 Hz [1]. In 2006, a previous study [2] using Canonical Correlation Analysis (CCA) to discriminate SSVEP detected a higher discrimination accuracy than that obtained using the conventional Fourier transform. This indicates that the analysis of SSVEP is more accurate than the conventional Fourier transform and that CCA is a useful method for analyzing SSVEP.

One factor that has drawn attention in CCA is that it does not require prior preparation, in contrast to analysis methods using machine learning and other methods. In 2015, Nakanishi et al. [3] reported the results of a comparison of various analysis methods based on CCA. In 2021, Li et al. [4] reported in a review article that there is a wide range of analysis methods based on CCA and that CCA is superior as a discrimination method for BCI using SSVEP.

Other EEGs used for BCI, such as the P300, generally require prior training on the task and data collection for machine learning. However, SSVEP does not require subject training because it is an exogenous visual–evoked potential. Therefore, SSVEP can exploit the previously mentioned benefits of requiring no prior preparation. In addition, compared to other EEG methods, SSVEP is easy to detect even when the measurement time is short, and has a high Signal–to–Noise ratio (S/N), rendering stable measurements relatively easy. In 2009, Parini et al. [5] reported that the Information Transfer Rate (ITR), a BCI evaluation index, is excellent. Furthermore, in 2017, Botani et al. [6] proposed an algorithm for a menu selection interface with SSVEP using six different visual stimuli, with an average correct response rate of 83.3 % and an average ITR of 30.5 bits/min. In 2018, a robot control method based on SSVEP, which can operate in virtual reality space, was proposed by Stawicki et al. [7], with an average correct response rate of 98.91 % and an average ITR of 32.00 bits/min.

As described above, BCIs using SSVEP have been actively studied in various settings. However, most current reports are based on head measurements using the international 10–20 method. Thus, electrodes must be applied to the scalp to measure SSVEP when using these systems. In 2017, Wang et al. [8] attempted to measure SSVEP in hairless areas such as the neck and behind the ears, and recently, ear EEG, wherein electrodes are applied around the ears, has been gaining popularity as a method for measuring SSVEP outside the head.

In 2011, Looney et al. [9] proposed a method to measure EEG signals from inside the ear, and in 2013, Kidmose et al. [10] developed an earpiece–type EEG measurement device. The signal measured inside the ear is also being investigated to determine whether it is similar to an EEG signal. In 2016, Zibrandsen et al. [11] used in–ear and on–head EEG to classify sleep stages and reported 90.9 % accuracy in discriminating between awake and REM sleep states.

However, the amplitude values of measurements inside and around the ears are lower than those of head measurements, and it is difficult to significantly improve the accuracy [12]. Here, we attempted to create a new signal by applying electrodes to both ears and performing additive averaging of EEG between the two ears. We expected the accuracy to improve as a results of using this new additive averaging method. In addition, we investigated the optimal location for detecting SSVEP from electrodes affixed around the ears when visual flashing stimuli are provided. The performance of the BCI was examined by comparing the monopolar induction electroencephalograms applied around the ears and the electroencephalograms based on the additive averaging of the electrodes around both ears.

The remainder of this paper is organized as follows. Section 2 describes the methods including experimental design and EEG data recording. Section 3 describes the EEG data analysis and evaluation methods. Section 4 presents the analytical results obtained in this study. Based on the results, a discussion of the binaural additive electrode method is presented in Section 5. Finally, the conclusions are presented in Section 6 .

## II. Methods

### A. Experimental Design

The subjects remained in a resting, sitting position. A display (27 in.) was placed 50 cm ahead of the subject for stimulus presentation. Stimuli were presented within 19.3° of the visual field.

For the SSVEP elicitation task, a black–and–white square (17 cm) was presented as a visual flashing stimulus on a display in front of the subject (Figure 1). Four types of flashing stimuli were selected in the low-frequency band [13] at 5, 7, 9, and 11 Hz, where high–amplitude values were easily recorded in the SSVEP. The stimuli were presented in the order described for 12 s with a 60 s rest between each stimulus (Figure 2). The subjects were instructed not to blink except for a minimum amount of blinking during the blinking stimuli, and to rest their eyes sufficiently during the rest period. This task was performed in one session, followed by two sessions of SSVEP–evoked tasks.

Figure 1. Image stimulation in SSVEP-induced experiment.

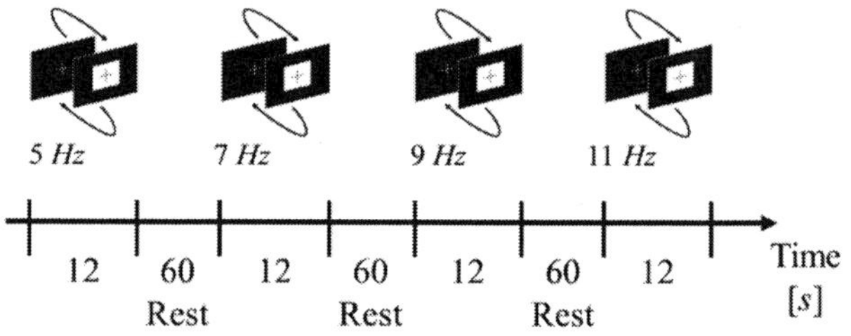


Figure 2. Experimental protocol.

### B. Data recording

BIO–NVX 52 (East Medic, Japan) was used to record the biometric data with a temporal resolution of 2000 Hz. A bandpass filter (0.50–70 Hz) was applied to eliminate noise. The electrode positions were Oz, O1, and O2 based on the extended 10–20 method [14]. The ground electrode was AFz and the reference electrode was the average value of both earlobes (A1 and A2). For the measurement around both ears, electrodes were affixed at eight locations around each ear, with the reference electrode for the electrode around the right ear being the right earlobe (A2) and that for the electrode around the left ear being the left earlobe (A1) (Figure 3(c, d)).

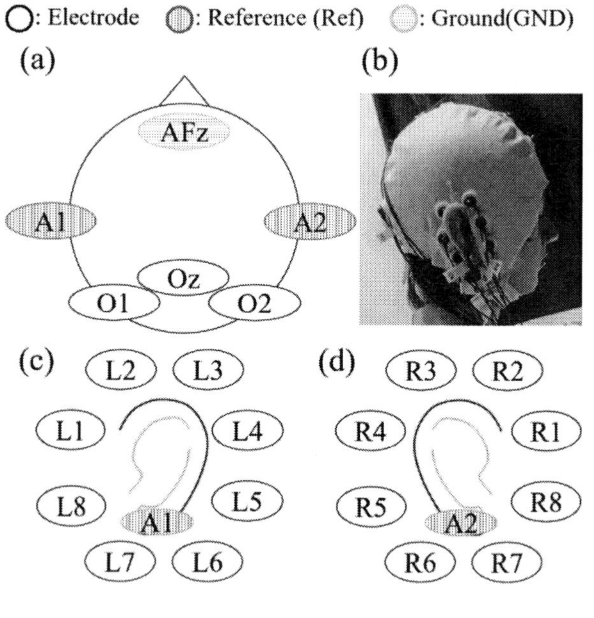


Figure 3. Electrode position.

The subjects were 14 healthy males and females (10 males, 4 females, Mean±SD: 21.93±0.83 years) enrolled in universities and graduate schools. Subjects with visual acuity problems were corrected to achieve normal vision. The subjects were given a thorough explanation of the experiment and their consent to participate was obtained. The experiment was conducted after obtaining approval (H31-9) from the Ethics Committee of Toyama Prefectural University.

## III. DATA ANALYSIS

### A. Pre-processing

In this experiment, each stimulus was measured for 12 s. Time-series data for 10 s were obtained by excluding data immediately after starting the stimulus presentation and data for 1.0 s before ending the stimulus presentation. The 10 s data were divided into ten segments with a time window of 1.0 s to avoid overlap of the data used. A bandpass filter of 4–35 Hz was applied. When performing additive averaging between left and right electrodes, the difference in amplitude between the electrodes may significantly affect the discrimination accuracy of one of the two electrodes. Therefore, we employed a robust z-score after applying the bandpass filter. The position of the electrodes to be averaged was between the electrodes with the same number of binaural peripheral electrodes, as shown in Figure 3.

### B. Analysis, discrimination method, and performance evaluation

The waveforms used in CCA were sine and cosine waves of the same length as the time window length, which were used for comparison. The sine and cosine waves started at 5, 7, 9, and 11 Hz, similar to visual stimuli. Those with frequencies that were two or three times higher than the harmonics were also used for discrimination. According to Bedard et al. [15], EEG also elicits harmonics that are multiples of the frequency of the visual-evoked stimulus. Therefore, using CCA without considering harmonics in the SSVEP analysis may result in them being classified as other frequencies [2]. Therefore, we classified the doubled and tripled frequencies as the same frequency as those provided as visual stimuli.

The Canonical Correlation Coefficient (CCC) calculated by CCA was used to discriminate the EEG signals by creating a 4×4– dimensional mixing matrix at 5, 7, 9, and 11 Hz. For discrimination, CCC was calculated from the frequencies of the four stimuli per data-set, and the highest CCC was predicted as the given stimulus. The discrimination index using this mixed matrix was evaluated by calculating the macro F-value, which is the average of the F-values of each of the four stimuli.

ITR was proposed by Wolpaw et al. [16], where N is the number of discriminations, P is the percentage of correct responses, and t is the time required per trial (min).

$$\mathrm{ITR} = \frac{\log_2 N + P\log_2 P + (1-P)\log_2\left(\frac{1-P}{N-1}\right)}{t} \quad \ldots (1)$$

The calculated CCCs, macro F-value, and ITR were compared between the left and right additive electrodes and the left and right unipolar electrodes by performing a Friedman test using the Bonferroni method in the EZR software [17]. The significance level for this study was set at p = 0.05.

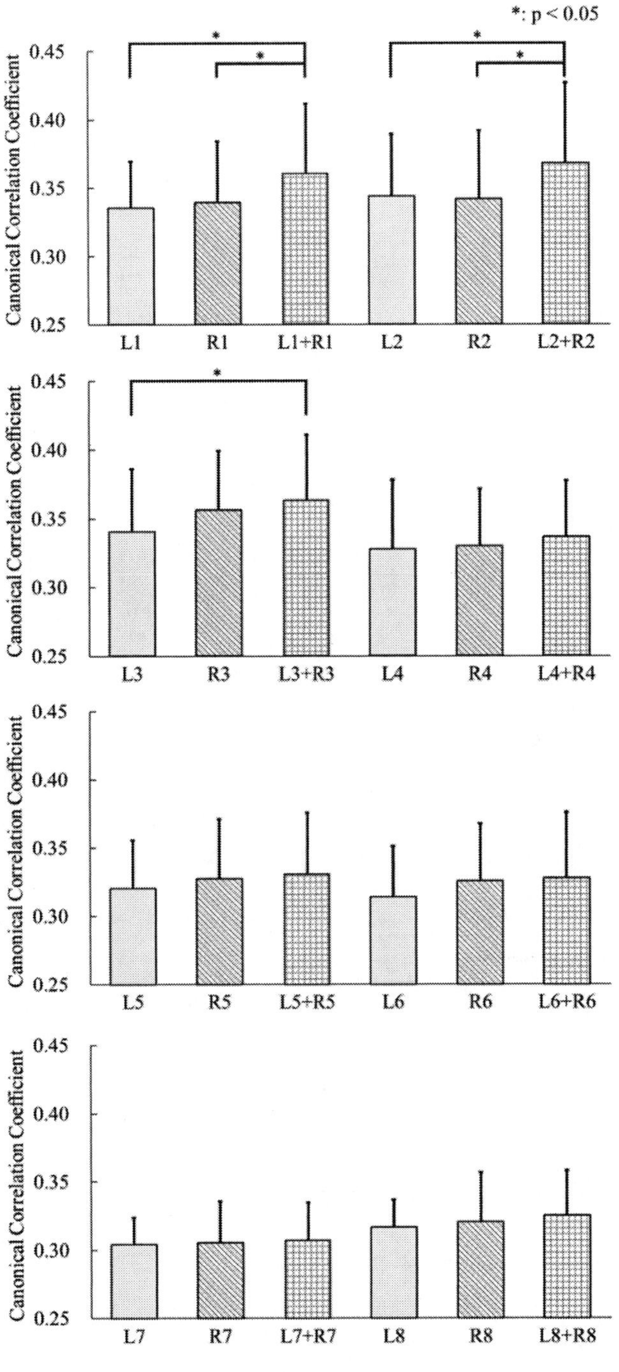


Figure 4. Canonical Correlation Coefficient of each position (Mean±SD).

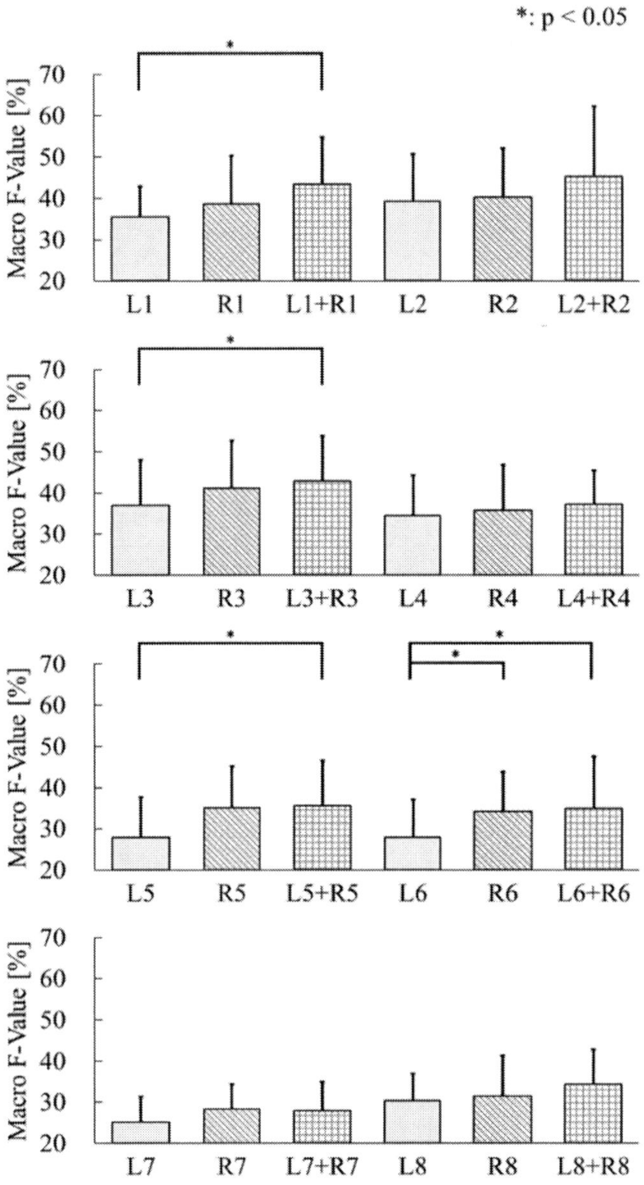


Figure 5. Macro F–value of each position (Mean±SD).

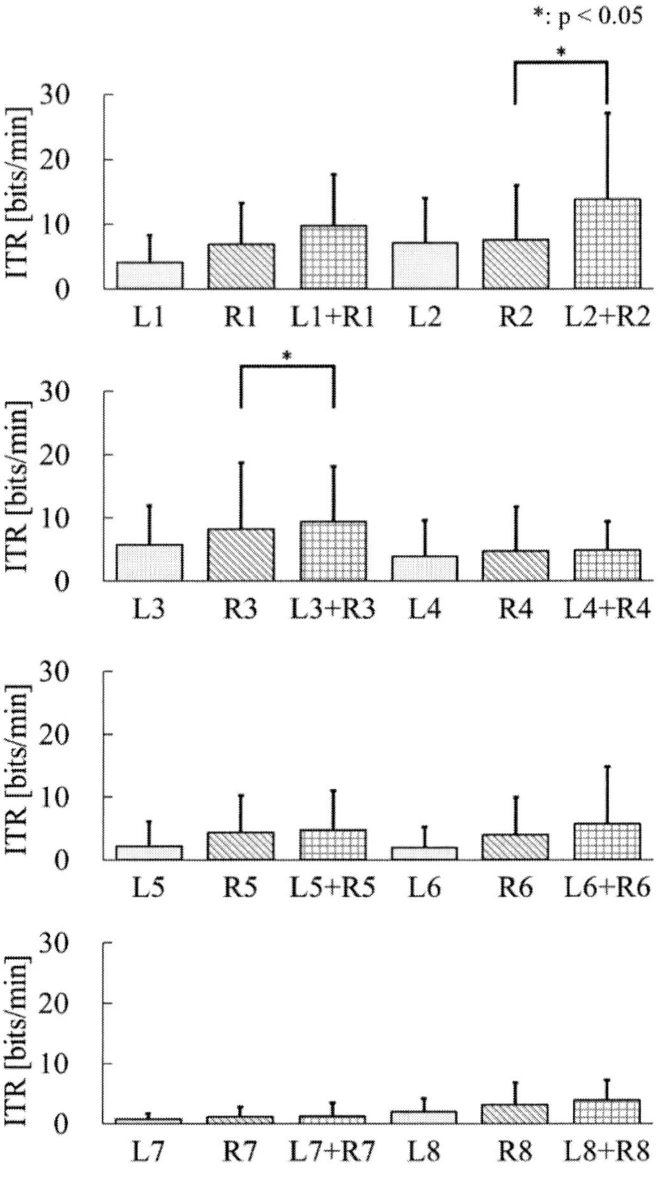


Figure 6. ITR of each position (Mean±SD).

## IV. Results

### A. Canonical correlation coefficient

The mean value of CCC was the highest at L2+R2, 0.37±0.06 (Mean±SD). Comparisons were made between the left, right, and added electrodes. Significant differences were found for electrodes 1, 2, and 3 as well as between the electrodes (Figure 4).

### B. Macro F–value and ITR

Figure 5 shows the macro F–value results. The highest mean value was obtained for the L2+R2 electrodes (45.33±16.84 %). Comparisons were made between the left, right, and added electrodes. Significant differences were found between electrodes 3, 5, 6, and 8 as well as between electrodes.

The highest mean ITR value was observed for L2+R2, at 13.86±13.21 bits/min. Comparisons were made using electrodes of the same number on the left, right, right, and left sides. The results showed a significant difference between the two electrodes at the 2– and 3–number electrodes (Figure 6).

## V. Discussion

In a previous study, Sun et al. [18] attached electrodes to the mirror legs of glasses and acquired data from the upper part of each ear. Data from the left and right ears were treated as separate signals with unipolar induction and were classified

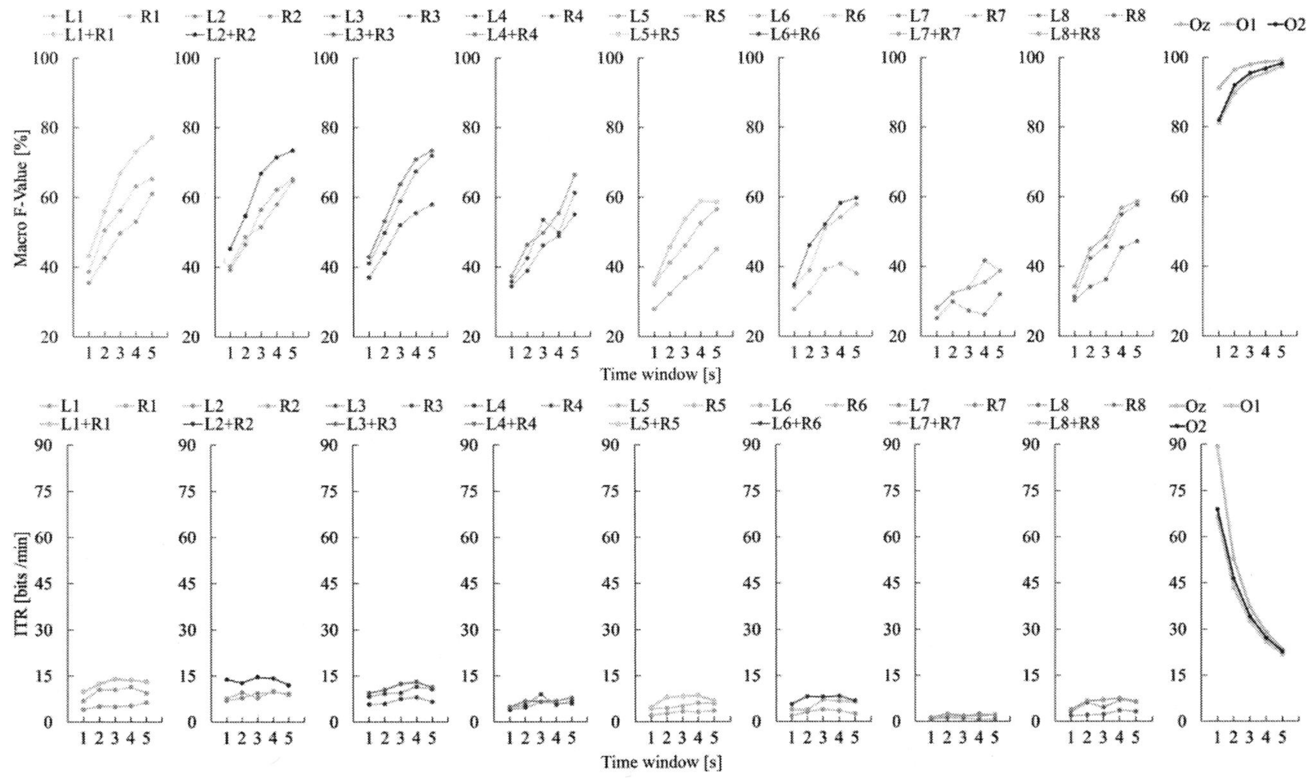


Figure 7. Macro F–value and ITR of change time window. (Mean).

using CCA. Thus, one stimulus of four different frequencies was presented on the screen, which was similar to the present study in terms of the presentation of visual stimuli. The results of the experiment by Sun et al. [18] showed that the estimated correct response rate for the gazing stimulus was 32.75 % when a simple CCA without prior learning was applied using a window length of 1.0 s. However, the estimated correct response rate increased to 43.75 % when the method was pre–trained with the participants' data. The estimated correct response rate based on binaural additive averaging in this study was 45.33 %, which is equivalent to that of the pretraining method proposed by Sun et al. [18]

Conventional CCA does not require prior learning, which is an advantage; however, Time–'Weighting Canonical Correlation Analysis (TWCCA) with prior learning reported by Sun et al. [18] boasts an accuracy equivalent to that of the present study, although it is a monopole induction. Therefore, further improvements in the accuracy of binaural additive averaging data can be a chieved by employing methods such as TWCCA and msetCCA [21], which perform prior learning.

We performed binaural additive averaging using only electrodes attached to the corresponding positions on the left and right sides of each ear. However, it has been reported that the accuracy of stimulus estimation also improves when multiple electrodes are used for binaural additive averaging using only electrodes in one ear [22]. From the above, we believe that by selecting areas with high CCCs and exhaustively applying various additive averaging methods in both ears, rather than between the corresponding positions on the left and right, electrode combinations that still improve the accuracy can be determined. In this study, the highest CCC was R3 for the right periapical electrode only, whereas L2+R2 was the highest when additive averaging was applied to both periapical electrodes. In ITR, R3 was the highest at 8.25±10.45 bits/min for the right periapical electrode alone, and L2+R2 was the highest at 13.86±13.22 bits/min when the bilateral periapical electrodes were added and averaged.

The results of the analysis with different time–window lengths showed that the F–value increased with the window length (Figure 7). In the occipital lobe area (Oz, O1, O2), a prominent peak was observed at a window length of 1 s in ITR. However, in the case of binaural additive averaging, ITR was not larger at a window length of 1 s.

In this experiment, only one type of flashing stimulus was presented, and there was a discrepancy with the actual use of the BCI. Therefore, in the future, we would like to measure and analyze SSVEP when two or more different flashing stimuli are simultaneously presented. In particular, the SSVEP component can change depending on the visual attention. By including the covert SSVEP [23], which does not involve eye movement, we can expect to detect visual attention in the ear's vicinity of the ear, which is impossible with eye–tracking devices. In such research, it is also imprtant to attach the electrodes easily. In the future, we will develop an earpiece–type sensor device to measure the electroencephalograms around the ear.

In this study, we included subjects who were younger in age. Previous studies have reported [24] an increase or decrease in accuracy with age, and the age range considered in this study was the one reported to exhibit high accuracy. In the future, it will be necessary to investigate whether the same level of accuracy can be achieved in older subjects by using periapical electrodes.

In addition, as mentioned above, when the number of subjects is increased, the accuracy converges in case the subjects are of the same age; therefore, the electrode addition method and the position of the attachment may be briefly discussed. However, the accuracy of SSVEP has been observed to change with age. Moreover, the change in accuracy when subjects are randomly selected is uncertain. Therefore, dividing the subjects into groups based on factors that affect accuracy, such as age, may aid in improving the accuracy of SSVEP around the ear.

## VI. Conclusion

Although BCIs have been extensively studied in healthy subjects, it is difficult to apply electrodes to the head of a single person. In this study, eight electrodes were applied around each ear and the potential activity induced by SSVEP was discriminated using CCA. To improve the accuracy, new waveforms were derived by adding and averaging the time–series data between the electrodes attached to the target sites in both ears and were compared with the single electrode results for the periapical electrodes.

The L2+R2 electrode exhibited the highest mean CCC of 0.37±0.06, with Macro F–value of 45.33±16.84 % and ITR of 13.86±13.21 bits/min. The CCC at L2+R2 was significantly higher than that at L2 and R2 monopoles. The CCC at other sites was also significantly higher for the additive electrodes than for the monopoles. In addition, when comparing the head and additive electrodes around the ears, there was no significant difference in the macro F–value for electrodes 1–3, and no significant difference in the ITR was observed only for Oz and L4+R4. In the future, we will examine the detailed electrode placement, time window length, and algorithms to improve the accuracy of measurements around the ear.

## Acknowledgements

The authors are grateful to M. Ito for conducting the experiments and recording data.

## References

[1] C. S. Herrmann, "Human EEG responses to 1–100 Hz flicker: Resonance phenomena in visual cortex and their potential," Experimental Brain Research, vol.137, no.3-4, pp.346-353, 2001.

[2] Z. Lin, C. Zhang, W. Wu, X. Gao, "Frequency recognition based on canonical correlation analysis for SSVEP-based BCIs," IEEE Transactions on Biomedical Engineering, vol.53, no.12, pp.2610-2614, 2006.

[3] M. Nakanishi, Y. Wang, Y. T. Wang, T. P. Jung, "A comparison study of canonical correlation analysis based methods for detecting steady-state visual evoked potentials," PLoS ONE, vol.10, no.10, e0140703, 2015.

[4] M. Li, D. He, C. Li, S. Qi, "Brain–Computer Interface Speller Based on Steady-State Visual Evoked Potential: A Review Focusing on the Stimulus Paradigm and Performance," brain science, vol.11, no.4, pp.1-25, 2021.

[5] S. Parini, L. Maggi, A. C. Turconi, G. Andreoni, "A Robust and Self-Paced BCI System Based on a Four Class SSVEP Paradigm: Algorithms and Protocols for a High-Transfer-Rate Direct Brain Communication," Computational Intelligence and Neuroscience, vol.2009, pp.1-11, 2009.

[6] H. Botani, M. Ohsuga, "Proposal of recognition algorithm for menu selection using steady state visual evoked potential," Japanese Journal of Ergonomics, vol.53, no.1, pp.8-15, 2017.

[7] P. Stawicki et al., "SSVEP-based BCI in virtual Reality - control of a vacuum cleaner robot," 2018 IEEE International Conference on Systems, Man, and Cybernetics, pp.534-537, 2018.

[8] Y. T. Wang, M. Nakanishi, Y. Wang, C. S. Wei, C. K. Cheng, T. P. Jung, "An online brain-computer interface based on SSVEPs measured from non-hair-bearing areas," IEEE Transactions on Neural Systems and Rehabilitation Engineering, vol.25, no.1, pp.11-18, 2017.

[9] D. Looney et al., "An in-the-ear platform for recording electroencephalogram," 2011 Annual International Conference of the IEEE Engineering in Medicine and Biology Society, pp.6882-6885, 2011.

[10] P. Kidmose, D. Looney, L. Jochumsen, D. P. Mandic, "Ear-EEG from generic earpieces: A feasibility study," 2013 35th Annual International Conference of the IEEE Engineering in Medicine and Biology Society, pp.543-546, 2013.

[11] I. Zibrandtsen, P. Kidmose, M. Otto, J. Ibsen, T. W. Kjaer, "Case comparison of sleep features from ear-EEG and scalp-EEG," Sleep Science, vol.9, no.2, pp.69-72, 2016.

[12] C. Athavipach, S. Pan-ngum, P. Israsena, "A wearable in-ear EEG device for emotion monitoring," Sensors, vol.19, no.18, 4014, 2019.

[13] D. Regan, "Human Brain Electrophysiology," Elsevier, New York, 1989.

[14] G. H. Klem, H. O. Luders, H. H. Jasper, C. Elge, "The ten-twenty electrode system of the International Federation. The International Federation of clinical neurophysiology," Electroencephalography and clinical neurophysiology. Supplement, vol.52, pp.3-6, 1999.

[15] C. Bedard, H. Kroger, A. Destexhe, "Modeling extracellular field potentials and the frequency-filtering properties of extracellular space," Biophysical Journal, vol.86, no.3, pp.1829-1842, 2004.

[16] J. R. Wolpaw, N. Birbaumer, D. J. McFarland, G. Pfurtscheller, T. M. Vaughan, "Brain–computer interfaces for communication and control," Clinical Neurophysiology, vol.113, no.6, pp.767-791, 2002.

[17] Y. Kanda, "Investigation of the freely available easy-to-use software 'EZR' for medical statistics," Bone Marrow Transplantation, vol.48, pp.452-458, 2013.

[18] Y. Sun et al., "Cross-subject fusion based on time-weighting canonical correlation analysis in SSVEP-BCIs," Measurement, vol.199, 111524, 2022.

[19] P. Israsena, S. Pan-Ngum, "A CNN-based deep learning approach for SSVEP detection targeting binaural ear-EEG," Frontiers in Computational Neuroscience, vol.16, 868642, 2022.

[20] D. O. Won, H. J. Hwang, S. Dähne, K. R. Müller, S. W. Lee, "Effect of higher frequency on the classification of steady-state visual evoked potentials," Journal of Neural Engineering, vol.13, 016014, 2015.

[21] Y. Zhang, G. Zhou, J. Jin, X. Wang, A. Cichocki, "Frequency recognition in SSVEP-based BCI using multiset canonical correlation analysis," International Journal of Neural Systems, vol.24, no.2, 1450013, 2014.

[22] M. Ito, F. Kinoshita, G. Cui, H. Touyama, "A study on electrode positions around the ear for BCI development using SSVEP," Transactions of the Institute of Electrical Engineers of Japan. C., vol.143, no.2, pp.178-184, 2023.

[23] S. P. Kelly, E. C. Lalor, R. B. Reilly, J. J. Foxe, "Visual spatial attention tracking using high-density SSVEP data for independent brain-computer communication," IEEE Transactions on Neural Systems and Rehabilitation Engineering, vol.13, pp.172-178, 2005.

[24] I. Volosyak, F. Gembler, P. Stawicki, "Age-related differences in SSVEP-based BCI performance," Neurocomputing, vol.250, no.9, pp.57-64, 2017.

# RCT-Net: TDNN based Speaker Verification with 2D Res2Nets on Frame Level Feature Extractor

*Note: Sub-titles are not captured in Xplore and should not be used

Razieh Khamsehashari
*Quality and Usability*
*Technical University of Berlin*
Berlin, Germany
email: razieh.khamsehashari@tu-berlin.de

Fengying Miao
*Quality and Usability*
*Technical University of Berlin*
Berlin, Germany
email: fengying.miao@campus.tu-berlin.de

Tim Polzehl
*Speech and Language Technology*
*German Research Center for Artificial Intelligence (DFKI)*
Berlin, Germany
email: tim.polzehl@dfki.de

Sebastian Möller
*Quality and Usability*
*Technical University of Berlin*
Berlin, Germany
email: sebastian.moeller@tu-berlin.de

***Abstract*—In speaker verification, Time Delay Neural Networks (TDNNs) and Residual Networks (ResNets) are currently achieving cutting-edge results. These architectures have very different structural characteristics, and development of hybrid networks appears to be a promising path forward. In this study, inspired by the combination of Convolutional Neural Network (CNN) blocks and multi-scale architectures we present a Residual-based CNN TDNN (RCT) system and evaluate the performance of integrating different residual blocks into a TDNN-based structure. We extend the state-of-the-art speaker embedding model for speaker recognition, namely Emphasized Channel Attention, Propagation, and Aggregation based CNN-TDNN (ECAPA CNN-TDNN), by gradually incorporating the proposed 2D convolutional stem with various bottleneck residual blocks. We evaluate the performance of our models on standard VoxCeleb1-O test set to investigate the performance of residual blocks and TDNN in the speaker verification domain. As a result, the proposed models significantly outperform the state-of-the-art by up to 14.6% of EER.**

***Index Terms*—ResNet, Residual blocks, TDNN, RCT-Net, speaker verification, automatic speaker verification (ASV)**

## I. Introduction

Current state-of-the-art speaker verification systems try to improve the most popular neural network topology based on ECAPA-TDNN by incorporating multiple ideas and techniques inspired by convolutional blocks, feature aggregation, and frequency-channel attention methods. ECAPA CNN-TDNN [6] introduced a 2D convolutional stem for the ECAPA-TDNN, incorporating frequency translational invariance in the four top layers of the network. Liu et al. [7] proposed MFA-TDNN, a Multi-scale Frequency-channel Attention (MFA) framework, that captures the local information and frame-level temporal information by the dual-pathway multi-scale module while emphasizing the important frequency and channel components in TDNN systems. Inspired by ECAPA CNN-TDNN, which enhances ECAPA-TDNN by incorporating a CNN-based front-end, the MFA module is created as a front-end module for TDNNs in order to learn multi-scale and extract high resolution feature representations from short utterances. [8] and [13] adapt the frame-level processing in ECAPA-TDNN. In [8], their experiments focus on bottleneck residual blocks, attention mechanisms, and feature aggregation based on ECAPA-TDNN. They replaced the Res2Block with SC-Block and proposed the hierarchical feature aggregation method to build their final model.

Many recent studies have focused on expanding the receptive field of the convolutional layer on Residual Network (ResNet) [1]. The first technique integrates the ResNet with the concept of inception [2] and proposes ResNext, a split-transform-merge strategy [3]. The introduced *cardinality* is intended for processing different sizes of receptive fields in order to obtain multi-scale features. Furthermore, Res2Net [4] improves multi-scale feature extraction capability by constructing hierarchical residual-like connections within one single residual block. The preceding ideas are similar to the TDNN, which obtains a wide range of time information through convolution with different dilation rates. We believe that development of hybrid networks to generate multi-scale features influences the final representation and appears to be a promising direction moving forward. The ECAPA-TDNN model [5], as an example, combines the benefits of Res2Net and TDNN.

Inspired by these recent progresses, we propose Residual-based CNN TDNN *RCT-Net* using 2D convolutions based on different residual blocks as the foundation for the initial network layers. We evaluate the performance of various residual blocks using the most recent speaker embedding model for

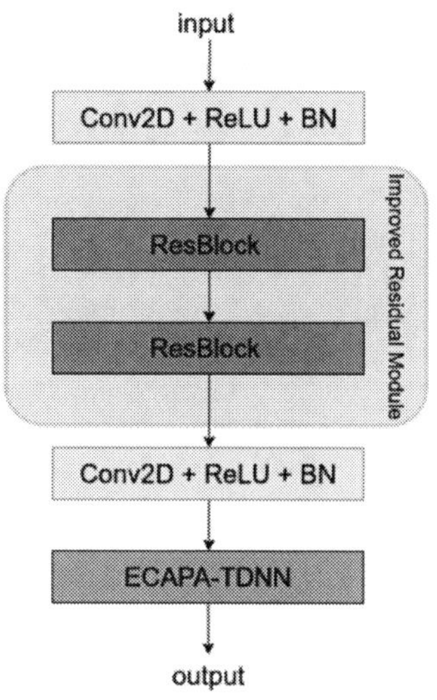


Fig. 1. The diagram of the proposed architecture.

speaker recognition, ECAPA CNN-TDNN [6], and experiment with the proposed 2D convolutional stem, including various bottleneck residual blocks such as Res2Net [4], Res2NeXt [3], standard ResNet [1], Improved ResNet [9] and ResTCN [10], [15].

This paper is organized as follows: In Section II, the baseline architectures are described. The structure of the proposed Residual-based CNN TDNN *RCT-Net* and different frame-level architectures are described in Section III. Section IV introduces the experimental setup including dataset, training the speaker embedding extractors, and evaluation protocol. Results and analysis are presented in Section V. In Section VI we discuss the potential justification for our best combination of two strong structures of TDNN and residual blocks. Finally, Section VII summarizes the findings.

## II. Baseline System Architectures

Two types of TDNN-based speaker embedding models are considered as reliable baselines to evaluate the performance of our suggested architecture: ECAPA-TDNN and ECAPA CNN-TDNN, which both currently provide state-of-the-art on speaker verification tasks.

The ECAPA-TDNN [5] model, which is based on the x-vector architecture [11], attempts to obtain exceptionally accurate x-vectors by introducing a number of enhancements to provide more robust speaker embeddings. First, channel- and context-dependent statistics pooling layer is used to aggregate all frame-level features to generate a fixed dimensional vector. Second, in order to add global context information to the locally operating convolutional blocks, the 1-dimensional Squeeze-Excitation (SE) block [17] is used and integrated with Res2Block [4], which has the advantage of multi-scale feature processing through group convolutions in hierarchical residual connections, and reduces the number of network parameters. Finally, the output features of all the SE-Res2Block for each frame are concatenated by multi-layer feature aggregation technique.

Inspired by 2D-CNNs, Thienpondt et al. [6] introduced a 2D convolutional stem in ECAPA-TDNN to transfer the advantages of ResNet architecture to the proposed hybrid CNN-TDNN network. Using ResNet in top layers allows the network to initially construct local, frequency-invariant features and then 1D convolutions are applied to incorporate the frequency position information of the features. The flattened output feature map subsequently is used to feed the ECAPA-TDNN network.

## III. Proposed RCT-Net Architecture

The neural network is used by the current speaker verification methods to derive speaker representations. The effective x-vector architecture [11] uses TDNN to project variable-length utterances into fixed-length speaker characterization embeddings by applying statistics pooling. On the task of speaker verification, we aim to obtain an extremely accurate version of x-vector topology and try to enhance the performance of the original TDNN-based architectures [12].

We investigate different deep residual unit variations, and we are particularly interested in whether the TDNN and the basic residual building blocks simplicity can be successfully combined with the advantages of standard residual-based architectures [1] [9] [10] [14], and how the performance of the resulting architectures compares to the more sophisticated multi-scale residual blocks [3] [4]. In this regard, our method integrates, extends, and generalizes the architecture of ASV we previously described [13]. The proposed architecture, as shown in Figure 1, follows an established multi-scale and frequency positional encoding structure, ECAPA CNN-TDNN. In this study, we propose enhancements to the frame-level feature extractor.

### A. Standard Residual Blocks

We shortly go over the key concepts underlying residual-based architectures like ResNet and Res-TCN [10] [15]. ResNet employs injected residual connections between processing streams to allow spatial-temporal interaction between them. Res-TCN redesigned the original TCN [14] by factoring out the deeper layers into additive residual terms that yielded both an interpretable hidden representation and model parameters. In contrast to the original ResNet, the basic residual unit of Res-TCN and improved ResNet [9] does not use ReLUs to support the element-wise additions $\bigoplus$ (see Figure 2(a-c)) and can therefore offer representations that are more interpretable. Additionally, such units create a direct path that enables the gradients and the signal to be transmitted directly in a backward pass through the entire network to any unit.

### B. Multi-Scale Residual Blocks

Multi-scale feature representation has been integrated from the beginning into the CNN architectural design with a stack

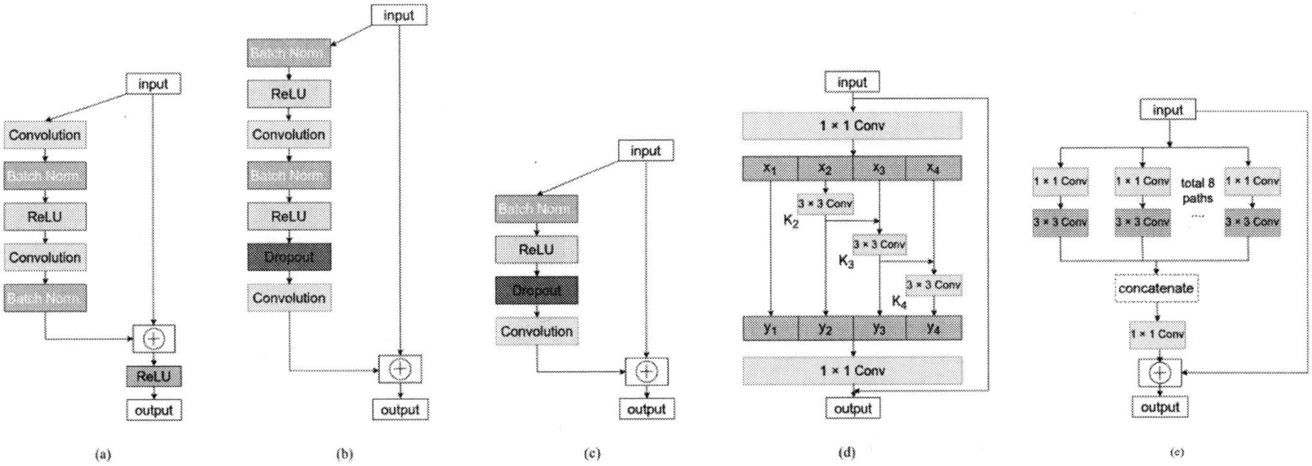


Fig. 2. The structures of bottleneck residual blocks in different architectures. Standard residual blocks in (a) ResNet [1], (b) Improved ResNet [9], and (c) Res-TCN [15]. Multi-scale residual blocks in (d) Res2Net [4] and (e) ResNeXt. [3]

of convolutional layers that automatically learn coarse-to-fine features [16]. The bottleneck module and shortcut connections to residual networks are effective at reducing the number of parameters and successfully addressing the gradient disappearance in deep CNN designs.

ResNeXt-50 [3] enhanced the bottleneck module by adding cardinal dimension and replacing conventional convolution with group convolution to perform more sophisticated transformations. Gao et al. [4] substituted the $3\times3$ convolution with a series of $3 \times 3$ convolution with smaller filter groups that are coupled hierarchically in order to incorporate the multi-scale capability of the feature representation into the module. This might be considered a network inside of a network. As a result, the range of receptive fields for each network layer is increased by the Res2NeXt, which also represents multi-scale features at a finer level. Res2NeXt-50 improved ResNeXt-50 by enabling multi-scale feature representation at both the global and local levels by integrating hierarchical multi-scale feature representation into the bottleneck module. SE-Res2NeXt-50 [4] integrated the SE block [17] to provide a channel-wise dynamic calibration of feature responses and provide enhanced feature representation capabilities.

Res2NeXt substitutes a set of $3 \times 3$ filters with smaller groups of filters, while connecting different filter groups in a hierarchical residual-like way, cf. Figure 2. $3 \times 3$ convolution is followed by the input being split into $s$ feature map subsets, indicated by the symbol $\mathrm{X}_i$, where $i \in \{1, 2, ..., s\}$. Each feature subset $\mathrm{X}_i$ differs from the input feature map only in that it has $1/s$ fewer channels but the same spatial extent. With the exception of $\mathrm{X}_1$, which is forwarded directly to the output, each $\mathrm{X}_i$ has a matching $3 \times 3$ convolution, indicated by $\mathrm{K}_i(\cdot)$. The output $\mathrm{K}_{i-1}(\cdot)$ from the earlier $3 \times 3$ convolution is then fed into $\mathrm{K}_i(\cdot)$ together with the feature subset $\mathrm{X}_i$. The output of the module is produced by concatenating the outputs of all groups and forwarding them to a $1 \times 1$ convolution. Thus, $\mathrm{Y}_i$ can be:

$$Y_i = \begin{cases} X_i & i{=}1 \\ K_i(X_i) & i{=}2 \\ K_i(X_i + Y_{i-1}) & 2 < i \leq s \end{cases}$$

## IV. Experimental Setup

We evaluate the performance of the proposed architecture on the ECAPA embedding on the development part of the VoxCeleb2 dataset with 5994 speakers as training data. VoxCeleb1 test set is taken into consideration as a validation set for hyperparameter optimization. As follow the baselines [5] [6], all models are trained using a standard Adam optimizer with cyclical learning rates ranging between 1e-8 and 1e-3. Using AAM-softmax with a margin of 0.2 and softmax prescaling of 30 for 4 cycles, all systems are trained.

### A. Dataset

We use the development part of the VoxCeleb 2 [18] as our training set. This dataset contains over 1 million utterances for 5,994 speakers extracted from YouTube. The MUSAN [19] and RIR [20] datasets are used to generate extra samples for online data augmentation. VoxCeleb1 [21] has three types of evaluation trials, which are VoxCeleb1-O, VoxCeleb1-E and VoxCeleb1-H. For fairness of comparisons, we keep consistent with the ECAPA-TDNN and ECAPA CNN-TDNN experiments and choose VoxCeleb1-O as the validation set, this dataset contains 4,708 utterances from 40 speakers.

### B. System Description

Both ECAPA-TDNN [5] and ECAPA CNN-TDNN [6] are used as baseline systems in this study. We can describe the proposed systems and the two baselines as follows:

- **ECAPA-TDNN (Re-implemented):** It follows the standard ECAPA-TDNN model from [5]. In the convolutional frame layers, there are 1024 channels, and the number of Res2Blocks is 3.

TABLE I
EER PERFORMANCE OF THE ECAPA-TDNN (ET) AND ECAPA CNN-TDNN (ECT) BASELINE MODELS AND PROPOSED ARCHITECTURES ON VOXCELEB1 TEST SET. PARAMETER $s$ DEPICTS THE VALUE OF SCALE, $g$ IS THE VALUE OF CARDINALITY, AND $c$ IS THE NUMBER OF FILTERS.

| Architecture | Residual Units | Setting | No. Params($Million$) | EER(%) | PRI-ET(%) | PRI-ECT(%) |
|---|---|---|---|---|---|---|
| ECAPA TDNN [5](Re-implemented) | Res2Net | 8s×1024$c$ | 14.73 | 1.03 | | |
| ECAPA CNN-TDNN [6](Re-implemented) | ResNet | 128c | 27.54 | 0.97 | | |
| Extended ECAPA-TDNN | Res2Net | 4s×1024$c$ | 15.43 | 1.12 | -8.7 | -15.5 |
| | | 6s×1024$c$ | 14.96 | 1.07 | -3.9 | -10.3 |
| | Res2NeXt | 4s×4$g$ × 1024$c$ | 14.17 | 1.02 | +0.97 | -5.2 |
| | | 6s×8$g$ × 1008$c$ | **14.06** | **0.94** | **+8.7** | **+3.1** |
| | | 8s×8$g$ × 1024$c$ | 13.87 | 1.03 | 0 | -6.2 |
| | ResNeXt | 4g×1024$c$ | 16.00 | 1.12 | -8.7 | -15.5 |
| | | 6g×1026$c$ | 15.23 | 1.13 | -9.7 | -16.5 |
| | | 8g×1024$c$ | 14.87 | 1.29 | -25.2 | -32.99 |
| **RCT-Net** | Improved ResNet | 128c | 27.54 | 0.98 | +4.9 | -1.03 |
| | Res-TCN | 128c | 27.26 | 0.95 | +7.8 | +2.06 |
| | Res2Net | 4s×128$c$ | 27.03 | 0.98 | +4.9 | -1.03 |
| | | 6s×128$c$ | 27.01 | 0.91 | +11.7 | +6.2 |
| | | 8s×128$c$ | 27.01 | 0.94 | +8.7 | +3.1 |
| | Res2NeXt | 4s×4$g$ × 128$c$ | 26.99 | 0.97 | +5.8 | 0 |
| | | 6s×8$g$ × 144$c$ | 27.01 | 0.90 | +12.6 | +7.2 |
| | | 8s×8$g$ × 128$c$ | **26.98** | **0.88** | **+14.6** | **+9.3** |
| | ResNeXt | 4g×128$c$ | 27.12 | 1.11 | -7.8 | -14.4 |
| | | 6g×132$c$ | 27.48 | 0.97 | +5.8 | 0 |
| | | 8g×128$c$ | 27.05 | 0.98 | +4.9 | -1.03 |

- **ECAPA CNN-TDNN (Re-implemented):** As proposed in [6] four layers of CNN are employed as a front-end for ECAPA-TDNN. Different from [6], we do not increase the intermediate channel dimension and depth in ECAPA-TDNN module, but the standard version with 3 SE-Res2Blocks and 1024 channels. This is for fair comparisons with ECAPA-TDNN and the proposed RCT-Net.
- **RCT-Net**: The standard ECAPA-TDNN with different residual blocks as a front-end.

### C. Training the speaker embedding extractors

The input features are 80-dimensional Mel-Frequency Cepstral Coefficients (MFCCs) extracted from a window length of 25 ms with a frame shift of 10 ms. Cepstral mean subtraction is used to normalize the two second random cropping of the MFCCs feature vectors. It is well known that data augmentation has great benefits for neural networks. So, we use the MUSAN (babble, music, noise, TV noise) corpora and the RIR corpora (reverb) for online data augmentation to generate five extra samples for each utterance. We apply SpecAugment [22] as the last step of augmentation, this algorithm randomly masks dimension of 10 and 8 in the temporal and frequency dimensions, respectively.

TABLE II
DIFFERENT SETTINGS OF *scale* AND *cardinality* DIMENSIONS ON MULTI-SCALE RESIDUAL BLOCKS

| Residual Units | Setting 1 | Setting 2 | Setting 3 |
|---|---|---|---|
| **Res2Net** | 4s | 6s | 8s |
| **ResNeXt** | 4g | 6g | 8g |
| **Res2NeXt** | 4s×4$g$ | 6s×8$g$ | 8s×8$g$ |

## V. RESULTS

A performance overview of the baseline systems described in Section II and our proposed architectures are summarized in Table I. We extend the baseline speaker embedding models by incorporating the proposed 1D and 2D convolutional stems with various bottleneck residual blocks. We then evaluate the Percent Relative Improvements (PRI) of the proposed models with the ECPA-TDNN and ECAPA CNN-TDNN baselines.

Results show that in general almost all RCT-based combinations (10 out of 11 combinations, i.e., around 91% of all combinations) lead to an improvement over standard ECAPA-TDNN. The results also demonstrate that all proposed models with potential to perform better than their corresponding baselines have fewer parameters. In the following, we analyze the performance in more detail wrt. to system combination constituents.

### A. Variations in CNN stems representation

Further analyzing the results, we assume a competitive threshold of EER=1, i.e., a high-performance system threshold where the amount of falsely rejected and falsely accepted speakers in an ASV system would be equally high, namely 1%. Accordingly, as shown in Table I, while 87.5% of any ECAPA-TDNN extension included in the experiments are above the threshold of 1%, 91% of RCT-Net proposed models are below it. We could therefore assume that overall the 2D convolutional stems are more optimally suited for the representation of speaker embeddings for ASV systems, compared to 1D representations.

### B. Dimension variations

Findings of prior benchmark experiments [4] imply that scale is an effective dimension to enhance model performance.

Moreover, scaling up is more efficient than other dimensions. In general, this finding can be confirmed, as for most system configurations s=4 results in inferior performance, compared to higher values. However, rising the scale from 6 to 8 does not always lead to gain. On this level, the overall performance also depends on the remaining parameters $c$ and $g$.

### C. Multi-scale residual blocks

In terms of EER, the best model using Res2NeXt$-8s \times 8g \times 128c$ surpasses both ECAPA-TDNN and ECAPA CNN-TDNN baselines by 14.6% and 8.7%, respectively. Remarkably, Res2NeXt$-6s \times 8g \times 1008c$ even outperforms the baseline, ResNet-128c, with only 51% of the number of parameters in the model (see Table I). As shown in Figure 3, for 1D representations the introduction of multi-scale blocks in ResNeXt alone does not lead to any improvement. However, when combining the advantages of it into the Res2NeXt model, the performance significantly improves, i.e., by 8.7% - a performance value even outperforming the ECAPA CNN-TDNN baseline operating on a 2D representation in the stem. For the RCT-Net based models, the introduction of multi-scale blocks clearly improves the overall performance, with only the exception of ResNeXt model with too small scale settings discussed above. All models show significant improvement, best of which improves performance by 14.6% using a Res2NeXt block. Eventually, we can hypothesize that the multi-scale feature setup greatly benefits from the 2D convolution processing in the entrance of the stem.

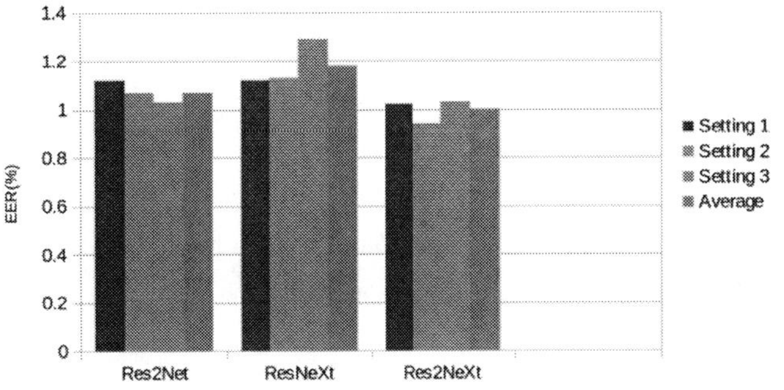


(a)

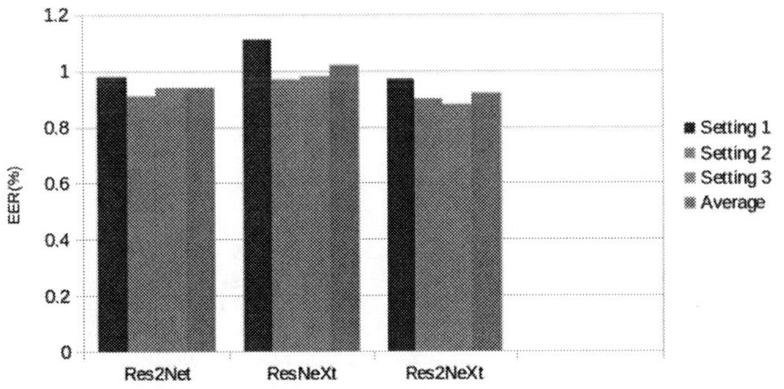


(b)

Fig. 3. Impact of various *scale* and *cardinality* dimensions with different settings as indicated in Table II. (a) ECAPA-TDNN based experiments, (b) ECAPA CNN-TDNN based experiments.

## VI. Discussions

Based on our results, we can conclude that integrating 2D Res2NeXt with TDNN is the best combination of two strong structures of TDNN and residual blocks. As a result, in our experiments representing features at multiple scales and constructing hierarchical residual-like connections within a single residual block in dimensions of both scale and cardinality is more performant than without or standalone dimensions of either scale or cardinality. A possible explanation could be the difference in the approach to obtaining multi-scale features in different residual-based architectures. Res2Net, for example, splits the original input into multiple groups according to the channels. The output of one group is fed into the next group, and so on, and all segments are concatenated as the final result. On the other side, Res2NeXt, repeats a building block that aggregates a set of transformations with the same topology and expands the range of receptive fields for each network layer, and depicts multi-scale features at a finer level. Accordingly, by integrating hierarchical multi-scale feature representation within the bottleneck module, the multi-scale feature representation is improved at both the global and local levels. Finally, in our experiment, the joint benefits of a parallel stacking layer of ResNeXt rather than sequential layers of standard ResNet architectures, multi-scaling features in Res2Net, and expanding the range of receptive fields show the potential to extract more invariant feature representations in a joint Res2NeXt architecture.

## VII. Conclusion

In this study, we adapt the frame-level layer architecture that integrates multiple ideas motivated by the convolutional block and multi-scale architectures. In our experiments, we evaluate the performance of integrating different residual blocks into TDNN-based structures. The best model using Res2NeXt improves current state-of-the-art by 14.6% relative on VoxCeleb1 test set.

These promising findings motivate us to investigate hybrid architectures in more detail and propose structures to reduce computational complexity in our upcoming studies. We will continue to evaluate the performance of various residual unit types as we integrate them with the 2D ECAPA-TDNN representation and explore several directions of multimodal fusion approaches. We will also provide speech-level interpretation of the proposed TDNN-based architectures for understanding our models. This includes visualizing the acoustic concepts the model has learned and comparing how they are represented in the model layers using [23] [24], etc, and generalizing our findings with more data utilizing additional datasets and evaluation metrics such as Minimum Value of Detection Cost Function (MinDCF).

## ACKNOWLEDGEMENT

[ This research has been partly funded by the Federal Ministry of Education and Research of Germany in the project

Emonymous (project number S21060A) and partly funded by the Volkswagen Foundation in the project AnonymPrevent (AI-based Improvement of Anonymity for Remote Assessment, Treatment and Prevention against Child Sexual Abuse).

## REFERENCES

[1] K. He, X. Zhang, S. Ren, and J. Sun, "Deep residual learning for image recognition," in 2016 IEEE Conference on Computer Vision and Pattern Recognition (CVPR), 2016, pp. 770–778.

[2] C. Szegedy, S. Ioffe, and V. Vanhoucke, "Inception-v4, inception-resnet and the impact of residual connections on learning," CoRR, vol. abs/1602.07261, 2016. [Online]. Available: http://arxiv.org/abs/1602.07261.

[3] S. Xie, R. Girshick, P. Dollar, Z. Tu, and K. He, "Aggregated residual transformations for deep neural networks," in Proceedings of the IEEE conference on computer vision and pattern recognition, 2017, pp. 1492–1500.

[4] S.-H. Gao, et al. "Res2net: A new multi-scale backbone architecture," IEEE transactions on pattern analysis and machine intelligence, vol. 43, no. 2, pp. 652–662, 2019.

[5] B. Desplanques, J. Thienpondt, and K. Demuynck, "ECAPA- TDNN: Emphasized Channel Attention, Propagation and Aggrega- tion in TDNN Based Speaker Verification," in Proc. Interspeech 2020, 2020, pp. 3830–3834.

[6] J. Thienpondt, B. Desplanques, and K. Demuynck, "Integrating frequency translational invariance in TDNNs and frequency positional information in 2d ResNets to enhance speaker verification," in Interspeech 2021. ISCA, aug 2021. [Online]. Available: $https : //doi.org/10.21437\%2Finterspeech.2021 - 1570$

[7] T. Liu, R. K. Das, K. A. Lee, and H. Li, "MFA: TDNN with multi-scale frequency-channel attention for textindependent speaker verification with short utterances," in IEEE International Conference on Acoustics, Speech and Signal Processing (ICASSP), 2022.

[8] Zhang, Y.-J., et al. (2021) Improving Time Delay Neural Network Based Speaker Recognition with Convolutional Block and Feature Aggregation Methods. Proc. Interspeech 2021, 76-80, doi: 10.21437/Interspeech.2021-356.

[9] H. Pham, L. Khoudour, A. Crouzil, P. Zegers, and S. A. Velastin, "Exploiting deep residual networks for human action recognition from skeletal data," CoRR, vol. abs/1803.07781, 2018. [Online]. Available: http://arxiv.org/abs/1803.07781

[10] R. Khamsehashari, K. Gadzicki, and C. Zetzsche, "Deep residual temporal convolutional networks for skeleton-based human action recognition," in Computer Vision Systems, D. Tzovaras, D. Gi- akoumis, M. Vincze, and A. Argyros, Eds. Cham: Springer International Publishing, 2019, pp. 376–385.

[11] D. Snyder, D. Garcia-Romero, G. Sell, D. Povey, and S. Khudanpur, "X-vectors: Robust DNN embeddings for speaker recognition," in Proc. ICASSP, 2018, pp. 5329–5333.

[12] D. Snyder, D. Garcia-Romero, G. Sell, D. Povey, and S. Khudanpur, "X-vectors: Robust dnn embeddings for speaker recognition," in 2018 IEEE International Conference on Acoustics, Speech and Signal Processing (ICASSP), 2018, pp. 5329–5333.

[13] R. Khamsehashari, et al. "Voice Privacy - leveraging multi-scale blocks with ECAPA-TDNN SE-Res2NeXt extension for speaker anonymization," in Proc. 2nd Symposium on Security and Privacy in Speech Communication, 2022, pp. 43–48.

[14] C. Lea, M. D. Flynn, R. Vidal, A. Reiter, and G. D. Hager, "Temporal convolutional networks for action segmentation and detection," CoRR, vol. abs/1611.05267, 2016. [Online]. Available: http://arxiv.org/abs/1611.05267

[15] T. S. Kim and A. Reiter, "Interpretable 3d human action analysis with temporal convolutional networks," CoRR, vol. abs/1704.04516, 2017. [Online]. Available: http://arxiv.org/abs/ 1704.04516

[16] K. Simonyan and A. Zisserman, "Very deep convolutional networks for large-scale image recognition," 2014. [Online]. Available: https://arxiv.org/abs/1409.1556

[17] J. Hu, L. Shen, and G. Sun, "Squeeze-and-excitation networks," in Proceedings of the IEEE conference on computer vision and pattern recognition, 2018, pp. 7132–7141.

[18] J. S. Chung, A. Nagrani, and A. Zisserman, "Voxceleb2: Deep speaker recognition," arXiv preprint arXiv:1806.05622, 2018.

[19] D. Snyder, G. Chen, and D. Povey, "MUSAN: A Music, Speech, and Noise Corpus," 2015, arXiv:1510.08484v1.

[20] T. Ko, V. Peddinti, D. Povey, M. L. Seltzer, and S. Khudanpur, "A study on data augmentation of reverberant speech for robust speech recognition," in 2017 IEEE International Conference on Acoustics, Speech and Signal Processing (ICASSP). IEEE, 2017, pp. 5220–5224.

[21] A. Nagrani, J. S. Chung, and A. Zisserman, "Voxceleb: a large-scale speaker identification dataset," arXiv preprint arXiv:1706.08612, 2017.

[22] D. S. Park, et al. "Specaugment: A simple data augmen- tation method for automatic speech recognition," arXiv preprint arXiv:1904.08779, 2019.

[23] O. Ozyegen, I. Ilic, and M. Cevik, Evaluation of interpretability methods for multivariate time series forecasting. Appl Intell 52, 4727–4743 (2022). https://doi.org/10.1007/s10489-021-02662-2

[24] R. R. Selvaraju, et al. "Grad-CAM: visual explanations from deep networks via gradient-based localization," in IEEE international conference on computer vision, 2017, pp. 618–626.

# Supervised Spatial Divide-and-Conquer Applied to Fish Counting

Gianna Arencibia-Castellanos
*CITSEM*
*Universidad Politécnica de Madrid*
Madrid, Spain
gianna.arencibia@upm.es

Alejandro González-Fernández
*CITSEM*
*Universidad Politécnica de Madrid*
Madrid, Spain
alejandro.gfernandez@alumnos.upm.es

María Castillo-Moral
*CITSEM*
*Universidad Politécnica de Madrid*
Madrid, Spain
maria.castillom@upm.es

Rubén Fraile
*CITSEM*
*Universidad Politécnica de Madrid*
Madrid, Spain
r.fraile@upm.es

Juana M. Gutiérrez-Arriola
*CITSEM*
*Universidad Politécnica de Madrid*
Madrid, Spain
juana.gutierrez.arriola@upm.es

Fernando Pescador
*CITSEM*
*Universidad Politécnica de Madrid*
Madrid, Spain
fernando.pescador@upm.es

***Abstract*—The estimation of fish biomass plays a crucial role in aquaculture. Performing this task automatically using machine learning algorithms has attracted the attention of the scientific community. This work describes the application of Supervised Spatial Divide-and-Conquer net to counting the number of larvae present in an image of an aquaculture tank. SS-DCNet is among the most robust object counters in the state of the art when applied to different datasets. It is trained with labeled images of turbots in breeding tanks, taking into account that the sizes can be variable and that they can be grouped and overlapped. Data augmentation is applied to obtain a greater number of training instances. The application of this model to counting turbots in images provides a mean relative error lower than 3.5%, which is an acceptable accuracy for this task. The main advantage of the model studied is its generalization ability, confirmed by its performance in counting objects in images where the density and the total number of objects are much higher than for the training images. Adapting the model for counting other types of fish, or turbot in other stages of growth, is straightforward since it is not necessary to build large training datasets.**

***Index Terms*—Image processing, Object detection, SS-DCNet, biomass estimation**

## I. INTRODUCTION

Biomass estimation, that is, knowing the number of fish and their weight, allows fish farmers to optimize the amount of feed, plan later stages of farming, and make decisions at the right times. Traditionally, biomass estimation has been carried out by people using invasive procedures that are usually slow and laborious and require great expertise, experience, and knowledge of the conditions of the farm and the environment [1].

Technological advances in recent decades have allowed the development of systems that offer automatic estimation of biomass based on artificial vision, acoustic signals, environmental deoxyribonucleic acid (DNA), or resistivity counters. These methods are objective, noninvasive and produce repeatable and reliable results. In contrast, they can be expensive and not easily adaptable to variations in the environment [1].

Recently, machine learning (ML) techniques have grown remarkably in applicability to the fields of industry, social networks, etc. In aquaculture, they have been used to predict water quality [2], identify and distinguish among fish types [3], diagnose diseases [4], estimate biomass [5], etc. Both image recording technology and computer services have been generalized and cheapened so that biomass estimation systems can currently be developed cheaply and reliably. The number of fishes in an image is among the parameters required for biomass estimation. For the purpose of estimating it, the algorithmic approaches used for counting objects in RGB images can be adapted.

To date, approaches used for counting objects in images can be grouped in roughly three types: counting by detection, regression, and density estimation [6]. Counting by detection is based on the position of each object in the image using the extracted image features. These methods have shown good results in datasets where the objects are separated from each other. However, in scenes where the objects are next to each other or even overlapping, the results have not been good. Some recent proposals in this area, using local features instead of global features, have improved counting results in images with high object density [6].

Alternatively, counting based on regression models attempts to establish a relationship between image features and the number of objects using supervised machine learning techniques. These models do not use datasets based on the location of individual objects but require only the total number of objects in the image. Thus, although the results of these models are generally better than those based on detection, they usually require large datasets to be trained [6].

The two model types previously described ignore the spatial information of the images; the solution proposed in [7] incorporates this information. In this work, a mapping of the features in the images and their corresponding density maps are developed that improves the accuracy of the counting

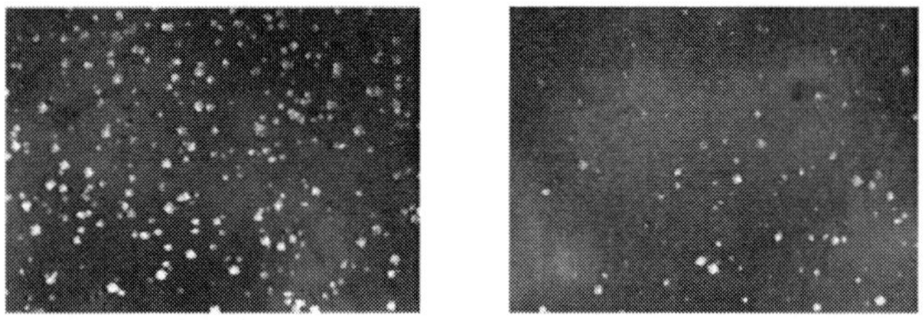

(a) (b)

Figure 1. Example of frames captured at a frequency of 15 f/s. (a) High density of turbots and (b) Low density of turbots.

results compared to previous approaches [8]. The advantages of this proposal are the following: the density maps provide more information about the distribution of the objects, and the algorithm is more adaptable to objects with different sizes and more tolerant to different images [8].

Aforementioned research suggests that the application of ML algorithms to images of fish larval tanks can enable the implementation of low-cost, accurate, and reliable biomass estimation systems. In this paper, we develop a system that allows obtaining an estimated number of turbot larvae present in RGB (red, green, blue) images. For this purpose, a deep learning algorithm is trained with labeled images of a fish larval tank, taking into account that fish sizes can appear to be variable in the image due to differences in depth, and that there can be grouped and overlapped objects.

The organization of the document is as follows: section II.A explains the experimental setting and construction of the dataset. Section II.B describes the implemented machine learning algorithm and the evaluation of several hyperparameters. Furthermore, the influence of different hyperparameter values on the prediction is measured with error metrics. The optimal values of the hyperparameters and the generalization capacity of the neural network were verified in section III: *Results and Discussion*. Finally, section IV presents the conclusions of the work.

## II. Materials and Methods

This section describes the neural network used to count the number of turbot larvae in an image, as well as the dataset used to train and test the model. In addition, the parameters that characterize a neural network and the metrics used to evaluate its performance and generalization capacity are explained.

### A. Dataset

The dataset consists of 156 RGB images with a resolution of $2560 \times 1920$ pixels. Two sample frames are shown in Figure 1. The images were manually annotated in the Group of Multimedia and Acoustic Applications (GAMMA) in our university with a Matlab® application specifically developed for this purpose.

Figure 1 shows two frames prototypical of two different cases: the left frame shows a high density of turbots while density is low in the right one. These images were captured in the same tank at different moments.The implemented algorithm must produce equally acceptable results in both cases, and also in intermediate ones.

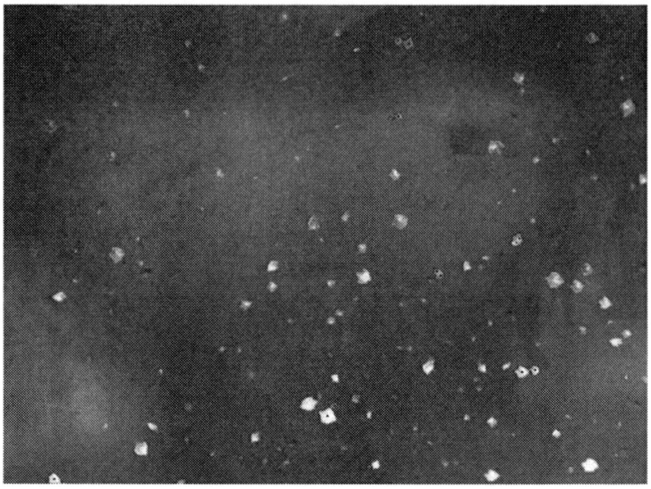

Figure 2. Segmentation of turbots, the red and blue boundaries stands out a single turbot and a group of turbots, respectively.

All images were taken from turbot larval tanks. The camera was located with the lens axis perpendicular to the water surface. In order to avoid the glaring of lighting reflections on the water, the camera focused only in part of the tank surface. Users of the annotation application were provided with images for which a segmentation by threshold had been applied to identify the objects present in the image (see Figure 2). Annotators were asked to check whether each object corresponded to a turbot larva or not. The process was made manually, and image by image, which is laborious and time consuming. But it is the most confident procedure to get a ground-truth fish count for each frame.

To train and test the neural network, the images were randomly divided into training and testing sets: 124 (80%) for training and 32 (20%) for testing. The distribution of turbots in both sets averaged 246 and 273 turbots per image, respectively.

### B. Machine learning algorithm

*1) Neural Network:* The convolutional neural network model implemented in our proposal for counting objects shows the best results in the application of counting people [6] [8]. The chosen model is the Supervised Spatial Divide-and-Conquer for Object Counting model (SS-DCNet) because it has been reported to produce low errors [9] and the applicability of the model beyond counting people has already been assessed: for counting vehicles [10], and grains of corn [11]. Thus, it is expected to be adaptable to alternative datasets too.

SS-DCNet learns from a closed set of counts and it generalizes to scenarios with open sets. This model was designed to approach the problem that only finite local patterns (a closed set) can be observed, but new scenes in the reality have a high probability of containing out of range objects (an open set). Specifically, SS-DCNet (see Figure 3) uses a 16-layer deep neural network (VGG16) as encoder and a Convolutional Networks for Biomedical Image Segmentation (UNet) like decoder to generate multi-resolution feature maps in frames of $64 \times 64$ pixels. All feature maps share the same counter, in

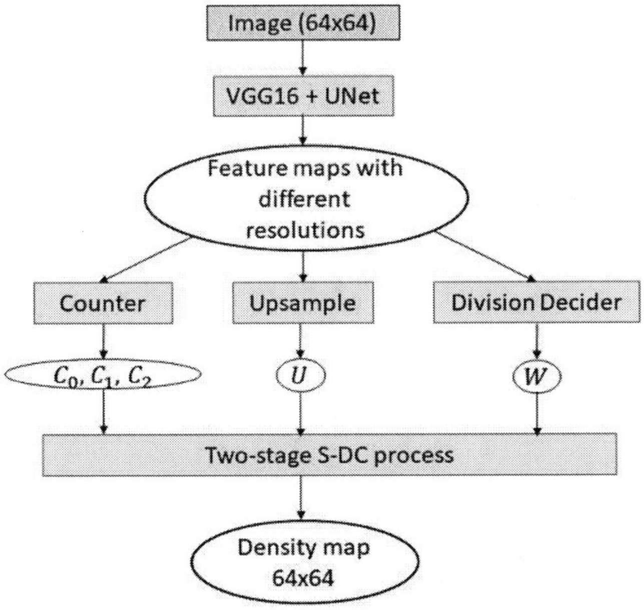


Figure 3. Diagram of SS-DCNet algorithm. $C_0$, $C_1$ y $C_2$ are the estimation counters for three different resolutions; the parameters $U$ y $W$ allows to combine the values of estimation counters to obtain the density map.

these are obtained $C_0$, $C_1$ y $C_2$ for three different resolutions. Then is applied two-stage spatial divide and conquer (S-DC) process to estimate the density map related to sub-image selected. The density map is used to calculate the local count. The final count of the image can be recovered by combining all sub-image counts into one count map with the same size as the test image. For each pixel, a normalization step is performed by dividing the number of sub-images that yield a prediction for the pixel [9]. In local counter modeling, one of the ways to define a counter in the closed set is [0, $C_{\max}$]. In practice, $C_{\max}$ should not be larger than the maximum local count observed in the training set. If the predicted counts are greater than $C_{\max}$, the predictions are simply truncated to $C_{\max}$.

Although the authors of the SS-DCNet model [9] have published source code to evaluate the accuracy of their model, their implementation only has the ability to evaluate an already trained model and does not have routines to train a model with a specific dataset. For this reason, the basic source code used in this project is that published by Dmitry Burdeiny [12] on the Github platform as free code. The code has been adapted to meet the design specifications and to make it compatible with the current dataset.

Analyzing the distribution of objects on $64 \times 64$ squares, it is observed in Table I that the 95$^{\text{th}}$ percentile corresponds to the value of 5 turbots per square. Therefore, following the recommendations of the model developers, a value of 5 was chosen as a starting point for model training. However, tests were performed with the lower and upper values to analyze their variation.

TABLE I. PERCENTILES OF TURBOTS COUNTED IN FRAMES OF $64 \times 64$ PIXELS

| Percentil | Value |
|---|---|
| 65 | 1 |
| 75 | 2 |
| 85 | 3 |
| 95 | 5 |

*2) Density map:* Density maps in SS-DCNet are generated using a Gaussian kernel. The density estimation based approach uses an adaptive geometric density mapping system. This implies that the standard deviation ($\sigma$) is calculated dynamically for each labeled point. This value is usually calculated as the product of the mean distance to nearest neighbors and a mitigation coefficient, usually 0.3 [13]. However, the adaptive calculation of the standard deviation is applied to images where the size of the object is evenly distributed among different image regions. For example, an image of a street where people's heads have similar size means that they are in the same image region (foreground, background, other). However, in our dataset, the turbot size is not distributed across the image regions, the size varies mainly with distance to the water surface. Turbots closer to the surface are larger than those in the depth, therefore neighbors in the same region can be in different planes. For this reason, a fixed standard deviation was chosen to create the density maps.

To measure how the value of $\sigma$ affects the accuracy of the model, the density map was created with different values of $\sigma$ between 3 and 15 in intervals of three, all with a kernel size of 30 pixels, as shown in Figure 4.

In Figure 4 can be seen that when the parameter $\sigma$ is increased, the algorithm detects objects where there are none, while at a low sigma of 3 it detects fewer objects.

*3) Train and validation test:* A random division of the training dataset is made to apply double cross validation: 90% of images for training and 10% for validation. Note that this validation is different from the final evaluation of the error on the test set. The goal of this evaluation is to check during training the evolution of accuracy after certain training iterations.

Moreover, the technique of data augmentation or artificial data generation is used to obtain a larger number of training instances. The strategy followed is to generate nine sub-images with a quarter of the total image resolution, as in [9] [14]. Four sub-images are drawn from the four corners without overlapping, and the other five are drawn randomly from the image. These images need to be normalized, so the average pixel value was calculated for each RGB channel using all images set. The calculated average pixel subtracted from pixels of each RGB channel, and then divided by 255 was the normalization process implemented.

The Stochastic Gradient Descent (SGD) optimization algorithm is chosen as the learning algorithm of the model. The implementation uses an initial learning rate of 0.0001, which is divided by a factor of 10 for each iteration of

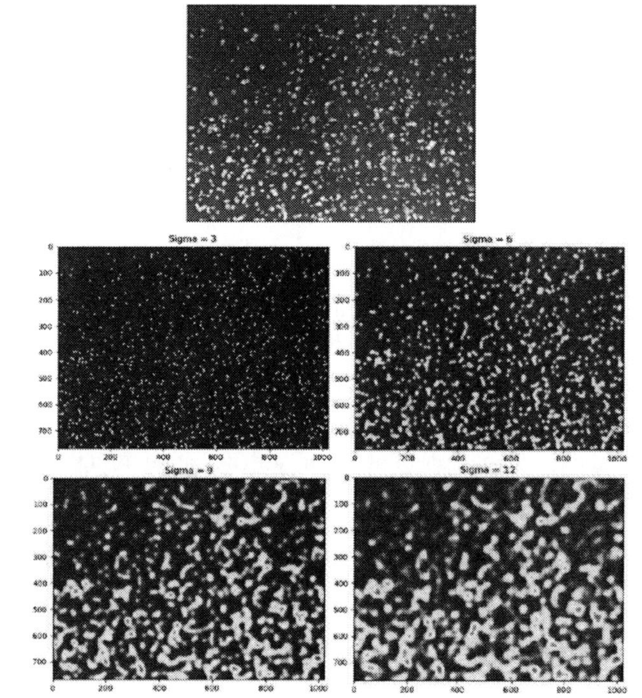


Figure 4. Examples of density maps for different values of $\sigma$. The original frame (top), maps with $\sigma$ equal to 3 (center-left), 6 (center-right), 9 (down-left) and 12 (down-right)

the training process. A random Gaussian initialization with a standard deviation of 0.01 is used to compute the weights. The convolutional neural network is pre-trained with the ImageNet dataset and the batch size is equal to 1 in our proposal.

In addition, the following techniques are used to improve the SGD optimization algorithm:

- Momentum: It is used to reduce excessive fluctuations in the weight changes in successive iterations and thus improve the learning rate [15]. The value used for this parameter is 0.9.
- Weight decay: This is a regularization technique whose main goal is to avoid overfitting that would affect generalization for new data. This technique introduces a penalty in the cost function to reduce the weights during the backward propagation of the error [16]. The value used for this parameter is $10^{-4}$.

## III. Results and discussion

In order to obtain the optimal parameters for the generation of the density maps and $C_{\max}$ of the classifier, experiments began with $\sigma$ equal to 12 and $C_{\max}$ equal to 5. The impact of these parameters was analysed training the system with their extreme values to appreciate the change of these parameters.

*1) Relationship between $\sigma$ and density map:* In order to evaluate how the choice of $\sigma$ for the Gaussian kernel affects the accuracy of the model when generating density maps, it was trained with a value of $C_{\max}$ equal to 5 and the density maps were generated for different $\sigma$ values, between 3 and 15 in steps of three. As can be seen in Table II, there is no significant effect on the model errors at small standard deviations.

TABLE II. ERRORS OBTAINED BY DIFFERENT DENSITY MAPS

| $\sigma$ | MAE | RMSE | MAPE (%) |
|---|---|---|---|
| 3 | 9.00 | 18.82 | 3.52 |
| 6 | 11.66 | 19.46 | 4.04 |
| 9 | 11.05 | 19.22 | 3.56 |
| 12 | 9.66 | 18.20 | 3.48 |
| 15 | 10.62 | 18.09 | 3.69 |

A value of 12 was used for $\sigma$ to create the density maps for the rest of tests. Although it has a slightly worse Mean Absolute Error (MAE) value than the map created with a $\sigma = 3$, the Mean Square Error (MSE) and Mean Absolute Percentage Error (MAPE) values are better and the deviations are therefore more homogeneous. The Root Mean Square Error (RMSE) is similar in all cases.

*2) Selection of $C_{\max}$ value:* The developers of the SS-DCNet model obtained the best model accuracy results for a $C_{\max}$ value corresponding to the 95th percentile of the objects distribution in $64 \times 64$ pixels. This value is 5 for the current dataset. The validity of that conclusion was verified training the model with $C_{\max}$ values below and above 5.

As can be seen in Table III, for $C_{\max} = 5$ , the smallest errors are obtained for both MAE and MAPE. However, for $C_{\max} = 6$, the RMSE is slightly smaller, meaning that there is less variation. Nevertheless, the difference between MAE and MAPE is considered to be more significant than RMSE, so a value of $C_{\max}$ equal to 5 is used for the further tests.

TABLE III. ERRORS OBTAINED BY DIFFERENT $C_{\max}$

| $C_{\max}$ | MAE | RMSE | MAPE (%) |
|---|---|---|---|
| 2 | 14.45 | 25.98 | 3.90 |
| 3 | 15.02 | 27.26 | 4.13 |
| 4 | 14.67 | 26.49 | 4.09 |
| 5 | 9.66 | 18.20 | 3.48 |
| 6 | 10.39 | 18.05 | 3.64 |

*3) Generalization capability / ability:* In order to evaluate how the model generalizes for frames with higher concentration of turbot larvae, it was re-trained with images that had a low density of individuals, less than 350 per frame, and tested with images that had a high density, between 350 and 898 individuals. For this experiment, 129 and 27 images were used for training and testing, respectively.

Figure 5 shows a low deviation for predictions in test images. Therefore, the model maintains an acceptable accuracy for images with a higher density and number of objects than that of the training set.

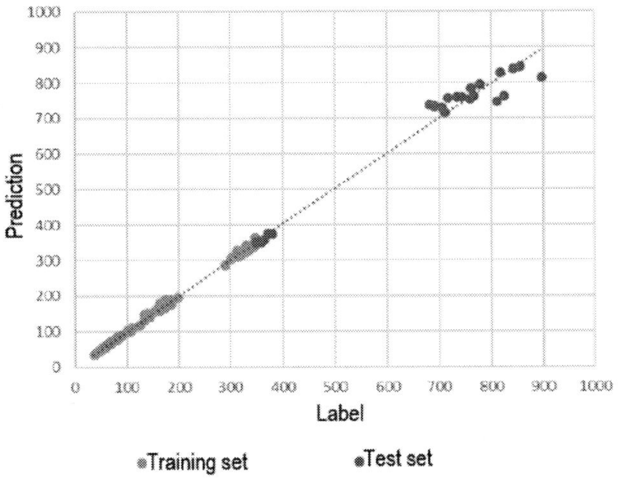


Figure 5. Generalization capability of SS-DCNet. The *Label* and *Prediction* axes represent the real and estimated number of turbots in a tank, respectively. The orange dots are the data of training set and the blue dots are the new data with high turbots density. The broken line shows the ideal estimation model

## IV. CONCLUSIONS

Applying a convolutional neural network model to count turbot larvae in breeding tanks from images yields a mean error lower than 3.5%, which is acceptable accuracy for this task. Adaptation of the model to count other fish species or turbot at other growth stages is feasible, as it is not necessary to use large datasets for training. The evaluated model exhibits a remarkable generalization ability, providing good counting estimates even when the density and total number of objects in test images is much larger than in the training images.

While the characteristics of the dataset used do not allow the application of the adaptive geometry strategies used in people counting, other strategies for creating the density maps can be explored, such as adjusting the value of $\sigma$ for each labeled point based on the morphological features extracted during the label segmentation process.

While using a pre-trained VGG16 encoding network helps in reducing the need for a large training dataset, it is possible that training the encoder from scratch with application specific images could improve accuracy, as there may be few or no images about larval turbot in the ImageNet dataset with that the encoder was pre-trained, despite its large expansion of images and categories.

## ACKNOWLEDGMENT

This work has been funded by Ministerio de Agricultura, Pesca y Alimentación, Plan de Recuperación, Transformación y Resiliencia, NextGenerationEU. Project: *Aplicación de tecnologías de visión e inteligencia artificial a la mejora del proceso productivo (Acuicultura 4.0)*

## REFERENCES

[1] D. Li, Y. Hao, and Y. Duan, "Nonintrusive methods for biomass estimation in aquaculture with emphasis on fish: a review," *Reviews in Aquaculture*, vol. 12, no. 3, pp. 1390–1411, 2020.

[2] A. Najah Ahmed, F. Binti Othman, H. Abdulmohsin Afan, R. Khaleel Ibrahim, C. Ming Fai, M. Shabbir Hossain, M. Ehteram, and A. Elshafie, "Machine learning methods for better water quality prediction," *Journal of Hydrology*, vol. 578, p. 124084, 2019.

[3] V. Kandimalla, M. Richard, F. Smith, J. Quirion, L. Torgo, and C. Whidden, "Automated detection, classification and counting of fish in fish passages with deep learning," in *Frontiers in Marine Science*, 2022.

[4] M. S. Ahmed, T. T. Aurpa, and M. A. K. Azad, "Fish disease detection using image based machine learning technique in aquaculture," *Journal of King Saud University - Computer and Information Sciences*, vol. 34, no. 8, Part A, pp. 5170–5182, 2022.

[5] N. Abinaya, D. Susan, and R. K. Sidharthan, "Deep learning-based segmental analysis of fish for biomass estimation in an occulted environment," *Computers and Electronics in Agriculture*, vol. 197, p. 106985, 2022.

[6] B. Li, H. Huang, A. Zhang, P. Liu, and C. Liu, "Approaches on crowd counting and density estimation: a review," *Pattern Analysis and Applications*, vol. 24, no. 3, pp. 853–874, 2021.

[7] R. Perko, M. Klopschitz, A. Almer, and P. M. Roth, "Critical aspects of person counting and density estimation," *Journal of Imaging*, vol. 7, no. 2, 2021.

[8] W. Li, Z. Fangbo, and H. Zhao, "Crowd density estimation based on global reasoning," *Journal of Robotics, Networking ,and Artificial Life*, vol. 7, no. 4, pp. 279–283, 2021.

[9] H. Xiong, H. Lu, C. Liu, L. Liu, C. Shen, and Z. Cao, "From open set to closed set: Supervised spatial divide-and-conquer for object counting," *ArXiv*, vol. abs/2001.01886, 2020.

[10] R. Guerrero-Gómez-Olmedo, B. Torre-Jiménez, R. López-Sastre, S. Maldonado-Bascón, and D. Oñoro-Rubio, "Extremely overlapping vehicle counting," in *Pattern Recognition and Image Analysis* (R. Paredes, J. S. Cardoso, and X. M. Pardo, eds.), (Cham), pp. 423–431, Springer International Publishing, 2015.

[11] H. Lu, Z. Cao, Y. Xiao, B. Zhuang, and C. Shen, "Tasselnet: counting maize tassels in the wild via local counts regression network," *Plant Methods*, vol. 13, no. 79, 2017.

[12] B. Dmitry, "Unofficial pytorch implementation of s-dcnet and ss-dcnet." https://github.com/dmburd/S-DCNet, 2020. (Accessed on 13/02/2023).

[13] Y. Zhang, D. Zhou, S. Chen, S. Gao, and Y. Ma, "Single-image crowd counting via multi-column convolutional neural network," in *2016 IEEE Conference on Computer Vision and Pattern Recognition (CVPR)*, pp. 589–597, 2016.

[14] Y. Li, X. Zhang, and D. Chen, "Csrnet: Dilated convolutional neural networks for understanding the highly congested scenes," *2018 IEEE/CVF Conference on Computer Vision and Pattern Recognition*, pp. 1091–1100, 2018.

[15] H. Shi, N. Yang, H. Tang, and X. Yang, "asgd: Stochastic gradient descent with adaptive batch size for every parameter," *Mathematics*, vol. 10, no. 6, 2022.

[16] H. Tessier, V. Gripon, M. Léonardon, M. Arzel, T. Hannagan, and D. Bertrand, "Rethinking weight decay for efficient neural network pruning," *Journal of Imaging*, vol. 8, p. 64, 03 2022.

# In-video Searching for Melody in Piano Lesson Videos

Tatsuya Oshiro, Megumi Wakao, Naoki Morita
School of Information Telecommunication Engineering
Tokai University
Tokyo, Japan
e-mail: {9bjt2136@cc, 9bjt2103@cc, wv062303@tsc}.u-tokai.ac.jp

Chiharu Nakanishi, Chiaki Sawada
Faculty of Music Studies
Kunitachi College of Music
Tokyo, Japan
e-mail: {nakanishi.chiharu,sawada.chiaki}@kunitachi.ac.jp

Kazue Kawai
Miyagi University
Miyagi, Japan
e-mail: kawaik@myu.ac.jp

Kenta Morita
Faculty of Medical Engineering
Suzuka University of Medical Science
Mie, Japan
e-mail: morita@suzuka-u.ac.jp

***Abstract*— In learning a musical instrument, such as the piano, it is beneficial for students to review their performances on video. However, it is difficult to search through a video for a part of a melody. This is because there is currently no way to search for a specific melody within a single piece of music. We are working towards the development of an in-video searching system for melodies. As a first step, in this study, we propose a method to detect the time when a particular melody is being played from the audio of a student practicing the piano, and test its feasibility.**

***Keywords: in-video searching; spectrogram; piano lesson; key melody.***

## I. Introduction

Reviewing oneself on video is effective in acquiring skills [1][2][3], and the same principle applies to piano practice. Students can review their performances objectively if they record them on video. In previous research, several learning methods have been proposed for filming lessons, such as systems that can analyze videos to detect bad habits [4] and methods that involve filming from multiple viewpoints [5].

However, it is difficult to search for a specific melody part in these videos. There are currently several ways to search for music. For example, humming searches, such as Google's hum to Search [6] search for metadata such as the song's title and genre based on the hummed melody. Songle [7] can graphically display the structure of a song, such as its chorus or refrain. Although there are various methods for this type of music retrieval, no method has been proposed for searching for parts of melodies contained within a single song.

Against this background, we are working towards the development of an in-video searching system for melodies that detects scenes in which students are practicing a specific melody part in a video showing them practicing the piano.

More specifically, first, students practice music and record their practicing in a video. After that, the same students perform a short melody that they want to review while watching the video and record it as a 'key melody'. Then, by using the system to detect the parts of the video that match the key melody, the student can immediately find and play back the scene in which they are practicing that same melody.

As a first step, this study proposes a method for detecting sounds that match the key melody from the audio of a video.

The structure of this paper is as follows. Section II describes the specific implementation. Section III verifies and evaluates the effectiveness of the proposed method. Section IV presents the conclusions of the paper.

## II. Method

This section describes an example of a system of in-video searching for melodies by comparing spectrograms.

(1) The system calculates the audio spectrogram of the captured video using a constant-Q [8] transform. This spectrogram will be described in a "salience representation [9]" that takes overtones into account to enhance the sound of harmonic instruments.

(2) The system stores the spectrogram obtained in (1) as an image. The frequency components with energies higher than the threshold value are drawn in white, and the rest are drawn in black. Figure 1 is an image created by the system from the processing steps (1) and (2) for a video recording of a performance of Twinkle Twinkle Little Star. The horizontal axis is time, and the vertical axis is scale.

(3) The system receives a key melody and generates a spectrogram using the same process described in (1) and (2). Figure 2 is an image generated from the first two bars of a performance of Twinkle Twinkle Little Star.

(4) The system overlaps the spectrogram of the video obtained in (2) with the spectrogram of the key melody obtained in (3) and counts the total number of overlapping white dots as the score. We can say that the higher the score is, the higher the similarity is. The

overlapping position is shifted to the right by 1 px from the left end of the spectrogram of the video until the entire recording has been covered. Figure 3 shows an example of how the system calculates the similarity between Figure 1 and Figure 2. Dots that are common to both images are shown in green, those that are only in Figure 1 are shown in white, and those that are only in Figure 2 are shown in red. The scores in the circles are the total number of green dots in the range of Figure 2. A higher number means a higher similarity to the key melody.

## III. Experiment

We evaluate whether multiple videos and key melodies show higher scores at times that include the melody being searched for.

### *i. Data used in the experiment*

Two recordings of piano practice at a music academy are used as the experimental video. In these videos, students practice their set pieces [11][12] repeatedly according to an instructor's comments. In each video, about two bars of a piece are repeatedly practiced.

As the key melody, the same melody as the one practiced in the video, performed by the same student after practice, is used.

### *ii. Generating spectrogram*

Scores are calculated every 10 milliseconds of the video. The spectrograms of the key melodies searched for in video 1 and video 2 had totals of 916 and 2635 white dots, respectively.

### *iii. Results and Discussion*

Figure 4 and Figure 5 show the changes in scores versus time. The horizontal axis is the number of seconds, and the vertical axis is the score. The gray area represents the time when the melody being searched for is actually being played in the video. The red line represents approximately 75% of the maximum score. Most of the scores were significantly higher at the beginning of the gray area. Thus, it was found that the scores were higher at the time when the melody being searched for was actually being played.

When a score exceeding 75% of the maximum was used as the threshold for similarity, it was found that all melodies being searched for could be extracted.

## IV. Conclusion

We proposed a melody retrieval method using spectrograms as a method to retrieve specific melodies from audio. Experimental results show that a melody being searched for can be successfully identified and extracted when the threshold is set to about 75% of the maximum score.

As this system uses only the sound of the video to find the time when a melody similar to the key melody is being played, we will develop a search engine in combination with a video viewer and recording functions in the future.

## Acknowledgment

This work was supported by the Japan Society for the Promotion of Science (JSPS) KAKENHI Grant Number 21K18528.

## References

[1] M. Kagawa, "Investigating the effects of video feedback using digital content on the acquisition and demonstration of motor skills," Journal of information education, Naruto University of Education, Vol.8, pp. 1-9, March 2011.

[2] K. Yomoda, K. Matsuda, T. Okimura and K. Saito, "The characteristic of students' reflections from video feedback on high-jump lessons in PE: Content analysis based on specificity, movement phases, and skill levels," Japanese journal of sports and health science, Vol. 43, pp. 87-101, 2021.

[3] H. Mihara et al., "Educational Practices of Medical Training via Video Learning and Video Assessment," Medical education, Vol. 52, No. 3, pp. 187-192, June 2021.

[4] R. Matsui, A. Hasegawa, Y. Takegawa, K. Hirata and Y. Yanagisawa, "Design, Implementation and Assessment of a Support System to Find Bad Fingering Habits for Piano Teachers," Transactions of Information Processing Society of Japan, Vol.61, No.4, pp. 789-797, April, 2020.

[5] R. Matsui, Y. Takegawa and K. Hirata, "Tel-Gerich:Remote Piano Lesson System Considering Joint Attention Camera Switching and Camera Switching," The Transactions of Human Interface Society, Vol. 20, No. 3, pp. 321–332, 2018.

[6] Google Inc. *Song stuck in your head? Just hum to search* [Online]. Available from: https://blog.google/products/search/hum-to-search/

[7] M. Goto, K. Yoshii, and T, Nakano, "Songle: active music appreciation service that uses music understanding technology to estimate the content of songs on the web," 2013-MUS-100 Vol. 16, pp1-9, August 2013.

[8] Judith C. Brown, "Calculation of a constant Q spectral transform, " The Journal of the Acoustical Society of America 89, 425, 1991.

[9] Nicholas Huang, "Auditory salience using natural soundscapes," The Journal of the Acoustical Society of America 141, 2163 ,2017.

[10] Atelier Music School. *Twinkle Twinkle Little Star* [Online]. Available from: https://atelier-music.com/sheetmusic/twinkle-twinkle-little-star

[11] Prokofiev, *Visions fugitives, Op.22*, Collected Works (Собрание сочинений), Vol.1 (pp.133-62), Moscow: Muzgiz, 1955. Plate M. 23404 Г

[12] Beethoven, *Piano Sonata No.15, Op.28*, Ludwig van Beethovens Werke, Serie 16: Sonaten für das Pianoforte (pp.27-44), Nr.138, Leipzig: Breitkopf und Härtel, n.d.[1862-90]. Plate B.138.

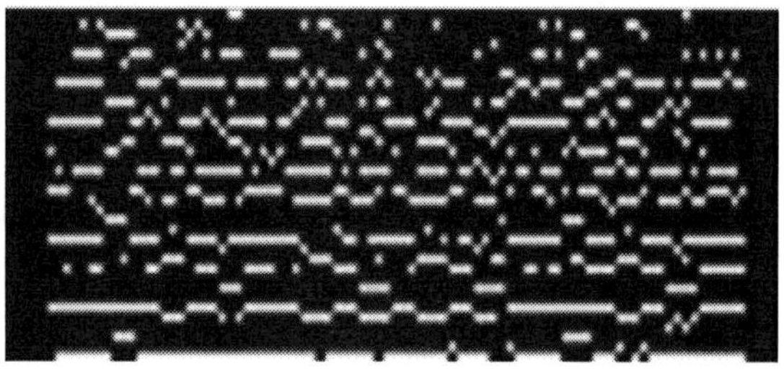

Figure 1. Image corresponding to Twinkle Twinkle Little Star

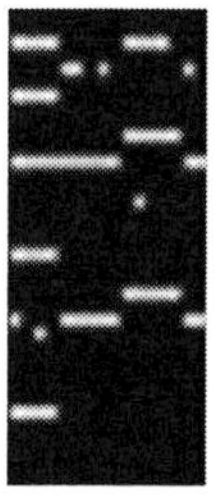

Figure 2. Image corresponding to key melody

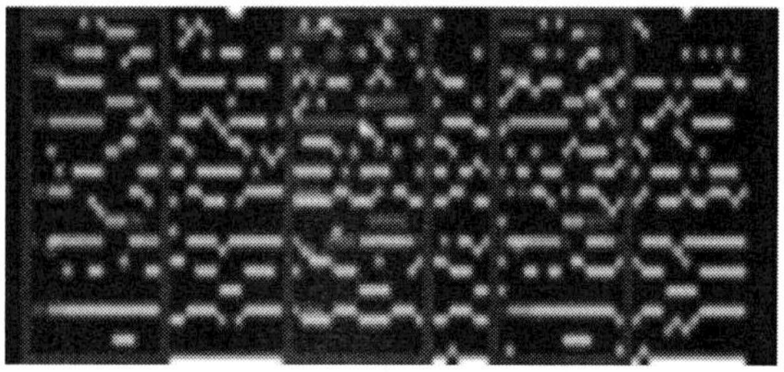

Figure 3. Example of similarity audio of a video and key melody

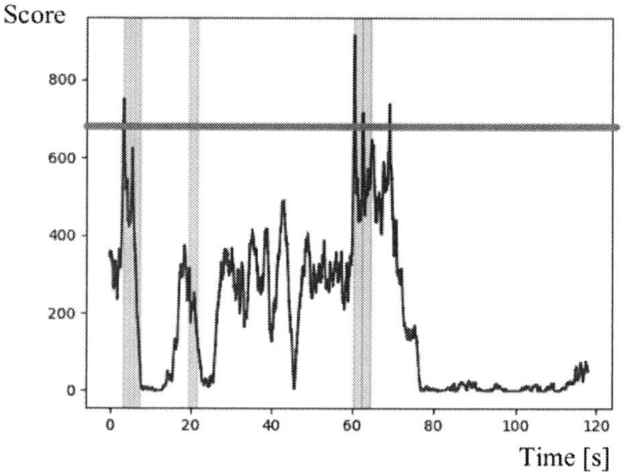


Figure 4. Score versus time of video 1

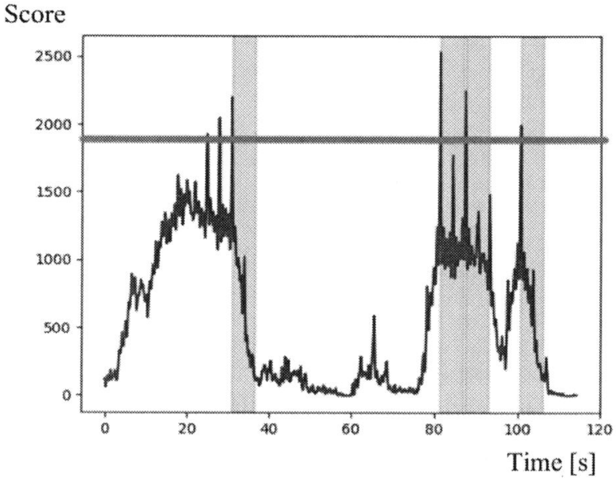


Figure 5. Score versus time of video 2

# SL(2,R) Multi-scale Contour Registration Based on Riemannian Calculation

Khaoula Sakrani
*CRISTAL Laboratory, GRIFT Group*
*National School of Computer Science*
Manouba university, Tunisia
Email. sakrani.khaoula@gmail.com

Sinda Elghoul
*CRISTAL Laboratory, GRIFT Group*
*National School of Computer Science*
Manouba university, Tunisia
Email. sinda.elghoul@ensi-uma.tn

Faouzi Ghorbel
*CRISTAL Laboratory, GRIFT Group*
*National School of Computer Science*
Manouba university, Tunisia
Email. faouzi.ghorbel@ensi-uma.tn

***Abstract*—We introduce a novel Affine multi-scale registration based on the Riemannian metric in the Lie group $SL(2,R)$ to estimate the best alignment between two planar curves. First, we smooth and re-simpling the input shapes. Then, in each level, we compute the special linear transformations $A_{\sigma_p}$ and translation vectors $B_{\sigma_p}$ using the pseudo-inverse algorithm. The obtained matrices $A_{\sigma_p}$ are then projected in the Lie algebra of $SL(2,R)$ which is $sl(2,R)$ to compute their average. In the final step, we register and calculate the $L_2$ distance.**

***Keywords*—*Multi-scale registration; Special affine transformation; Riemannian metric; Affine Spacial group $SA(2,R)$.***

## I. Introduction

The comparison process between images is complicated and restricted when the images were captured using multiple sensors and poses and were not shot simultaneously. Most of the time, a machine will not be able to find the same thing in different pictures because it can change. In this situation, it is challenging to integrate two comparable forms. To address these issues, researchers created different curve registration methods. The main goal of this method is to find the geometric transformation between two or more images in order to get the most desirable alignment. The registration of the planar curves' shapes is the optimum solution that has been presented for a great number of applications, including motion tracking [1], mosaicing [2] [3], object recognition [4], remote sensing [5], 3D curve reconstruction [6] [7] and medical image analysis [8] [9]. Different methods of shape registration have been proposed in recent years to estimate motion and align two shapes. Thus, 2D affine shapes can be registered using techniques that rely on the Riemannian calculation. The authors in [10] introduce a subspace method for aligning two 2D shapes and estimating the affine transformation between them. By minimizing the projection error in the subspace spanned by the two shapes, the affine transformation is estimated in the proposed 2D signal method. Bryner et al. [11] propose a broad Riemannian framework for shape analysis of planar objects, whose metrics and related quantities are invariant under the action of affine and projective groups. Within the framework of landmark-based shape analysis, Sparr [12] develops affine shape theory through the use of subspace computations. Begelfor and Werman [13] provide a Riemannian geometric metric for computing the averages and distributions of point configurations, such that configurations up to affine transformations are regarded as equivalent. Also, authors in [14] introduce a framework for contour-based shape analysis based on Riemannian geometry that is robust against affine transformation and contour re-parameterization. By integrating the Iwasawa decomposition of $GL(2,R)$ and Lie group parametrization into the regular Iterative Closest Point (ICP) method, Ying et al. [17] introduce new techniques for 2D affine shape registration. Moreover, authors in [18] show how to find a geodesic that is invariant to scale, translation, rotation, and re-parameterization using a Riemannian quasi-Newton approach. YI MA [28] highlights how multiple-view geometry can be studied in three-dimensional spaces with constant curvatures, like Euclidean space, spherical space, and hyperbolic space. In [29], the authors talk about the manifold and Lie group SO(n) of special orthogonal related to the non-negative independent component analysis (ICA). Huang et al. [30] come up with a new way to use Riemannian optimization to align curves in elastic shape analysis.

The purpose of this paper is to introduce a novel Affine Multi-Scale Curve Registration that employs Riemannian geometry. For this technique, two curves are taken as input (the source image and the target image), and then they are sequentially smoothed and reparametrized with affine arc-length. The pseudo-inverse algorithm is then used to compute the special linear transformations $A_{\sigma_p}$ and translation vectors $B_{\sigma_p}$ for each smoothed and reparametrized shape. These matrices $A_{\sigma_p}$ belong to the affine spacial group $SA(2,R)$. The average of these matrices, $A$, is then found using Riemannian calculation in $SA(2,R)$. Finally, the alignment process is done.

The following is the outline for this paper: In Section II, we present the affine multi-scale curve registration based on the Riemannian calculation that we propose. In Section III, we assess the performance of the suggested methods for shape retrieval with MCD. Ultimately, a final conclusion is reached.

## II. Affine Multi-Scale Curve Registration based on Riemannian calculation

Here, we will talk about the main parts of the proposed method, which is called Affine Multi-Scale Curve Registration based on Riemannian calculation. In this new method, the input normalized contours are filtered over and over again, and the Riemannian calculation in the special linear group SL(2, R) is used to find the best transformation. Fig. 1 demonstrates the Affine Multi-Scale Curve Registration based on the Riemannian calculation procedure.

- A-1: Normalize the input shapes $f$ and $h$ using the affine arc-length normalization [15]. Fig.2 shows two shapes that have been normalized with affine arc-length.
- A-2: Convolve each of the two re-sampling curves using the Gaussian calculation [15], where the resulting curve is depicted in Fig.3.
- A-3: The obtained $p$ systems at each level are formed by the following $2N$ linear equations.

$$\begin{cases} h_{\sigma_1}(l_1) = A_{\sigma_1} f_{\sigma_1}(l_1) + B_{\sigma_1} \\ h_{\sigma_1}(l_2) = A_{\sigma_1} f_{\sigma_1}(l_2) + B_{\sigma_1} \\ \quad \cdots \\ h_{\sigma_1}(l_N) = A_{\sigma_1} f_{\sigma_1}(l_N) + B_{\sigma_1} \end{cases} \begin{cases} h_{\sigma_2}(l_1) = A_{\sigma_2} f_{\sigma_2}(l_1) + B_{\sigma_2} \\ h_{\sigma_2}(l_2) = A_{\sigma_2} f_{\sigma_2}(l_2) + B_{\sigma_2} \\ \quad \cdots \\ h_{\sigma_2}(l_N) = A_{\sigma_2} f_{\sigma_2}(l_N) + B_{\sigma_2} \end{cases} \quad (1)$$

$$\ldots \begin{cases} h_{\sigma_p}(l_1) = A_{\sigma_p} f_{\sigma_p}(l_1) + B_{\sigma_p} \\ h_{\sigma_p}(l_2) = A_{\sigma_p} f_{\sigma_p}(l_2) + \hat{B}_{\sigma_p} \\ \quad \cdots \\ h_{\sigma_p}(l_N) = A_{\sigma_p} f_{\sigma_p}(l_N) + B_{\sigma_p} \end{cases}$$

- A-4, A-5: The $A_{\sigma_p}$ matrices, which contain the elements of the special affine group $SA(2, R)$, and the $B_{\sigma_p}$ translation vectors, are obtained by performing the pseudo-inverse calculation [16] on each system.
- A-6: **Riemannian calculation in** $SA(2, R)$.
  We provide a brief introduction to the Special Affine $SA(2)$, which is the underlying geometric space for non-rigid registration. In affine space, the special affine group consists of transformations by scaling, rotation, and then translation. Specifically, it is the semi-direct product of the Special Linear group $SL(2)$ and $R^2$.

$$SA(2) = SL(2) \times R^2 \quad (2)$$

It is worth remembering that a Lie group is both a group and a differential manifold, and that a Lie algebra is a vector space on which a Lie bracket is defined.

The $SL(2, R)$ special linear group contains all determinants of unit size that are real matrices of size 2 by 2.

$$SL(2, R) = \{A \in R^2 / det(A) = 1\} \quad (3)$$

An Iwasawa decomposition exists for this 2-dimensional Lie group $SL(2, R)$ of real matrices.

$$SL(2, R) = A_{shear} A_{scale} A_{rotation} \quad (4)$$

In our case, the affine transformation matrices $A_{\sigma_p} \in SL(2, R)$ and $A_{shear}$ represent shears, $A_{scale}$ is for scales and $A_{rotation}$ list the rotation matrices.

$$A_{\sigma_p} = \begin{pmatrix} a_{11_{\sigma_p}} & a_{12_{\sigma_p}} \\ a_{21_{\sigma_p}} & a_{22_{\sigma_p}} \end{pmatrix}$$

$$A_{\sigma_p} = A_{shear} A_{scale} A_{rotation} \quad (5)$$

$$A_{\sigma_p} = \begin{pmatrix} 1 & b \\ 0 & 1 \end{pmatrix} \times \begin{pmatrix} a & 0 \\ 0 & 1/a \end{pmatrix} \times \begin{pmatrix} cos\,\theta & -\,sin\,\theta \\ sin\,\theta & cos\,\theta \end{pmatrix} \quad (6)$$

$$= \begin{pmatrix} a\,cos\,\theta & b\,a\,cos\,\theta - (1/a)\,sin\,\theta \\ a\,sin\,\theta & b\,a\,sin\,\theta + (1/a)\,cos\,\theta \end{pmatrix}$$

with $det(A_{\sigma_p}) = 1$, $a \in R^*$ and $\theta, b \in R$.
The Lie algebra of $SL(2, R)$ is denoted by $sl(2, R)$, and is identified with the set of $2 \times 2$ matrices and they have a basis provided by $e_n{:}n = 1, 2, 3$.

$$e_1 = \begin{pmatrix} 1 & 0 \\ 0 & -1 \end{pmatrix}, \quad e_2 = \begin{pmatrix} 0 & 1 \\ 0 & 0 \end{pmatrix}, \quad e_3 = \begin{pmatrix} 0 & 0 \\ 1 & 0 \end{pmatrix} \quad (7)$$

Lie group theory relies heavily on the Lie algebra of a Lie group since it encodes many of the group's global topological features. Exp, a local diffeomorphism, is also known as exponential mapping.

In the first step, we do the projection in the space tangent of the $A_{\sigma_p}$ matrices using the following equation Eq (8) [19].
Once calculated, the logarithm map of matrices belonging to the lie algebra elements $\ln(A_{\sigma_p}) \in sl(2, R)$ is projected in the tangent space, and we are in the vector space where the matrices must satisfy the following conditions Eq(9):

$$\{\ln(A_{\sigma_p}) \in sl(2, R) / Tr(\ln(A_{\sigma_p})) = 0\}. \quad (9)$$

Therefore the exponential mapping of the logarithm mapping $\ln(A_{\sigma_p})$ is expressed as below in Eq(10) [19]:

- A-7: The registration is then performed using the special linear transformation $A$ obtained after the Riemannian calculation and the translation vector B deduced after applying average arithmetic.

$$A = \begin{pmatrix} a_{11} & a_{12} \\ a_{21} & a_{22} \end{pmatrix} \quad B = \begin{pmatrix} B^x \\ B^y \end{pmatrix} \quad (11)$$

Finally, we calculate the euclidean distance $L_2$, which is denoted by:

$$L^2 = \min_{(A,B)} = \|Af(l_a) + B - h(l_a)\|^2 \approx e \quad (12)$$

## III. EXPERIMENTS

In this section, we compare the proposed Affine Multi-Scale Curve Registration based on Riemannian metrics to the currently available shape alignment methods and present the recognition rates of each. The MCD dataset is used for testing.

### A. MCD image database retrieval

One of the most important uses of the proposed algorithm is in shape registration. Therefore, we will evaluate the Affine Multi-Scale Curve Registration based Riemannian metrics on the Multiview Curve Dataset (MCD) [20], which is made up of 40 shape classes from the MPEG-7 database. Figure

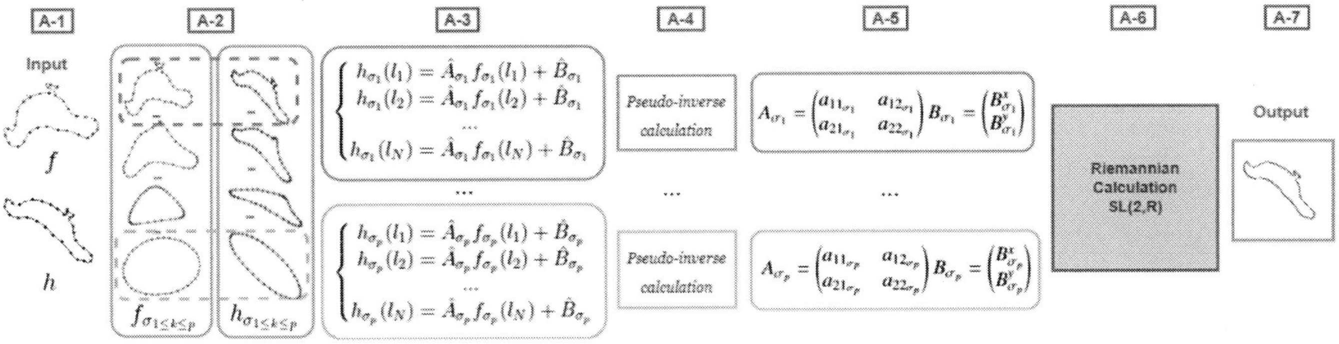


Fig. 1. Workflow of multi-scale contour registration using Riemannian calculation

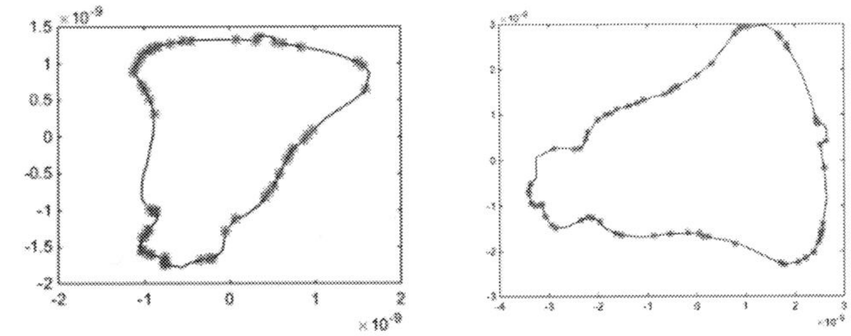

(a) (b)

Fig. 2. Example of re-sampling shapes with affine arc-length parametrization

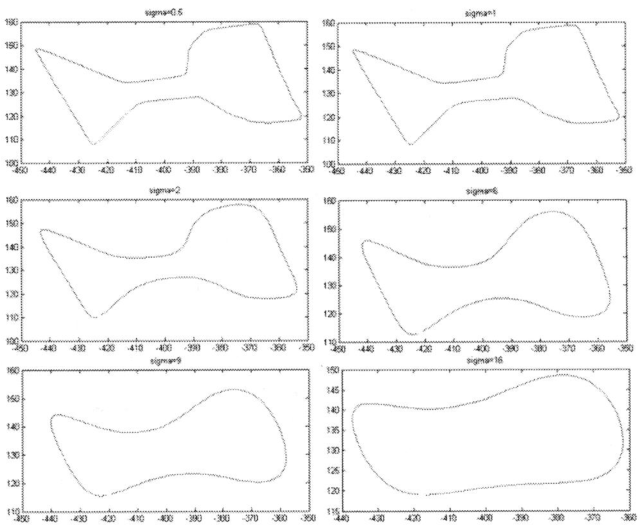

Fig. 3. Example of a convolved shape

4 shows that there are 14 different curves in each of these categories that are distorted in the same way as the original curve.

In Table 1, we compare our methods to some of the current state-of-the-art studies. We discovered that our technique (89.21%) performs better than Arber (41%) [21], SC (56.29%) [22] , Huang (71%) [23], Rube (79%) [24], and Mai (89%)

TABLE I. Retrieval results on the entire MCD dataset

| Methods | Average |
|---|---|
| Arber [21] | 41% |
| SC [22] | 56.29% |
| Huang [23] | 71 % |
| Rube [24] | 79 % |
| Mai [25] | 89 % |
| **Our method** | **89.21%** |
| Fast and non-rigid global registration [26] | 92.8% |
| ACMA [16] | 94 % |
| Partial Contour Matching Based on ACSS [27] | 95.98% |
| **AMSCR** [15] | **96.36 %** |
| **AMSCR with Binary-EM** [15] | **96.58 %** |

[25]. Our method, on the other hand, is less effective than the methods of fast and non-rigid global registration (92.8%) [26] and ACMA (94%) [16]. Moreover, when compared to AMSCR (96.36%) [15] and AMSCR with Binary-EM (96.58%) [15], our technique demonstrated its limits. The difficulty of the computation in $SL(2, R)$, which will be resolved in future work, demonstrates this limitation clearly.

In Figure 5 we see an example of successfully registered shapes made with our approach.

## IV. Conclusion and future work

In this paper, we suggested a new affine multi-scale curve registration method based on the Riemannian calculation that deals with occlusion and affine transformations. First, the two curves are normalized and smoothed out on different scales. So, for each level, we have several rectangular linear systems. The pseudo-inverse computation is used for each level to compute the special linear transformations $A_{\sigma_p}$ and translation vectors $B_{\sigma_p}$. Afterward, the average of the $A_{\sigma_p}$ matrices is then calculated using the Riemannian metric in the spatial affine group $SA(2, R)$. After that, the two shapes are lined up, and the euclidean distance $L_2$ is calculated.

Despite the novelty of the proposed method, the obtained results are not always as good as those of other methods since several numerical challenges remain, such as the choice of the point in the tangent space and the shape's starting point. So, in the future, we will be working to resolve these issues.

$$if \quad a_{11_{\sigma_p}} + a_{22_{\sigma_p}} \geqslant 2$$

$$\ln(A_{\sigma_p}) = \frac{\ln\left[\left(a_{11_{\sigma_p}} + a_{22_{\sigma_p}} + \sqrt{(a_{11_{\sigma_p}} + a_{22_{\sigma_p}})^2 - 4}\right)/2\right]}{\sqrt{(a_{11_{\sigma_p}} + a_{22_{\sigma_p}})^2 - 4}} \begin{pmatrix} a_{11_{\sigma_p}} - a_{22_{\sigma_p}} & 2a_{12_{\sigma_p}} \\ 2a_{21_{\sigma_p}} & a_{22_{\sigma_p}} - a_{11_{\sigma_p}} \end{pmatrix}$$

$$if - 2 < a_{11_{\sigma_p}} + a_{22_{\sigma_p}} \leq 2$$

$$\ln(A_{\sigma_p}) = \frac{\arccos\left[\left(a_{11_{\sigma_p}} + a_{22_{\sigma_p}}\right)/2\right]}{\sqrt{4 - (a_{11_{\sigma_p}} + a_{22_{\sigma_p}})^2}} \begin{pmatrix} a_{11_{\sigma_p}} - a_{22_{\sigma_p}} & 2a_{12_{\sigma_p}} \\ 2a_{21_{\sigma_p}} & a_{22_{\sigma_p}} - a_{11_{\sigma_p}} \end{pmatrix} \quad (8)$$

$$if \quad a_{11_{\sigma_p}}^2 + a_{12_{\sigma_p}} a_{21_{\sigma_p}} \geq 0$$

$$A_{\sigma_p} = \cosh\left[\sqrt{a_{11_{\sigma_p}}^2 + a_{12_{\sigma_p}} a_{21_{\sigma_p}}}\right] I + \ln\left(A_{\sigma_p}\right) \frac{\sinh\left[\sqrt{a_{11_{\sigma_p}}^2 + a_{12_{\sigma_p}} a_{21_{\sigma_p}}}\right]}{\sqrt{a_{11_{\sigma_p}}^2 + a_{12_{\sigma_p}} a_{21_{\sigma_p}}}}$$

$$if \quad a_{11_{\sigma_p}}^2 + a_{12_{\sigma_p}} a_{21_{\sigma_p}} \leq 0$$

$$A_{\sigma_p} = \cos\left[\sqrt{-a_{11_{\sigma_p}}^2 - a_{12_{\sigma_p}} a_{21_{\sigma_p}}}\right] I + \ln\left(A_{\sigma_p}\right) \frac{\sin\left[\sqrt{-a_{11_{\sigma_p}}^2 - a_{12_{\sigma_p}} a_{21_{\sigma_p}}}\right]}{\sqrt{-a_{11_{\sigma_p}}^2 - a_{12_{\sigma_p}} a_{21_{\sigma_p}}}} \quad (10)$$

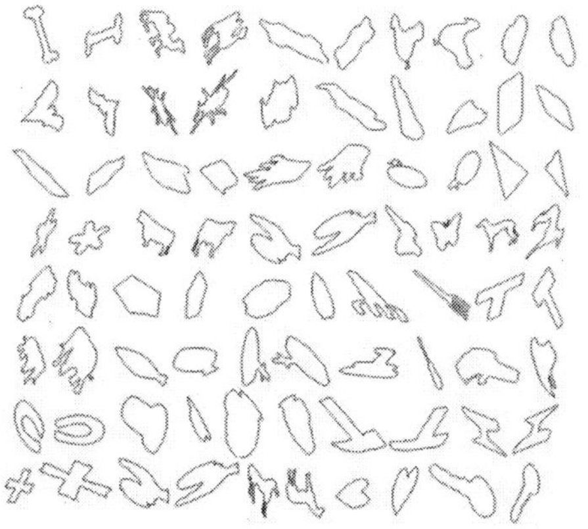

Fig. 4. Different shape images from the MCD dataset, two images from each class.

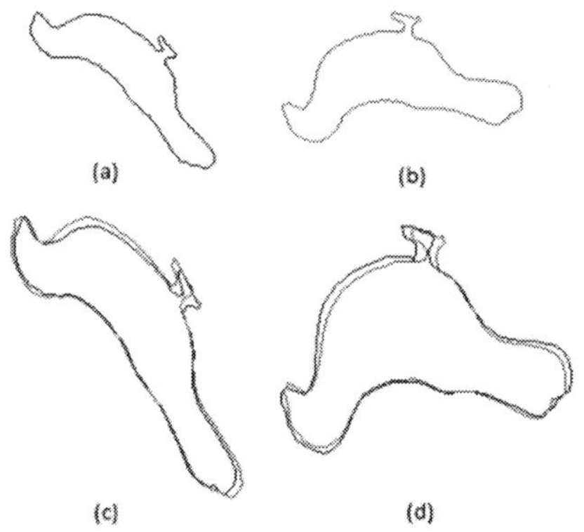


Fig. 5. a and b are the original curves, c, and d display the aligned shapes

## REFERENCES

[1] Cheng, P., & Menq, C. H. (2013). Real-time continuous image registration enabling ultraprecise 2-D motion tracking. IEEE Transactions on Image Processing, 22(5), 2081-2090.

[2] Majumdar, J., Vinay, S., & Selvi, S. (2004, December). Registration and mosaicing for images obtained from UAV. In 2004 International Conference on Signal Processing and Communications, 2004. SPCOM'04. (pp. 198-203). IEEE.

[3] Elghoul, S., Saidani, M., & Ghorbel, F. (2017). An interactive Tunisian virtual museum through affine reconstruction of gigantic mosaics and antic 3-D models.

[4] Sebastian, T. B., & Kimia, B. B. (2005). Curves vs. skeletons in object recognition. Signal processing, 85(2), 247-263.

[5] Ernst, M. D., & Flinchbaugh, B. E. (1989, March). Image/map correspondence using curve matching. In AAAI Symposium on Robot Navigation (pp. 15-18).

[6] Berthilsson, R., Åström, K., & Heyden, A. (2001). Reconstruction of

general curves, using factorization and bundle adjustment. International Journal of Computer Vision, 41(3), 171-182.

[7] Mai, F., Hung, Y. S., & Chesi, G. (2010). Projective reconstruction of ellipses from multiple images. Pattern Recognition, 43(3), 545-556.

[8] Roche, A., Pennec, X., Malandain, G., & Ayache, N. (2001). Rigid registration of 3-D ultrasound with MR images: a new approach combining intensity and gradient information. IEEE transactions on medical imaging, 20(10), 1038-1049.

[9] Rui, W., & Minglu, L. (2003, September). An overview of medical image registration. In Proceedings Fifth International Conference on Computational Intelligence and Multimedia Applications. ICCIMA 2003 (pp. 385-390). IEEE.

[10] Mai, F., Chang, C. Q., & Hung, Y. S. (2011). A subspace approach for matching 2D shapes under affine distortions. Pattern Recognition, 44(2), 210-221.

[11] Bryner, D., Klassen, E., Le, H., & Srivastava, A. (2013). 2D affine and projective shape analysis. IEEE transactions on pattern analysis and machine intelligence, 36(5), 998-1011.

[12] Sparr, G. (1992). Depth computations from polyhedral images. Image and Vision Computing, 10(10), 683-688.

[13] Begelfor, E., & Werman, M. (2006, June). Affine invariance revisited. In 2006 IEEE Computer Society Conference on Computer Vision and Pattern Recognition (CVPR'06) (Vol. 2, pp. 2087-2094). IEEE.

[14] Bryner, D., Srivastava, A., & Klassen, E. (2012, June). Affine-invariant, elastic shape analysis of planar contours. In 2012 IEEE Conference on Computer Vision and Pattern Recognition (pp. 390-397). IEEE.

[15] Sakrani, K., Elghoul, S., Falleh, S., & Ghorbel, F. (2021, December). SA (2, R) Multi-scale contour registration based on EM Algorithm. In 2021 International Conference on Visual Communications and Image Processing (VCIP) (pp. 1-5). IEEE.

[16] Elghoul, S., & Ghorbel, F. (2022). A fast and robust affine-invariant method for shape registration under partial occlusion. International Journal of Multimedia Information Retrieval, 11(1), 39-59.

[17] Ying, S., Peng, Y., & Wen, Z. (2011). Iwasawa decomposition: a new approach to 2D affine registration problem. Pattern Analysis and Applications, 14(2), 127-137.

[18] You, Y., Huang, W., Gallivan, K. A., & Absil, P. A. (2015, December). A Riemannian approach for computing geodesies in elastic shape analysis. In 2015 IEEE Global Conference on Signal and Information Processing (GlobalSIP) (pp. 727-731). IEEE.

[19] Qiao, Z.,& Dick, R. (2019). Matrix logarithms and range of the exponential maps for the symmetry groups, and the Lorentz group. Journal of Physics Communications, 3(7), 075008.

[20] Zuliani, M., Bhagavathy, S., Manjunath, B. S., & Kenney, C. S. (2004, October). Affine-invariant curve matching. In 2004 International Conference on Image Processing, 2004. ICIP'04. (Vol. 5, pp. 3041-3044). IEEE.

[21] Arbter, K., Snyder, W. E., Burkhardt, H., & Hirzinger, G. (1990). Application of affine-invariant Fourier descriptors to recognition of 3-D objects. IEEE Transactions on pattern analysis and machine intelligence, 12(7), 640-647.

[22] Mori, G., Belongie, S., & Malik, J. (2005). Efficient shape matching using shape contexts. IEEE Transactions on Pattern Analysis and Machine Intelligence, 27(11), 1832-1837.

[23] Huang, X., Wang, B., & Zhang, L. (2005). A new scheme for extraction of affine invariant descriptor and affine motion estimation based on independent component analysis. Pattern Recognition Letters, 26(9), 1244-1255.

[24] El Rube, I., Ahmed, M., & Kamel, M. (2005). Wavelet approximation-based affine invariant shape representation functions. IEEE transactions on pattern analysis and machine intelligence, 28(2), 323-327.

[25] Mai, F., Chang, C. Q., & Hung, Y. S. (2010, September). Affine-invariant shape matching and recognition under partial occlusion. In 2010 IEEE international conference on image processing (pp. 4605-4608). IEEE.

[26] Elghoul, S., & Ghorbel, F. (2021). Fast global SA (2, R) shape registration based on invertible invariant descriptor. Signal Processing: Image Communication, 90, 116058.

[27] Elghoul, S., & Ghorbel, F. (2021). Partial Contour Matching Based on Affine Curvature Scale Space Descriptors. In New Approaches for Multidimensional Signal Processing (pp. 73-81). Springer, Singapore.

[28] Ma, Y. (2004). A differential geometric approach to multiple view geometry in spaces of constant curvature. International Journal of Computer Vision, 58, 37-53.

[29] Plumbley, M. D. (2005). Geometrical methods for non-negative ICA: Manifolds, Lie groups and toral subalgebras. Neurocomputing, 67, 161-197.

[30] Huang, W., Gallivan, K. A., Srivastava, A., & Absil, P. A. (2016). Riemannian optimization for registration of curves in elastic shape analysis. Journal of Mathematical Imaging and Vision, 54, 320-343.

# Comparison of Different Speech Features for Connected Number Recognition of Indian Vernacular Languages

Mayurakshi Mukherji
*Research and Development Centre*
*Hitachi India Private Limited*
Bengaluru, India
Email: mayurakshi.mukherji@hitachi.co.in

Shreyas Kulkarni
*Research and Development Centre*
*Hitachi India Private Limited*
Bengaluru, India
Email: shreyas.kulkarni@hitachi.co.in

Vivek Kumar
*Research and Development Centre*
*Hitachi India Private Limited*
Bengaluru, India
Email: vivek.kumar@hitachi.co.in

Senthil Raja G, Senior Member, IEEE
*Research and Development Centre*
*Hitachi India Private Limited*
Bengaluru, India
Email: senthil.raja@hitachi.co.in

Thiruvengadam Samon
*Research and Development Centre*
*Hitachi India Private Limited*
Bengaluru, India
Email: thiruvengadam.s@hitachi.co.in

Kingshuk Banerjee
*Research and Development Centre*
*Hitachi India Private Limited*
Bengaluru, India
Email: kingshuk.banerjee@hitachi.co.in

Yuichi Nonaka
*Research and Development Centre*
*Hitachi India Private Limited*
Bengaluru, India
Email: ynonaka@hitachi.co.in

***Abstract*— This paper presents the experimental results and comparative analysis of Connected Number Speech Recognition (CNR) models trained using four feature combinations: Mel Frequency Cepstral Coefficient (MFCC), MFCC+Pitch, Perceptual Linear Prediction (PLP), and PLP+Pitch. The set of experiments is conducted for five Indian Native Languages-Bengali, Hindi, Tamil, Kannada, and Marathi. We have collected connected number speech datasets for all five languages and have trained speech recognition models. The Kaldi speech recognition toolkit was used to train acoustic model and the SRILM toolkit was used to build an N-gram language model to prepare a speech recognition system. The model performances were compared and analyzed using Word Error Rate (WER) and Sentence Error Rate (SER) as accuracy metrics. Although, above mentioned Indian languages are atonal in nature, our experiments show that adding pitch features along with MFCC features show overall improvements in WER and SER Values for connected number speech recognition. Moreover, all the speech recognition models are trained under identical conditions but show significantly different WER and SER for different languages.**

***Keywords-MFCC; PLP; speech features; pitch; Indian Langauge.***

## I. Introduction

Speech is a natural and effective way of communication between human beings, which can be used to communicate with machines since it can be captured by a microphone as a vibration signal with respect to time. This signal can be processed, and the speech content of the signal can be recognized and understood to perform further downstream tasks. Automatic Speech Recognition (ASR) system has two types of architectures broadly classified as (a) conventional acoustic model plus language model-based ASR and (b) End to End ASR. The conventional architecture makes use of statistical, neural network based, or hybrid (of both) models to develop ASR systems [1]. These models are typically trained on speech features extracted from speech data. Even though diverse types of representations are available in terms of extracted features, extensive robustness is still being investigated. In ASR systems, every speech feature vector extracted from the audio is classified as a particular phoneme (smallest unit of sound). This step is carried out by the acoustic model, which learns the characteristics of each phoneme using the speech features extracted from the audios in the training set. The acoustic model is often built using a hybrid method consisting of Hidden Markov Models (HMM), Gaussian Mixture Model (GMM), and Neural Networks. Several data augmentation techniques are employed at this stage to generate variations in the pronunciation of phonemes, such as speed perturbation, volume perturbation, frequency perturbations, etc. Phonemes, as recognized by the acoustic model are grouped together to form words, which are then grouped to form sentences. This is achieved by the language model, which can be a simple N-gram language model, or a Neural Network based language model, trained on some text corpus to learn the grammar. The acoustic model and the language model are used in combination to build a decoding graph which is used for model inference. The second architecture, End-to-End speech recognition [2] has gained significant attention in recent years. The End-to-End neural networks are trained to learn directly from raw audio data, without the need for feature-engineering or complex modeling and show state of the art performance on a wide range of speech recognition tasks. However, End-to-End models have limited interpretability as they operate as black boxes. One of the objectives of the presented work is to gain comparative insights over multiple Indian language speech recognition models when trained under identical conditions. Therefore, we decided to experiment with the conventional architecture over End-to-End architecture.

In this paper, we present our experiments on Connected Number Recognition (CNR) – a domain-specific task in ASR – we have primarily used Hitachi Dataset–I consisting of connected number samples from 1000 speakers for each of the five languages (Hindi, Bengali, Marathi, Tamil, Kannada), with speakers contributing approximately 56 connected number samples each. ASR models for CNR using different speech feature combinations, namely – MFCC, PLP, MFCC+Pitch, and PLP+Pitch, have been built and tested using the Kaldi Speech Recognition Toolkit. The business use-case and market significance of CNR are detailed in Section II. Data collection process for our work is included in Section III. The discussion on different speech features for ASR is elaborated in Section IV. Further experimental details are mentioned in Section IV. Experimental evaluation results for Connected Number recognition and following discussion are Section VI and VII respectively. Finally, we have concluded the best features for CNR, as well as future directions, in Section VIII.

## II. Use Case

Connected numbers are at the heart of financial transactions of every kind, be it withdrawing cash, transferring money, conducting offline transaction with merchants, etc. In a country like India with a large rural population with limited literacy, a large Section of the society is excluded from many financial services, creating an ecosystem where people often have to depend on others to access the respective services. In order to truly democratize financial services, there is an immense need of voice-aided financial applications either over smartphones or feature phones, ideally combined with multi-modal user interface (possible with smartphone) and available in a variety of Indian languages. To realize such systems, ASR capability for several Indian languages, particularly in this domain, needs to be built. Our experiments with connected number recognition on five Indian languages aims to identify the best type of speech feature to build such a system. This investigation will be useful for any use case surrounding connected number recognition, for instance, a voice-aided number based electronic device, use-cases involving vehicle numbers, ticket booking etc.

## III. Data Collection

Since our objective is to build highly accurate speech recognition systems for various Indian vernacular languages in the finance domain, we collected data from various parts of the country following a systematic and planned approach. Most vernacular Indian languages can be considered resource-poor languages, which is why data collection is especially necessary for this project.

Speech data was collected mainly in the form of connected numeral samples between zero to one million. Ten Indian languages were targeted and most major states in the country were covered along with seventy percent coverage being given to rural areas, i.e., the places where we believe our vernacular language speech recognition system will have the most amount of positive impact. Data from five out of these ten languages have been used for the presented work. The data collection was performed in natural setting hence contains native environmental noise and background sounds. Collection was done in a way that number of samples for connected numerals most likely to be used during financial transactions are maximized and have diverse representations in the dataset. Volunteers within the age group of eighteen to fifty willing to record audio samples were taken through a guided data collection process which resulted in approximately 56 samples per volunteer. Therefore, per language we have collected 56000 samples. The data was collected from thousand such volunteers for each of the ten languages. The volunteers' data privacy and security measures were taken during this entire exercise.

## IV. Speech Features

In ASR, every speech audio is processed to extract speech features, which are then used for training and testing purposes. The popular speech features are- Linear Prediction Cepstral Coefficients (LPCC), Mel-Frequency Cepstral Coefficients (MFCC), and Perceptual Linear Prediction (PLP).

The human speech generation system can be broadly represented as shown in Figure 1. The vocal folds generate periodic excitation input which passes through vocal tracts that convert it into speech. The MFCC/PLP features aim to model the vocal tracts and pitch features aim to learn about the excitation signal. We aim to present a comparative study of the performance achieved by four speech feature combinations- MFCC, PLP, MFCC+Pitch and PLP+Pitch when tested on five different Indian vernacular languages- Hindi, Bengali, Marathi, Tamil, and Kannada. The performance of various speech features has been tested in past studies, for instance a study published in 2019 concluded the superior performance of MFCC compared to PLP in case of Spanish language [5]. However, a study specifically focused on Indian languages is yet to be seen. In 2014, a study on pitch features introduced Kaldi Pitch tracker, a modified version of a previously existing pitch extractor, and claimed an improvement for both tonal and atonal languages, the former showing a larger reduction in WER [6].

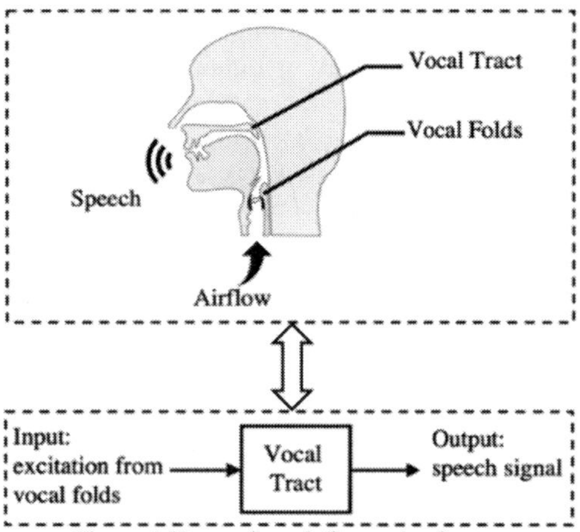


Figure. 1 Human Speech Generation System

We hope to provide further insights on the performance of pitch features when combined with both MFCC and PLP features for a small vocabulary domain-specific ASR task for Indian languages. A short overview of some common speech features and the pitch features is included in this Section.

### A. Mel-frequency Cepstral Coefficients

Calculating MFCC of short audio segments in frequency domain is one of the most popular methods of extracting speech features for speech processing. It utilizes the concept of Mel-scale, a non-linear frequency scale which is based on human auditory perception. Mel-filter bank maps the actual frequency, $f$ to Mel-scale frequency, $f^*$ , i.e., the perceived frequency [7] as in (1). Audio segments of 25 ms with an overlap of 10 ms are windowed (Hamming window of length N with coefficients $W(n)$, (2)) and represented in frequency domain using FFT, and subsequently the Mel-filter bank is applied to the log of the amplitude spectrum to represent the frequency measurements on the Mel-scale.

$$f^* = 2595 \log\left(\frac{1+f}{700}\right) \quad (1)$$

$$W(n) = 0.54 - 0.46 \cos\left(\frac{2\pi n}{N-1}\right), 0 \le n \le N-1 \quad (2)$$

Discrete Cosine Transform (DCT) of the output from the previous step is calculated to obtain MFCC coefficients [8]. Typically, along with the first 12 coefficients and the energy of the segment, the first order derivatives and the second order derivatives of these 13 features are also included to form a 39-feaures MFCC feature vector of a short audio segment. The first 12 MFCC features are phonetically significant features which are critical for analysis of speech signal.

### B. Predictive Coding

Linear Predictive Coding (LPC) is a method commonly used for estimating speech parameters such as spectra and pitch formants [9]. It is used to faithfully encode speech for low bit-rate transmission. It is based on the principal that the value of a sample $\tilde{s}(n)$ can be estimated by a linear combination of all $p$ previous samples as displayed in (3). The first method to calculate LPC coefficients is by minimizing the estimation error and solving a system of linear equations by autocorrelation method, covariance method, or lattice method. The LPC coefficients $\alpha_k$ define the formants of the signal, i.e., the frequencies at which there is an occurrence of resonant peaks, same as the peaks in the spectrum of the linear prediction filter resulting from the transfer function (5) [7][8][10].

The coefficients are calculated over the entire speech signal by using sliding time window with overlap of 10 ms and multiplying the frame with the Hamming window. The set of LPC coefficients of each frame constitute the feature vector for the respective audio segment.

$$\tilde{s}(n) = \sum_{k=1}^{p} a_k s(n-k) \quad (3)$$

$$e(n) = s(n) - \tilde{s}(n) \quad (4)$$

$$\frac{S(z)}{E(z)} = \frac{1}{1 - \sum_{k=1}^{p} \alpha_k z^{-k}} \quad (5)$$

### C. Perceptual Linear Prediction

PLP is similar to LPC, but it takes into account the human auditory perception. It uses critical bands, intensity-to-loudness compression, and equal loudness pre-emphasis to remove irrelevant information and extract feature vectors. It utilizes the non-linear frequency scale called Bark scale to map frequency in Hertz, $f$, to frequency in Bark scale, $f^b$ (6).

$$f^b = 7 \log\left(\frac{f}{650} + \sqrt{1 + \left(\frac{f}{650}\right)^2}\right) \quad (6)$$

The speech signal segment is windowed using the Hamming window and the power spectrum is calculated, post which the Bark filter bank is applied. The Bark filter bank incorporates the process of frequency warping to the Bark scale, smooths the spectrum using the simulated critical-band masking curve, and down-samples the smoothened spectrum to ~ 1 bark intervals. It essentially compresses the higher frequencies into a narrow band. The filter bank outputs are weighted using equal loudness pre-emphasis weights to reflect human sensitivity of hearing. Linear prediction is applied to this warped spectrum to obtain predictor coefficients. From these coefficients, the cepstral coefficients are calculated by performing an inverse Fourier transform over the log of linear prediction model spectrum [7][8][11].

### D. Pitch Features

MFCC+Pitch features and PLP+Pitch are combinations of the regular MFCC/PLP coefficients with pitch features. There are various pitch feature extraction methods such as Yin [12], Getf0 (get fundamental frequency) [13], SAcC [14],

Wu [15], SWIPE [16], and YAAPT [17] to extract pitch features from speech signal, however all of them process voiced and unvoiced audio frames separately [18]. All pitch trackers aim to get an estimate of the fundamental frequency (F0) of a signal, which is a property of all periodic signals and is a good indicator of perceived pitch. Estimating F0 requires the classification frames as voiced or unvoiced. This estimation has 3 steps- pre-processing, generation of estimate candidates for the true period, and post-processing to select the best estimate [13].

Pre-processing is carried out to perform high-pass and low-pass filtering, and to remove the DC-offset, noise, vocal-tract filter influences, etc. Subsequently to generate period candidates, various methods such as auto-correlation, cross-correlation, and cestrum can be used, although the best approach is using normalized cross-correlation function (NCCF). It overcomes the issues of the other methods but with the caveat of higher computational complexity.

$$\emptyset_{i,\ k} = \frac{\sum_{j=m}^{m+n-1} s_j s_{j+k}}{\sqrt{e_m e_{m+k}}} \tag{7}$$

$$e_j = \sum_{l=j}^{j+n-1} s_l^2 \tag{8}$$

NCCF (7) of voiced samples tend towards 1.0 (maxima) for lags corresponding to integer multiples of 'true period' whereas NCCF of unvoiced samples has maximum values at zero lag. In post-processing, dynamic programming is used for voicing decision and selection of the 'true period', consequently determining F0 [13].

The Kaldi pitch tracker used in our experiments is based on the Getf0 pitch extractor. While the original Getf0 makes hard decisions on whether a frame is voiced or unvoiced, the Kaldi pitch extractor treats all frames as voiced and uses Viterbi search to interpolate over unvoiced frames naturally. It is based on finding lag values that maximize the Normalized Cross Correlation Function (NCCF). Instead of just the local maxima, the search is conducted over a fine grid. A 'ballast' term is added to the NCCF formula such that it tends to zero for quieter regions of the signal. NCCF in combination with the raw pitch feature is used to compute the three default output features of the Kaldi pitch tracker, namely the Probability Of Voicing (POV) feature, mean-subtracted-log-pitch, and delta-of-raw-pitch. $c$ being the NCCF of an audio frame, $a = abs(c)$ and $l = -5.2 + 5.4\exp(7.5(a-1)) + 4.8a - 2\exp(-10a) + 4.2\exp(20(a-1))$. POV, $p$, is given by (9). The POV feature, $f$ , is described by (10).

$$p = \frac{1}{1-\exp(-l)} \tag{9}$$

$$f = 2((1.0001 - c)^{015} - 1) \tag{10}$$

It gives a gaussian distribution to the feature. For the mean-subtracted-log-pitch, at time t, the average of pitch value over a window of width 151 frames, centered at t and weighted by POV, is subtracted from log pitch value to normalize it. The third default feature, delta-of-raw-pitch, is calculated from the unnormalized log pitch in the standard way using ±2 frames of context [6]. The three extra pitch features are added to the standard MFCC/PLP coefficients, and the first and second derivatives are calculated for the MFCC/PLP coefficients plus the three additional features as per the standard procedure, to form the speech feature vector for MFCC+Pitch and PLP+Pitch.

## V. Model Training

All experiments on the comparison of speech features for spoken CNR were performed using the Kaldi Speech Recognition Toolkit. ASR model training for all five languages was performed using 80% connected number dataset and 20% general dataset. The connected number data collection was outsourced to an external party by Hitachi India Pvt. Ltd. and resulted in the Hitachi Dataset-I. The general data is obtained from various opensource datasets such as OpenSLR [19][20], CommonVoice, and Shrutilipi [21]. For a given language, all training conditions except speech feature type was ensured to be identical. We used a distribution of 70% train, 20% dev, and 10% eval for all model training and testing. Additionally, mutual exclusivity with regards to speakers was maintained for train, dev, and eval datasets to avoid bias towards any speaker. The details of model training are explained in following Subsections.

### A. Data Pre-processing

To train the acoustic model, the initial pre-processing of audio training data included volume pre-normalization and volume perturbation. An ASR model should be robust against volume/amplitude variations of audio signals, thus requiring a dataset with a variety of amplitudes. The range of volume levels selected for our experiments was 0.125 to 1.

Before the extraction of speech features, a dataset of speed-perturbed audios was created, such that the model could learn diverse representations of each phoneme. Speed perturbation simply involves resampling the signals to change the tempo and pitch. Typically, speed-perturbation-based data augmentation improves the ASR performance [22]. We selected 0.9, 1, and 1.1 as the three speeds to create the speed-perturbed dataset, thus increasing the effective data size for feature extraction to three times its previous size.

To prepare the language dictionary with phoneme representations, a transliteration tool based on ILSL 2.0 was used. Indian languages, in general, have one-to-one grapheme to phoneme mapping, unlike the English language. ILSL 2.0 consists of unified transliteration standards specifically designed for Indian languages, which define common phoneme representations for corresponding graphemes in respective Indian languages. This is not necessarily an IPA-like representation of phonemes but a way to represent the most similar sounding phonemes in multiple Indian languages by a common representation. This step is critical to perform the comparison of ASR models in multiple languages.

### B. Speech Features Extraction

For our experiments, we tested two primary speech features: MFCC and PLP. Furthermore, we combined both MFCC and PLP with pitch features to test for MFCC+Pitch and PLP+Pitch, respectively. The speech feature extraction scripts are a part of Kaldi. For CNR experiments, a 39-dimensional feature vector was generated for each frame of audio, which had a duration of 25ms and was shifted by 10ms. The first 13 dimensions of the feature vector consisted of 12 speech features along with the energy of the spectrum, while the remaining 26 dimensions were constituted by the first and second order derivatives of the same. This architecture was maintained for both MFCC and PLP feature vectors.

Pitch feature extraction and combining them with MFCC and PLP features were done using the scripts for Kaldi pitch-tracker, which is based on the concepts introduced in "A pitch extraction algorithm tuned for automatic speech recognition" [6]. However, to maintain the 39-dimensional structure of the feature vectors, we considered 11 speech features and the energy of the spectrum, along with their first and second order derivatives for the first 36 dimensions of the feature vector. The last 3 dimensions were dedicated to the three pitch features extracted using the Kaldi pitch tracker. After extracting the features, Cepstral Mean and Variance Normalization (CMVN) was applied to reduce differences in feature representation of different speakers and enhance the noise robustness of speech recognition [23].

### C. Phoneme Alignment Training

As a part of conventional speech recognition model training, the next step involved alignment of phonemes. We implemented Montreal Force Alignment (MFA) [24] for phoneme alignment. MFA trains HMM-GMM model in consecutive steps, i) Monophone training, ii) Triphone training (tri-1), iii) Triphone + LDA + MLLT training (tri-2), iv) Triphone + LDA + MLLT + SAT training (tri-3). The final alignments generated from tri-3 are passed to the TDNN-LSTM network to train the acoustic model. The hyperparameters tuned during the training process are listed Table 1. The 'numleaves' and 'totgauss' decide the number of triphones which can be modelled and their fine-grained nature. The hyper parameter values were obtained as per Kaldi community guidelines. Further, we performed Bayesian optimization to tune hyper parameters, but it showed insignificant improvements. We fixed identical values of these hyper parameters for all experiments to compare the model performances based on speech feature type and language.

### D. TDNN-LSTM Model training

Once phoneme alignments are learnt, next step is to learn the temporal sequences of speech signals. Recurrent Neural Network (RNN) is a popular approach to learn sequential information; however, it suffers from the vanishing gradient problem. Hence, Long Short-Term Memory (LSTM) neural networks were invented. Furthermore, Time Delay Neural Networks (TDNN) can learn the localized temporal patterns better than traditional Deep Neural Networks (DNN). We integrated TDNN with LTSM, instead of integrating DNN, thus making it a TDNN-LSTM network. Moreover, our objective is to compare the speech recognition performance for multiple speech features over multiple languages. Therefore, we did not necessarily investigate the network with the best performance and the best tuning parameters. Rather, we opted for a standard network architecture and trained multiple models to derive comparative insights. The hyperparameters used in the training are listed in Table 1. These hyperparameters were set as per IIT Madras Speech Lab ASR Challenge demo Kaldi recipe [25] and further modified as per Kaldi community guidelines. Again, these hyperparameters were set to be identical for all the experiments to compare the model performances.

### E. Language Model training

The connected number language models were built for all the languages separately using the SRILM toolkit. The corpus for training the language model consisted of the text representation of connected numbers from 1 to 100,000 in the respective language. 3-gram language models showed the best perplexity scores and were thus selected for decoding.

The model inference of test data is achieved by combining the results of the acoustic model and the language model.

## VI. Experimental Evaluation

The investigation of speech features with and without pitch for five Indian language for CNR has been presented with the standard metrics, i.e., Word Error Rate (WER) and Sentence Error Rate (SER). The connected number samples in the eval set are used to display the results of our investigation with the mentioned metrics in Figure 2 and Figure 3. The training, dev, and eval set are identical for all experiments pertaining to a specific language. The eval set connected number audio samples have been collected in a natural environment, therefore contain various types of background noises native to the environment.

On average, MFCC+Pitch yields the least WER and SER among all the speech features. Inclusion of pitch features with MFCC features reduces WER for all languages except Bengali, where it shows a slight increase by 0.58%. MFCC+Pitch shows 0.68% average reduction of WER and 1.27% average reduction of SER when compared with MFCC. The highest improvement was observed in Hindi language in this case. However, adding pitch features with PLP shows a slight increase in WER (~0.8%) across three languages.

TABLE I. RANGE OF HYPERPARAMETER AND TRAINING CONDITION USED AT DIFFERENT STAGES OF TRAINING

| Training Stage | Hyperparameters | Range |
|---|---|---|
| Monophone | iterations | 40 |
| Triphone (tri-1) | iterations | 35 |
| | numleaves | 2750 |
| | totgauss | 50000 |
| Triphone + LDA + MLLT (tri-2) | iterations | 35 |
| | numleaves | 2750 |
| | totgauss | 50000 |
| Triphone + LDA + MLLT + SAT (tri-3) | iterations | 35 |
| | numleaves | 2750 |
| | totgauss | 50000 |
| TDNN-LSTM | Epochs | 6 |
| | Hidden layers | 13 |
| | Dimension of layers | 1024 |
| | Non- linearity | ReLU |
| | Initial learning rate | 0.0001 |
| | Final learning rate | 0.00001 |

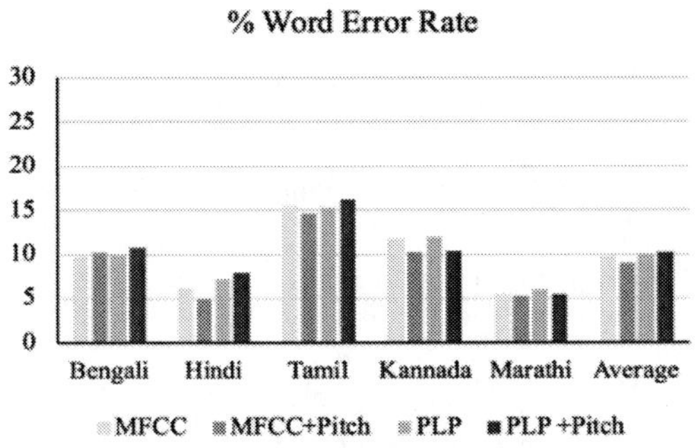


Figure. 2 Comparison of % WER for CNR models built for 5 Indian languages with 4 feature combinations

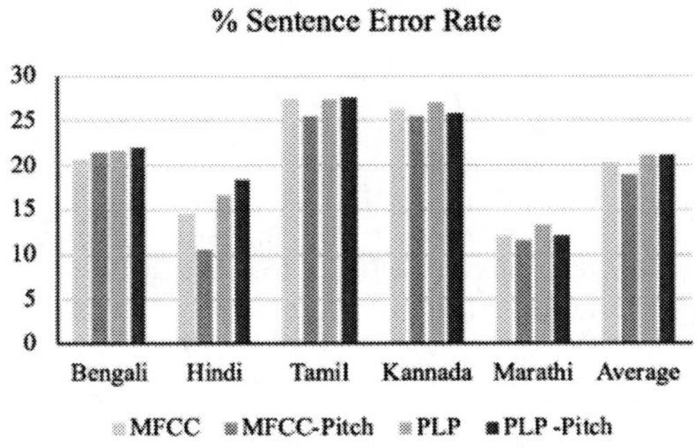


Figure. 3 Comparison of % SER for CNR models built for 5 Indian languages with 4 feature combinations.

The PLP and PLP+Pitch based models show comparable results overall. MFCC features with and without pitch show better performance than PLP features with and without pitch features.

## VII. DISCUSSION

India is a diverse country with multiple languages spoken in different regions. The presented experimental work helps in building a single acoustic model for multiple languages. The aim is to gather insights regarding the tuning of a multilingual ASR model to meet different recognition criteria depending on the part of the country where the model is to be deployed. Therefore, the model should ultimately show higher accuracy for the region-specific language, while also supporting multiple other languages.

For example, if the model needs to be deployed in the West Bengal region, it should meet the high accuracy criteria for Bengali and Hindi languages and also support other languages like Marathi or Kannada. The experimental results show that for same amounts of training and testing data, and identical training conditions, the Hindi model shows better performance as compared to the Bengali model. Therefore, while training the multilingual ASR model, one can think of including more data for Bengali than for Hindi to get decent performance over both languages. Also, using MFCC features can be helpful since it shows the best performance in Bengali. The presented work provides such heuristics for multilingual ASR developments, without which we lose out on language-specific nuances of training conditions. This leads to higher resource requirements in terms of data, infrastructure, and time to get the desired performance.

This study also provides language-specific learnings. The five Indian languages in this experimentation are broadly classified into two language families; The Indo-Aryan language family to which Hindi, Bengali, and Marathi belong, and the Dravidian language family to which Tamil and Kannada belong. Amongst these languages, Marathi and Hindi are phonetically similar, moreover, they use the same 'Devanagari' script. As mentioned in Section V.A., we use an ILSL 2.0 transliteration tool for grapheme-to-phoneme representation. For both Hindi and Marathi, the grapheme-to-phoneme map is one-to-one, hence both languages show similar and relatively better performance as per Figure 2 and Figure 3. On the other hand, Bengali language has some elements in the grapheme-to-phoneme map which exhibit many-to-one mapping, leading to relatively poorer recognition performance. Tamil and Kannada languages belong to the same language family, and show similar and relatively poorer performance. Therefore, one needs to tune their training conditions differently to get better performance from the models.

## VIII. CONCLUSION

In this paper, we have presented the experimental results for building Connected Number Speech Recognition (CNR) models in multiple Indian languages. The experiments were conducted for five Indian languages Bengali, Hindi, Tamil, Kannada, and Marathi. Different speech recognition models were trained for four feature combinations: MFCC, MFCC+Pitch, PLP, and PLP+Pitch features. The

MFCC+Pitch features offers the best result on average; however, results may vary from one language to another. Such comparative analysis can help select the best feature combination for any given training conditions and dataset. The presented work provides language specific insights and heuristics for building multilingual ASR models.

In future, we hope to build a single speech recognition model for multiple languages for Connected Number recognition (CNR), which can be more adaptive for language switching and have a smaller memory footprint.

## REFERENCES


[1] M.A.Anusuya and S.K. Katti, "Speech Recognition by Machine: A Review", International Journal of Computer Science and Information Security, vol. 6, no. 3, 2009

[2] Wang Dong, Xiaodong Wang, and Shaohe Lv,"An Overview of End-to-End Automatic Speech Recognition", Symmetry, vol.11, no.8, 1018, 2019

[3] H. Hirsh, P. Meyer, and H.W. Ruehl, "Improved speech recognition using high-pass filtering of sub-band envelopes", Proc. EUROSPEECH 91, pp. s413-416, Genova, Italy, 1991

[4] A. Acero, "Acoustical and environmental robustness in automatic speech recognition", PhD thesis, CMU, 1990.

[5] J. M. R. Sánchez, M. Bereau, and J. R. C. de Lara, "Feature selection for automatic speech recognition in noisy Scenarios," In 2nd International Conference of Information Processing , vol. 40, pp. 51-71, Dec. 2019.

[6] P. Ghahremani et al., "A pitch extraction algorithm tuned for automatic speech recognition," 2014 IEEE International Conference on Acoustics, Speech and Signal Processing (ICASSP), pp. 2494-2498, 2014

[7] D. Namrata, "Feature extraction methods LPC, PLP and MFCC in speech recognition", International Journal For Advance Research in Engineering And Technology (ISSN 2320-6802), vol. 1, pp. 1-6 , 2013

[8] S. A. Alim and N. K. A. Rashid, "Some commonly used speech feature extraction algorithms", in From Natural to Artificial Intelligence - Algorithms and Applications. London, United Kingdom: IntechOpen, 2018 [Online]. Available: https://www.intechopen.com/chapters/63970 doi: 10.5772/intechopen.80419

[9] O. Buza, G. Toderean, A. Nica, and A. Caruntu, "Voice signal processing for speech synthesis," IEEE InternationalConference on Automation, Quality and Testing Robotics, vol. 2, pp. 360-364, 25-28, May 2006.

[10] H. Gupta and D. Gupta, "LPC and LPCC method of feature extraction in speech recognition system." 2016 6th International Conference - Cloud System and Big Data Engineering (Confluence), pp. 498-502, 2016.

[11] L. Xie and Z. -q. Liu, "A comparative study of audio features for audio-to-visual conversion in Mpeg-4 compliant facial animation," 2006 International Conference on Machine Learning and Cybernetics, pp. 4359-4364, 2006, doi: 10.1109/ICMLC.2006.259085.

[12] A. de Cheveigné and H. Kawahara, Eds., "YIN, a fundamental frequency estimator for speech and music," The Journal of the Acoustical Society of America, vol. 111 4, pp. 1917–30, Apr. 2002.

[13] D. Talkin and W. Bastiaan Kleijn. "A robust algorithm for pitch tracking (RAPT)." Speech coding and synthesis, pp. 497-518, 1995

[14] B. S. Lee, "Noise Robust Pitch Tracking by Subband Autocorrelation Classification.", Ph.D. dissertation, Columbia University, Ann Arbor, 2012.

[15] M. Wu, D. Wang, and G. J. Brown, "A multi-pitch tracking algorithm for noisy speech," 2002 IEEE International Conference on Acoustics, Speech, and Signal Processing, pp. I-369-I-372, 2002, doi: 10.1109/ICASSP.2002.5743731.

[16] A. Camacho and J. G. Harris, "A sawtooth waveform inspired pitch estimator for speech and music," The Journal of the Acoustical Society of America, vol. 124, no. 3, pp. 1638–1652, Sep. 2008, doi: 10.1121/1.2951592.

[17] K. Kasi and S. A. Zahorian, "Yet another algorithm for pitch tracking," 2002 IEEE International Conference on Acoustics, Speech, and Signal Processing, pp. I-361-I-364, 2002, doi: 10.1109/ICASSP.2002.5743729.

[18] X. Lei. "Modeling lexical tones for mandarin large vocabulary continuous speech recognition.", Ph.D. dissertation, University of Washington, 2006.

[19] O. Kjartansson, S. Sarin, S. Pipatsrisawat, M. Jansche, and L. Ha, "Crowd-sourced speech corpora for Javanese, Sundanese, Sinhala, Nepali, and Bangladeshi Bengali", Proc. 6th Workshop on Spoken Language Technologies for Under-Resourced Languages (SLTU 2018), 2018, pp. 52-55, doi: 10.21437/SLTU.2018-11.

[20] F. He et al., 'Open-source multi-speaker speech corpora for building Gujarati, Kannada, Malayalam, Marathi, Tamil and Telugu Speech synthesis systems', Proc. The 12th Language Resources and Evaluation Conference (LREC), pp. 6494–6503, 2020.

[21] K. S. Bhogale et al., 'Effectiveness of mining audio and text pairs from public data for improving ASR systems for low-resource languages'. arXiv, 2022.

[22] G. Chen, et al., "Data augmentation for children's speech recognition", The "Ethiopian" System For The SLT 2021 Children Speech Recognition Challenge, arXiv preprint arXiv:2011.04547, 2020.

[23] N. V. Prasad and S. Umesh, "Improved cepstral mean and variance normalization using Bayesian framework", 2013 IEEE Workshop on ASRU, pp. 156–161, 2013

[24] M. McAuliffe, M. Socolof, S. Mihuc, M. Wagner, and M. Sonderegger, 'Montreal Forced Aligner: Trainable Text-Speech Alignment Using Kaldi', Proc. Interspeech 2017, pp. 498–502, 2017.

[25] "IITM Hindi Speech Corpus: a corpus of native Hindi Speech Corpus" – Speech signal processing lab, IIT Madras, 2020.

# On Machine Integers and Arithmetic

Pavel Loskot
*ZJU-UIUC Institute*
Haining, China
e-mail: *pavelloskot@intl.zju.edu.cn*

***Abstract*—All signal and data processing is performed on computing machines. However, the computing efficiency requires that numbers are represented in a finite memory space. It is claimed that all such numbers can be considered to be integers, and that decimal point has purely syntactical meaning to align numbers in arithmetic operations. This subtle, but fundamental observation seems to have been ignored so far. As an introductory exploration of integer arithmetic, this paper introduces a dual modulo operator to select digits in string representations of machine numbers. Moreover, it is proposed that natural integers offset by a real-valued constant satisfy Peano axioms. The Fermat last theorem is then considered as an example of Diophantine equation. It is shown how it can be modified to allow the solutions to exist. A Fermat metric is newly introduced to define distances between integers to allow their partitioning into subsets. These results point at the importance of investigating integer arithmetic, integer algebra, and integer analysis in designing and modeling computing systems.**

***Keywords*—*dual modulo arithmetic; Fermat last theorem; Fermat metric; natural numbers.***

## I. INTRODUCTION

Numbers are abstract mathematical objects that can also carry semantic meaning of quantity. The former leads to rich axiomatic algebraic systems, and the latter enables performing arithmetic operations in computing problems. Since computing machines have limited resources, and must execute numerical algorithms in a time and memory efficient manner, they have to represent numbers as constant size objects. This limits the largest and the smallest number values as well as precision, which can be considered. Therefore, any algorithm described or implemented in a programming language can only compute numbers from a finite set, $\mathcal{N} = \{N_1 < N_2 < \ldots\}$, such that,

$$\forall i: \ -\infty < \inf(\mathcal{N}) \leq N_i \leq \sup(\mathcal{N}) < \infty. \qquad (1)$$

Thus, two machine numbers, $N_i$, and, $N_j$, can be compared, i.e., ordered, and the difference, $\min_{i \neq j} |N_i - N_j| = \varepsilon_0$, represents the precision. The set, $\mathcal{N}$, is necessarily computable [1].

Most machine number systems use floating point and fixed point number representations. These representations including basic arithmetic operations are precisely defined by the IEEE 754 standard [2]. They enable efficient utilization of hardware and software resources to achieve the time and space efficiency in implementing computing algorithms. Some languages (e.g., Python) support infinite-precision integer arithmetic, or perform computations at the user-defined precision (e.g., Mathematica). The GNU library [3] is a popular and efficient implementation in C programming language of the multi-precision arithmetic for integer and floating-point numbers; this library is also used in several commercial software products (e.g., Mathematica and Maple). The smallest and the largest integers and single and double precision floating point numbers are defined in Matlab toolbox, Elementary Matrices, and in the C standard libraries, limits.h and float.h.

The algorithms described in various programming languages represent numbers as strings of digits in a given basis. In particular, the number, $N \in \mathcal{N}$, in basis, $B$, is represented as,

$$\begin{aligned} N = & \sum_{i=i_{\min}}^{i_{\max}} D_i \times B^i \\ \leftrightarrow \quad & D_{i_{\max}} D_{i_{\max}-1} \cdots D_1 D_0 \,.\, D_{-1} \cdots D_{i_{\min}} \end{aligned} \qquad (2)$$

where the digits, $D_i \in \{0, 1, \ldots, 9, \mathrm{A}, \mathrm{B}, \mathrm{C}, \ldots B-1\}$, and the orders, $i_{\min} \leq 0 \leq i_{\max}$. It is customary to place decimal point between the digits $D_0$ and $D_{-1}$, which divides the digits into the integral and the fractional part, respectively. More importantly, the decimal point allows aligning digits of numbers when performing arithmetic operations and comparisons.

The most common bases are decimal ($B = 10$), hexadecimal ($B = 16$), and binary ($B = 2$). However, internally, the numbers are stored much more efficiently in a byte-size basis, i.e., $B = 2^{8 \times \#\text{bytes}-1}$, with one bit reserved for the sign. The total number of bytes used for each number is usually fixed for different number classes (types) such as short and long integers, and single and double precision floating point numbers. The conversions between the string notation and the internal representation are performed automatically by compilers.

The textbook [2] provides a comprehensive overview of the number systems used on computers. The computability of functions of natural numbers is established in [4]. The mismatch between exact mathematical description and practical implementation of algorithms with approximate number representations has been studied in [5] including the methods how to mitigate such a discrepancy. The construction of large-scale real numbers, which are suitable for software implementations is considered in [6]. Binary approximations of real-numbers are investigated in [7]. Other representations of real numbers such as binary expansion, Dedekind cut and Cauchy sequence are compared in [1]. The $p$-adic number systems allow defining real-numbers as an arithmetic of rational numbers [8]. Logical statements involving comparisons of real-numbers are evaluated in satisfiability modulo theories [9]. The article [10] conclusively argues that a finite precision is usually sufficient in practical engineering applications. Many number-theoretic theorems and conjectures can be found in [11].

In this paper, it is argued that the number systems commonly used on computers can be assumed to be integer-valued, which also includes single and double precision floating point numbers and the corresponding arithmetic operations. Consequently, computing machines are inherently governed by integer algebras and arithmetic. The paper contributions are formulated as four claims and one proposition. In particular, in Section II, dual modulo operator is introduced to select digits in string representations of numbers. It can be exploited to define equivalences between numbers in integer arithmetic. In addition, it is proposed that natural numbers can be offset by a real-valued constant, and still be considered as being integers. In Section III, several modifications of Fermat last theorem (FLT) are devised to allow the solutions to exist. A Fermat metric is newly defined, which is then used to compute distances between natural numbers, and to divide the numbers into subsets. The paper is concluded in Section IV.

## II. Machine Integers and Arithmetic

Constraining machine computations to numbers, $\mathcal{N}$, has several fundamental consequences. First, the results of arithmetic operations can overflow the limits, $\inf(\mathcal{N})$, or, $\sup(\mathcal{N})$. Second, the results of arithmetic operations can underflow the precision, $\varepsilon_0$, so the results may have to be truncated, rounded, or otherwise approximated. Third, the decimal point to align numbers can be arbitrarily placed in-between any digits as long as the placement is consistent in the number system and arithmetic used. This is formalized as the following claim.

**Claim 1.** *The machine numbers allocated a predefined memory space are integers, $\mathcal{N}$, isomorphic to a finite set of finite integers, $Z = \{\ldots,-1,0,+1,\ldots\}$.*

The important consequence is that (without a formal proof) any machine arithmetic is isomorphic to integer arithmetic. However, implementing such integer arithmetic at large scale and precision to be efficient and also error-free is non-trivial.

The memory allocated by compilers of programming languages allows adding only a finite number of digits before and after a decimal point. If the numbers are padded by zero-digits from both ends, all numbers are represented by strings of the same length, and the decimal point becomes a hypothetical construct. The non-zero digits at the right end of the number string represent the precision (resolution), whereas the first non-zero digits from the left represent the scale.

The algorithms usually contain many logical statements (predicates). These statements involve comparisons of numerical values. The two integers are said to be exactly equal, provided that all digits in their string representations are the same. The exact comparison can be rather restrictive in some applications, where the differences in scale and precision could be or must be tolerated. Specifically, if the differences are tolerated in precision (the right-end sub-strings), it is equivalent to comparing quantized numbers. If the differences are tolerated at scale (the left-end sub-strings), it is equivalent to comparing periodically repeated values.

Mathematically, removing the right-end or the left-end sub-strings from the string representations of numbers can be expressed by a canonical modulo operator. In particular, for any integer $a$, and any positive integer $b$, let, $(a \bmod b) = (|a| \bmod b) \in \{0,1,\ldots,b-1\}$, to be a reminder after the integer division of $a$ by $b$. Note that this can be readily extended to real numbers as, $0 \leq (a \bmod b) = (|a| \bmod b) < b$, assuming a real division of, $a \in \mathcal{R}$, by integer, $b$. Then, the numbers, $a_1$, and, $a_2$, are said to be equivalent in a sense of congruence, provided that, $a_1 \equiv a_2 \pmod{b}$. Both equality (indicated by symbol, $=$) and equivalence (indicated by symbol, $\equiv$) satisfy axiomatic properties of reflexivity, symmetry, and transitivity, and the equality implies equivalence.

If the machine numbers, $N_i = \sum_{i=0}^{L-1} D_i B^i$, are represented by strings of $L$ digits in some basis $B$, then the first $L_1$ digits and the last $L_2$ digits, $(L_1 + L_2) < L$, can be zeroed by applying a dual modulo operator introduced next.

**Definition 1.** *The dual modulo operator has two parameters, $m_1$, and, $m_2$, and it is defined as the difference,*

$$\begin{aligned} N_i \operatorname{Mod}(m_1,m_2) &= (N_i \bmod m_1) - (N_i \bmod m_2) \\ &= \underbrace{0\cdots0}_{L_1} D_{L-L_1-1} \cdots D_{L_2+1} D_{L_2} \underbrace{0\cdots0}_{L_2}. \end{aligned} \quad (3)$$

*where $m_1 = B^{L-L_1}$, and $m_2 = B^{L_2}$.*

Modular arithmetic with dual modulo operator has similar properties as the arithmetic involving canonical modulo operator. In particular, given integers $a$, $b$, $m_1$, and $m_2$, then,

$$\begin{aligned} a \operatorname{Mod}(0,m_2) &= a - (a \bmod m_2) \\ a \operatorname{Mod}(m_1,1) &= a \bmod m_1 \\ a \operatorname{Mod}(m_1,m_1) &= 0. \end{aligned} \quad (4)$$

Furthermore, it is straightforward to prove that,

$$\begin{aligned} a+b &\equiv a \operatorname{Mod}(m_1,m_2) + b \operatorname{Mod}(m_1,m_2) \ (\operatorname{Mod}(m_1,m_2)) \\ a-b &\equiv a \operatorname{Mod}(m_1,m_2) - b \operatorname{Mod}(m_1,m_2) \ (\operatorname{Mod}(m_1,m_2)) \\ a \cdot b &\equiv a \operatorname{Mod}(m_1,m_2) \cdot b \operatorname{Mod}(m_1,m_2) \ (\operatorname{Mod}(m_1,m_2)). \end{aligned} \quad (5)$$

However, in general, for integer division with a reminder,

$$a/b \not\equiv a \operatorname{Mod}(m_1,m_2)/b \operatorname{Mod}(m_1,m_2) \ (\operatorname{Mod}(m_1,m_2)). \quad (6)$$

The Chinese reminder theorem [11] can be restated for dual modulo operator as follows. If $m_{11}$ and $m_{12}$ are co-prime, and,

$$\begin{aligned} N_i &\equiv a_1 \ (\operatorname{Mod}(m_{11},m_2)) \\ N_i &\equiv a_2 \ (\operatorname{Mod}(m_{12},m_2)) \end{aligned} \quad (7)$$

for some integers, $N_i$, and, $m_2$, then there is a unique integer, $a$, such that,

$$N_i \equiv a \ (\operatorname{Mod}(m_{11}m_{12},m_2)). \quad (8)$$

The proof is based on the property that, if $N_i \equiv a \pmod{m_1}$, then also, $N_i \equiv a \ (\operatorname{Mod}(m_1,m_2))$.

Furthermore, it is useful to consider how the machine integers used in algorithms are approximations of infinite precision real-numbers obtained from mathematical analysis.

The dual modulo operator defined in (3) produces a finite-size integer, $x \text{ Mod}(m_1, m_2)$, from a real number, $x \in \mathcal{R}$. This introduces a periodicity due to truncation from the left (specified by the parameter, $m_1$), and the quantization due to truncation from the right (specified by the parameter, $m_2$).

It is also useful to define countably infinite integer sets,

$$\tilde{\mathbb{N}}_x = \{x, x+1, x+2, \ldots\} \tag{9}$$

parameterized by finite constants, $x \in \mathcal{R}$, so that, $\tilde{\mathbb{N}}_0$, is the set of natural numbers. Such integer sets can provide exact solutions to some integer (Diophantine) problems, which otherwise do not have any solution. More importantly, for all finite $x$, the integers, $\tilde{\mathbb{N}}_x$, satisfy Peano axioms [11].

## III. Case Study: FLT Problems

The FLT states that there are no positive integers $a$, $b$, $c$, and $n > 2$, such that, $a^n + b^n = c^n$. This has been first verified numerically until the proof was obtained only recently [11]. Note also that, $|a^n + b^n - c^n| \leq 1$, has a trivial solution, $a = 1$, and, $b = c$, for $\forall n > 1$. The Fermat Number Transform (FNT) resembles Discrete Fourier Transform, however, the former assumes the sums modulo a prime [12].

More importantly, the original formulation of FLT can be modified to allow the solutions to exist.

**Claim 2.** *For every $n$, there exist infinitely many natural integers $a$, $b$, $c$, $m_1$ and $m_2$ satisfying the congruence,*

$$a^n + b^n \equiv c^n \ (\text{Mod}(m_1, m_2)). \tag{10}$$

For example, assuming the first 100 natural numbers as strings of $l = 9$ digits in the number basis, $B = 8$, and, $B = 10$, the total number of solutions, $n_l$, and, $n_r$, respectively, of (10) for the first $l_1$ digits and the last $l_2 = l - l_1$ digits is given in Table I. It can be observed that, always, $n_l > n_r$, since the number strings often contain zeros at the left to make up the given width, $l$.

TABLE I. The number of solutions of (10)

| | $B=8$ | | | | $B=10$ | | | |
|---|---|---|---|---|---|---|---|---|
| | $n=3$ | | $n=4$ | | $n=3$ | | $n=4$ | |
| $(l_1, l_2)$ | (3,6) | (4,5) | (3,6) | (4,5) | (3,6) | (4,5) | (3,6) | (4,5) |
| $n_l$ | 69627 | 22278 | 5505 | 2318 | 1284 | 44532 | 10666 | 3622 |
| $n_r$ | 212 | 644 | 730 | 2076 | 198 | 207 | 230 | 596 |

**Claim 3.** *For any integer, $n \geq 1$, the equation,*

$$a^n + b^n = c^n \tag{11}$$

*has infinitely many solutions among the integers, $\cup_x \tilde{\mathbb{N}}_x$, for specific real-values (from some set), $x > 0$.*

*Proof.* Let $c = y \in \mathcal{R}$, $a = y - d_1$, and, $b = y - d_2$, where $d_1$ and $d_2$ are arbitrarily chosen positive natural integers. Then, for any $n$, the polynomial (11) has at least one real-valued solution, $y > \max(d_1, d_2)$. Let $d_0 = \lfloor y \rfloor$ (floor function), so that $x = (y - d_0) < 1$. This defines the positive integers, $c = d_0 + x$, $a = d_0 - d_1 + x$, and $b = d_0 - d_2 + x$, from the set, $\tilde{\mathbb{N}}_x$. □

**Proposition 1.** *For any natural integer, $n$, there exists an integer, $m \geq n$, such that the expression,*

$$\sum_{i=1}^{m} a_i^n = b^n \tag{12}$$

*is satisfied for a set of natural integers, $\{a_1, a_2, \ldots, a_m\} \cup \{b\}$.*

The proof of Proposition 1 appears to be rather non-trivial, except when $n = 1$ and $n = 2$ (Pythagorean theorem). However, it is easy to find examples satisfying the expression (12), e.g.,

$$\begin{aligned} 3^2 + 4^2 &= 5^2 \ (m = n = 2) \\ 3^3 + 4^3 + 5^3 &= 6^3 \ (m = n = 3) \\ 2^4 + 2^4 + 3^4 + 4^4 + 4^4 &= 5^4 \ (m = n + 1 = 5) \\ 19^5 + 43^5 + 46^5 + 47^5 + 67^5 &= 72^5 \ (m = n = 5). \end{aligned} \tag{13}$$

In general, the sequence, $a^n + b^n$, obtained by enumerating all natural integers, $a$, and, $b$, becomes rapidly very sparse as the exponent, $n$, is increased. Given $n$, it is easy to show that the best approximation of $(a^n + b^n)$ by $c^n$ is obtained when, $c = \lfloor (a^n + b^n)^{1/n} \rceil$ (rounding function). This motivates the following Fermat metric.

**Definition 2.** *The Fermat metric for positive numbers, $a$, and, $b$, is computed as,*

$$\mathcal{F}_n(a, b) = a^n + b^n - \lfloor (a^n + b^n)^{1/n} \rceil^n \tag{14}$$

*where $n = 2, 3, \ldots$ is a natural number, and always, $\mathcal{F}_1(a, b) = 0$. The Fermat distance between the numbers, $a$, and, $b$, is the absolute value of the Fermat metric, i.e.,*

$$D_n(a, b) = |\mathcal{F}_n(a, b)|. \tag{15}$$

The distribution of Fermat metric values by enumerating all pairs of natural integers up to $10^5$ are shown in Figure 1 for $n = 2$ and $n = 3$, respectively. It can be observed that the Fermat metric values are spread much more evenly when $n = 2$, and the distributions are asymmetric about 0.

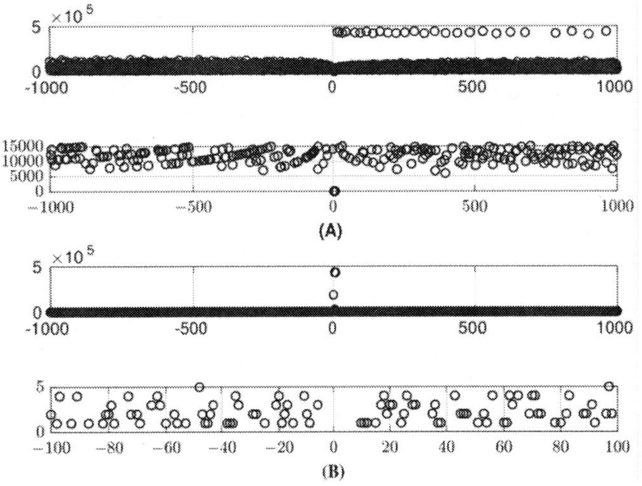

Figure 1. The counts of Fermat metric values for all pairs of natural integers up to $10^5$, for the exponents $n = 2$ (A), and $n = 3$ (B).

The Fermat distance can be used to cluster natural numbers into subsets. Figure 2 shows the dendrogram assuming the distance, $\mathcal{F}_2(a,b)$. The corresponding assignment of the first 50 natural numbers into four subsets based on the distances, $\mathcal{F}_2$, $\mathcal{F}_3$, $\mathcal{F}_4$, and $\mathcal{F}_5$ are shown in Figure 3.

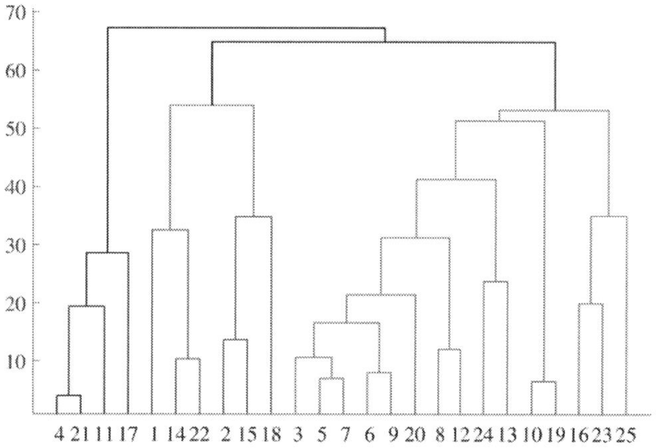


Figure 2. The dendrogram of natural numbers constructed assuming the Fermat distance, $\mathcal{F}_2(a,b)$, defined in (15).

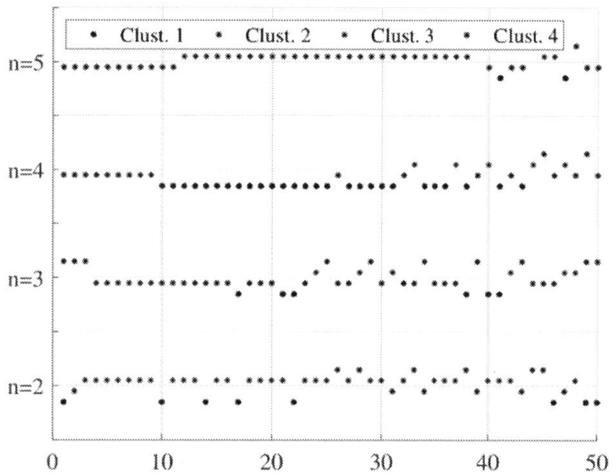


Figure 3. The first 50 natural numbers partitioned into four clusters (subsets) using the Fermat distances, $\mathcal{F}_n(a,b)$, for $n = 2,3,4$, and 5.

## IV. Discussion and Conclusion

This paper investigated modular arithmetic and introduced dual modulo operator under the premise that all machine numbers can be assumed to be integers, when they are pre-allocated a fixed space in a computer memory. This is the case with fixed point as well as floating point number representations. The meaning of a decimal point is mainly syntactical to allow aligning the operands in arithmetic operations. This leads to another fundamental claim.

**Claim 4.** *Any computing algorithm utilizing finite number representations can be represented by a system of Diophantine equations.*

Hence, there is a large gap between mathematical description based on real analysis, and the actual implementation of corresponding algorithms on computers [5].

Improving accuracy of machine numbers by $p$-adic representations [8] and by Diophantine approximations [13] is impractical, since the underlying arithmetic operations require more time and more memory. More efficient multi-precision arithmetic is available as a $C$-library [3]. In many practical applications, finite accuracy is often sufficient [10]. On the other hand, the full accuracy is required in cryptography [14].

The FLT can be modified to allow the solutions to exist. The key ideas introduced in this paper are to define equivalences between numbers assuming only a subset of digits in their number string representations, and to consider sets of natural numbers offset by real-valued constants. In addition, the Fermat metric can be used to define distances between natural and other numbers.

Future work can define and prove further properties of machine numbers and arithmetic, which are explicitly considered to be integers. This can lead to more efficient design of integer-based models and architectures for large-scale computing machines, and improved approximations of real-valued systems.

## Acknowledgment

This work was funded by a research grant from Zhejiang University.

## References

[1] X. Zheng and R. Rettinger, "Weak computability and representation of reals," *Mathematical Logic Quarterly*, vol. 50, no. 4–5, pp. 431–442, Sep. 2004.

[2] R. T. Kneusel, *Numbers and Computers*, 2nd ed. Springer International Publishing, Cham, Switzerland, 2017.

[3] T. Granlund, "The GNU multiple precision arithmetic library, GNU MP 6.2.1," https://gmplib.org, Jan. 2020, accessed: 2023-01-30.

[4] M. Wrocllawski, "Representations of natural numbers and computability of various functions," in *Conference on Computability in Europe*, 2019, pp. 298–309.

[5] R. Krebbers and B. Spitters, "Type classes for efficient exact real arithmetic in Coq," *Logical Methods in Computer Science*, vol. 9, no. 1:01, pp. 1–27, Feb. 2013.

[6] R. O'Connor, "A monadic, functional implementation of real numbers," *Mathematical Structures in Computer Science*, vol. 17, no. 1, pp. 129–159, 2007.

[7] J. van der Hoeven, "Computations with effective real numbers," *Theoretical Computer Science*, vol. 351, pp. 52–60, 2006.

[8] F. Q. Gouvêa, *p-adic Numbers: An Introduction*, 3rd ed. Springer, Cham, Switzerland, 2020.

[9] G. Kremer, F. Corzilius, and E. Ábrahám, "A generalised branch-and-bound approach and its application in SAT modulo nonlinear integer arithmetic," in *Computer Algebra in Scientific Computing*, vol. 9890, 2016, pp. 315–335.

[10] NASA/JPL Edu, "How many decimals of Pi do we really need?" https://www.jpl.nasa.gov/edu/news/2016/3/16/how-many-decimals-of-pi-do-we-really-need, Oct. 2022, accesssed: 2023-01-30.

[11] T. Gowers, J. Barrow-Green, and I. Leader, *The Princeton Companion to Mathematics*. Princeton University Press, Princeton, NJ, USA, 2008.

[12] M. Křížek, , F. Luca, and L. Somer, *17 Lectures on Fermat Numbers: From Number Theory to Geometry*. Springer New York, USA, 2001, ch. Fermat Number Transform and Other Applications, pp. 165–186.

[13] B. Church, "Diophantine approximation and transcendence theory," Apr. 2019, lecture Notes.

[14] J. Hoffstein, J. Pipher, and J. H. Silverman, *An Introduction to Mathematical Cryptography*, 2nd ed. Springer, New York, NY, USA, 2014.

# A Refined ERR-based Method for Nonlinear System Identification. Application to Epilepsy.

Marc Greige Ahmad Karfoul Isabelle Merlet Régine Le Bouquin Jeannès
Univ Rennes, INSERM, LTSI - UMR 1099, F-35000 Rennes, France
email: marc.greige@univ-rennes.fr ahmad.karfoul@univ-rennes.fr
isabelle.merlet@univ-rennes.fr regine.le-bouquin-jeannes@univ-rennes.fr

***Abstract*—The goal of this paper is to refine the solution of the Error Reduction Ratio (ERR)-based method for nonlinear system identification in the context of epilepsy. Based on a predefined dictionary, the ERR-based method is composed of two main steps: (i) identifying the most relevant candidates that are required to fit the signal at hand, and (ii) estimating their respective weights in a least squares sense. However, the used candidate selection criterion, which is based on a fixed threshold, often leads to an overestimation of the number of retained candidates. This consequently affects the quality of the system identification. This point is of particular interest in epilepsy especially for the identification of brain networks involved in the seizure onset. To deal with this issue, a refined ERR-based solution is proposed in this paper. It relies on the assumption that a few number of the retained candidates using the ERR-based method are really the most significant ones. This leads to consider a sparse representation of the associated estimated coefficient vector. The well-known Proximal Alternating Linearized Minimization (PALM) is used in this paper to solve the proposed optimization problem. To guarantee good estimation results, the used regularization parameter is, at each iteration, optimally computed using the discrepancy principle. Results on simulated and real iEEG data confirm the efficacy of the proposed method.**

***Keywords*—Error Reduction Ratio; Orthogonal Least Squares; proximal optimization; epilepsy; effective connectivity**

## I. Introduction

Epilepsy is a group of neurological disorders that cause temporary dysfunctions of the brain electrical activity. It is characterized by repetitive seizures - called ictal periods - whose frequency and duration may vary. Epileptic seizures are induced by abnormal excessive or synchronous neuronal activity in certain regions of the brain, known as epileptogenic [1]. Around 30% of epileptic patients are drug-resistant, for whom alternative therapies, such as surgery or neural stimulation, must be considered. Satisfactory outcomes of these therapies require beforehand a reliable identification of the epileptic network underlying the initiation and/or the propagation of the epileptic seizures. Identifying the epileptic network involves not only its nodes (brain regions) but also the direction of the information flow among them leading to the concept of brain effective connectivity [2]. Intracerebral electroencephalographic (iEEG) recording is a commonly used invasive technique to record brain electrical activity [3], [4]. Albeit invasive, it provides recordings with relatively high Signal-to-Noise Ratio (SNR) and free from the volume conduction effect. Neural activities are generally the result of nonlinear processes, and hence interactions between brain regions can be qualified as nonlinear. Consequently, analyzing interactions among brain regions in a linear way is sub-optimal. The Error Reduction Ratio (ERR)-based method [5]–[9] has already shown promising results in identifying nonlinear systems and inferring effective connectivity between brain regions. It is a dictionary based approach comprising two main steps: (i) identifying from a predefined dictionary the most relevant candidates that are required to fit the signal at hand; this is performed through an orthogonal least squares (OLS) scheme combined with a threshold-based candidate selection criterion [5] [6], and (ii) estimating their respective weights (model coefficients) in a least squares sense. Despite its efficiency, the ERR-based method suffers from the presence of spurious terms whose number is subject to the predefined threshold. This often leads to low system identification quality and consequently induces errors in the inference of effective connectivity. To cope with this limitation, a refined ERR-based method, denoted by rERR, is proposed in this paper. The solution relies on the assumption that, among those retained dictionary candidates using the original ERR-based method, a few number is really contributing to the signal at hand. These few but relevant candidates are found by simply prompting a sparse representation on the retained dictionary. To this end, the Proximal Alternating Linearized Minimization (PALM) [10] method is used. Besides, an optimal computation of the regularization parameter is also performed at each iteration of the proposed iterative approach leading to a more reliable identification quality. The behavior of the proposed rERR-based approach is compared to the original ERR-based one using both simulated signals and real epileptic iEEG recordings. In this contribution, Section II is devoted to the methodology before presenting the dataset in Section III. Results are given in Section IV where the rERR-based approach is compared to the original one. Some concluding remarks are given in Section V.

## II. Methodology

Assume that a set $\{\boldsymbol{y}_m\}_{m\in 1,\cdots,M}$ of $M$ epileptic iEEG signals are recorded over a $T$ period of time. The $m$-th iEEG signal $\boldsymbol{y}_m$ denotes the neural activity of the $m$-th brain region. As brain is a complex network of distributed interconnected regions, epileptic seizures can be initiated and propagated due to a specific brain epileptic network whose nodes are the involved brain regions and edges reflecting how these brain regions interact. Thus, the activity of the $m$-th brain region, $\boldsymbol{y}_m$, is linked to the ones of other brain regions. More precisely, assume that $\boldsymbol{y}_m$ can be decomposed as a linear combination of a set of $N_m$ time series, denoted by $\tilde{\boldsymbol{y}}_i^{(m)}, 1 \leq i \leq N_m$. Assume also that each of these time series is a linear and/or nonlinear combination of a subset of delayed versions of the acquired iEEG signals $\{\boldsymbol{y}_k^{\tau_k}\}_{\forall k \in \Omega_i^{(m)}, \forall \tau_k \in \Phi_i^{(m)}}$ where the indices of these time series and their related time lags are defined in the sets $\Omega_i^{(m)}$ and $\Phi_i^{(m)}$, respectively. Then, we write:

$$\begin{aligned} \boldsymbol{y}_m &= \sum_{i=1}^{N_m} \alpha_i^{(m)} \tilde{\boldsymbol{y}}_i^{(m)} + \boldsymbol{w}_m \\ \boldsymbol{y}_m &= \sum_{i=1}^{N_m} \alpha_i^{(m)} f_i^{(m)}(\{\boldsymbol{y}_k^{\tau_k}\}_{\forall k \in \Omega_i^{(m)}, \forall \tau_k \in \Phi_i^{(m)}}) + \boldsymbol{w}_m (1) \end{aligned}$$

where $f_i^{(m)}$ is the $i$-th unknown linear or nonlinear function, $\alpha_i^{(m)}$ is the $i$-th decomposition coefficient and $\boldsymbol{w}_m$ is the model residual related to $\boldsymbol{y}_m$. Understanding linear/nonlinear interactions among brain regions can be summed up to (i) the identification of the set of signals $\{\boldsymbol{y}_k^{\tau_k}\}_{\forall k \in \Omega_i^{(m)}, \forall \tau_k \in \Phi_i^{(m)}}$, (ii) the estimation of the $N_m$ functions $f_i^{(m)}$ and (iii) the identification of the coefficients vector $\boldsymbol{\alpha}_m = [\alpha_1^{(m)}, \cdots, \alpha_{N_m}^{(m)}]^\intercal$ associated to $\boldsymbol{y}_m$. A compact representation of the aforementioned decomposition problem is expressed as follows:

$$\begin{aligned} \boldsymbol{y}_m &= \boldsymbol{D}_m \boldsymbol{\alpha}_m + \boldsymbol{w}_m, \quad \forall m \in \{1, \cdots, M\} \\ &= \boldsymbol{D}\boldsymbol{\Pi}\boldsymbol{\Pi}^{-1}\boldsymbol{\theta}_m + \boldsymbol{w}_m \end{aligned} \quad (2)$$

where $\boldsymbol{D}_m = \boldsymbol{D}\boldsymbol{\Pi}$ is a matrix collecting the $M$ times series constituting the signal $\boldsymbol{y}_m$. These times series stand for the most relevant candidates that can be selected from a predefined dictionary $\boldsymbol{D} \in \mathbb{R}^{T \times N}$ using a selection matrix $\boldsymbol{\Pi}$, $N$ being the total number of candidates. This predefined dictionary encodes all possible time series candidates (comprising possible linear and/or nonlinear functions) and $\boldsymbol{\theta}_m \in \mathbb{R}^N$ is a coefficient vector. The matrix $\boldsymbol{\Pi}$ is binary with exactly one entry of 1 in each row and each column. More particularly, as initially suggested in [6], the most relevant candidates required to fit properly the signal $\boldsymbol{y}_m$, up to an ERR criterion [6], are found using an OLS scheme combined with a threshold-based candidate selection criterion [5] [6]. To this end, the matrix $\boldsymbol{D}$ is decomposed as $\boldsymbol{D} = \boldsymbol{U}\boldsymbol{W}$ where $\boldsymbol{U} \in \mathbb{R}^{T \times N}$ and $\boldsymbol{W} \in \mathbb{R}^{N \times N}$ are orthogonal and upper triangular matrices, respectively. For the sake of readability, the subscript $m$ will be dropped from now on keeping in mind that the $m$-th, $m \in \{1, \cdots, M\}$, signal $\boldsymbol{y}_m$ is being processed. This leads to rewrite equation (2) as follows:

$$\boldsymbol{y} = \boldsymbol{D}\boldsymbol{\theta} = \boldsymbol{U}\tilde{\boldsymbol{\theta}} = \sum_{n=1}^{N} \tilde{\theta}_n \boldsymbol{u}_n \quad (3)$$

where $\tilde{\boldsymbol{\theta}} = \boldsymbol{W}\boldsymbol{\theta}$, $\boldsymbol{u}_n$ is the $n$-th column of $\boldsymbol{U}$ and $\tilde{\theta}_n$ stands for the $n$-th component of the coefficients vector $\tilde{\boldsymbol{\theta}}$. Then, decomposing $\boldsymbol{y}$ requires the identification of a subset $\Gamma = \{\boldsymbol{u}_{k_\ell}\}_{k_\ell \in \{1 \cdots, N\}, \ell \in \{1, \cdots, N_m\}}$ of the most $N_m$ relevant column vectors of $\boldsymbol{U}$ contributing to $\boldsymbol{y}$ together with their corresponding coefficients $\tilde{\theta}_\ell, 1 \leq \ell \leq N_m$. The elements of $\Gamma$ are found successively according to their contribution (from the highest to the lowest) to $\boldsymbol{y}$ [5]–[9]. To this end, for the sake of convenience, let us define $\boldsymbol{D}^{-(0)} = \boldsymbol{D}$ as the initial dictionary matrix that is used to estimate the first relevant vector, $\boldsymbol{u}_{k_1}$, in $\Gamma$. Then, the matrix $\boldsymbol{D}^{-(k_i-1)} \in \mathbb{R}^{T \times N - k_i + 1}$ is a reduced dictionary matrix to be used to estimate $\boldsymbol{u}_{k_i}, k_i > 1$. The matrix $\boldsymbol{D}^{-(k_i-1)}$ is obtained by excluding one column vector from $\boldsymbol{D}^{-(k_i-2)}$. The excluded column vector in $\boldsymbol{D}^{-(k_i-2)}$ stands for the most relevant candidate model defining the vector $\boldsymbol{u}_{k_i-1}$. To find this most relevant column vector in $\boldsymbol{D}^{-(k_i-1)}$, a grid search over the columns of $\boldsymbol{D}^{-(k_i-1)}$ is applied. More precisely, let $\tilde{\boldsymbol{U}}_{k_i} = [\boldsymbol{u}_{k_i}^1, \cdots, \boldsymbol{u}_{k_i}^{N-k_i+1}] \in \mathbb{R}^{T \times N - k_i + 1}$ be defined as

$$\tilde{\boldsymbol{U}}_{k_i} = \boldsymbol{D}^{-(k_i-1)} - \boldsymbol{H}_{k_i}\tilde{\boldsymbol{U}}_{k_i-1} \quad (4)$$

where $\tilde{\boldsymbol{U}}_{k_i-1} = \boldsymbol{u}_{k_i-1}\mathbf{1}^\intercal{}_{N-k_i+1}$ and $\boldsymbol{H} \in \mathbb{R}^{N-k_i+1 \times N-k_i+1}$ is a diagonal matrix that can be obtained by solving the following optimization problem:

$$\boldsymbol{H}_{k_i}^* = \arg\min_{\boldsymbol{H}_{k_i}} ||\boldsymbol{D}^{-(k_i-1)} - \tilde{\boldsymbol{U}}_{k_i-1}\boldsymbol{H}_{k_i}||_F^2 \ s.t. H_{k_i, \underset{\forall i \neq j}{i,j}} = 0 \quad (5)$$

where $H_{k_i,i,j}$ is the $(i,j)$-th entry of $\boldsymbol{H}_{k_i}$ and $\mathbf{1}_N$ is a $N$-dimensional column vector of ones. Once the vector $\boldsymbol{u}_{k_i}$ is estimated, the vector $\tilde{\boldsymbol{\theta}}_{k_i}$ is computed also in a least squares sense:

$$\tilde{\boldsymbol{\theta}}_{k_i}^* = \arg\min_{\tilde{\boldsymbol{\theta}}_{k_i}} ||\boldsymbol{y} - \tilde{\boldsymbol{U}}_{k_i}\tilde{\boldsymbol{\theta}}_{k_i}||_2^2 \quad (6)$$

Then, the $(N - k_i + 1)$-dimensional ERR vector, denoted here by $\boldsymbol{e}$, is defined by:

$$\boldsymbol{e}_{k_i} = \boldsymbol{\Lambda}\boldsymbol{\Psi}\tilde{\boldsymbol{\theta}}_{k_i}^{\odot 2} \quad (7)$$

where $\boldsymbol{\Lambda}$ is a diagonal matrix whose main diagonal is the vector $[||\boldsymbol{u}_{k_i}^1||_2^2, \cdots, ||\boldsymbol{u}_{N-k_i+1}^1||_2^2]$, $\boldsymbol{\Psi} = \frac{1}{||\boldsymbol{y}||_2^2}\boldsymbol{I}_{N-k_i+1}$, $\odot$ stands for the Hadamard product (element-wise matrix product, $\tilde{\boldsymbol{\theta}}_{k_i}^{\odot 2} = \tilde{\boldsymbol{\theta}} \odot \tilde{\boldsymbol{\theta}}$ and $\boldsymbol{I}_K$ is a $(K \times K)$ identity matrix. Note that the $\ell$-th component, $e_\ell$, $1 \leq \ell \leq N - k_i + 1$, of the vector $\boldsymbol{e}_{k_i}$ quantifies the contribution strength of the $\ell$-th candidate model, $\boldsymbol{d}_\ell^{-(k_i-1)} \in \mathbb{R}^T$, in the current dictionary $\boldsymbol{D}^{-(k_i-1)}$. Once the $N - k_i + 1$ ERR values are computed, the index of the highest ERR value, $e_{max}^{(k_i)}$, in the vector $\boldsymbol{e}_{k_i}$ refers to the position of the most relevant candidate in $\boldsymbol{D}^{-(k_i-1)}$. The above mentioned steps are repeated until $N_m$ candidate models are selected and for which the inequality $1 - \sum_{i=1}^{N_m} e_{\max}^{(i)} < \epsilon$, where $\epsilon$ is a predefined threshold chosen heuristically, becomes true. Let us now define $\boldsymbol{D}_1 \in \mathbb{R}^{T \times N_m}$ as the dictionary collecting the $N_m$ retained column vectors of the initial dictionary $\boldsymbol{D} \in \mathbb{R}^{T \times N}$. Then, in order to avoid some spurious retained models in $\boldsymbol{D}_1$ that could be raised due to the choice of the threshold $\epsilon$, we propose to refine the obtained dictionary $\boldsymbol{D}_1$. To this end, we assume that, among all retained models, few of them are relevant to reconstruct the signal $\boldsymbol{y}$. This formally leads to consider a sparse representation of the coefficient vector, $\boldsymbol{\theta}$. Then, the refined representation of $\boldsymbol{y}$ can be obtained by solving the following optimization problem:

$$\boldsymbol{\theta}^* = \arg\min_{\boldsymbol{\theta}} \frac{\lambda}{2}||\boldsymbol{y}-\boldsymbol{x}||_2^2 + ||\boldsymbol{z}||_1 \text{ s.t. } \boldsymbol{x} = \boldsymbol{D}_1\boldsymbol{\theta} \text{ and } \boldsymbol{z} = \boldsymbol{\theta} \tag{8}$$

where $\lambda$ is a regularization parameter and $||.||_1$ is the $L1$-norm. Such optimization problem can be solved using the PALM method [10]. The choice of the PALM method is justified by its good convergence properties [11]. PALM minimizes the augmented Lagrangian function associated to (8) given by:

$$\begin{aligned}\mathcal{L}(\boldsymbol{x},\boldsymbol{z},\boldsymbol{\theta},\boldsymbol{v},\boldsymbol{g},\lambda) = &\frac{\lambda}{2}||\boldsymbol{y}-\boldsymbol{x}||_2^2 + ||\boldsymbol{z}||_1 + \frac{\rho_1}{2}||\boldsymbol{\theta}-\boldsymbol{z}||_2^2 \\ &+\boldsymbol{v}^{\intercal}(\boldsymbol{\theta}-\boldsymbol{z}) + \frac{\rho_2}{2}||\boldsymbol{D}_1\boldsymbol{\theta}-\boldsymbol{x}||_2^2 + \boldsymbol{g}^{\intercal}(\boldsymbol{D}_1\boldsymbol{\theta}-\boldsymbol{x})\end{aligned} \tag{9}$$

where $\boldsymbol{x}$ and $\boldsymbol{z}$ are auxiliary variables, $\boldsymbol{v}$ and $\boldsymbol{g}$ stand for the Lagrange multipliers and $\rho_1, \rho_2 \in \mathbb{R}_+^*$. The update rules of variables $\boldsymbol{\theta}$ and $\boldsymbol{x}$ are computed by looking for the stationary points of $\mathcal{L}$ in these two variables. This leads to :

$$\boldsymbol{\theta} = (\rho_1\boldsymbol{I}_N + \rho_2{\boldsymbol{D}_1}^{\intercal}\boldsymbol{D}_1)^{-1}(\boldsymbol{v} + \rho_1\boldsymbol{z} + {\boldsymbol{D}_1}^{\intercal}(\rho_2\boldsymbol{x} - \boldsymbol{g})) \tag{10}$$

$$\boldsymbol{x} = \frac{\lambda\boldsymbol{y} + \boldsymbol{g} + \rho_2\boldsymbol{D}_1\boldsymbol{\theta}}{\lambda + \rho_2} \tag{11}$$

As far as the Lagrangian multipliers $\boldsymbol{v}$ and $\boldsymbol{g}$ are concerned, they are updated through a gradient-ascent scheme as follows:

$$\Delta\boldsymbol{v} = \rho_1(\boldsymbol{\theta}-\boldsymbol{z}), \quad \Delta\boldsymbol{g} = \rho_2(\boldsymbol{D}_1\boldsymbol{\theta}-\boldsymbol{x}) \tag{12}$$

where $\Delta\boldsymbol{v} = \boldsymbol{v}_{i+1} - \boldsymbol{v}_i$ and $\Delta\boldsymbol{g} = \boldsymbol{g}_{i+1} - \boldsymbol{g}_i$ ($i$ represents the iteration index). Besides, the update rule of the dual variable $\boldsymbol{z}$ is performed by:

$$\boldsymbol{z} = prox_{\phi,\lambda c_{\boldsymbol{z}}}\left(\boldsymbol{z} - \frac{1}{c_{\boldsymbol{z}}}\nabla_{\boldsymbol{z}}\mathcal{L}(\boldsymbol{x},\boldsymbol{z},\boldsymbol{\theta},\boldsymbol{v},\boldsymbol{g},\lambda)\right) \tag{13}$$

where $\nabla_{\boldsymbol{z}}\mathcal{L}(\boldsymbol{x},\boldsymbol{z},\boldsymbol{\theta},\boldsymbol{v},\boldsymbol{g},\lambda) = \frac{\partial\mathcal{L}(\boldsymbol{x},\boldsymbol{z},\boldsymbol{\theta},\boldsymbol{v},\boldsymbol{g},\lambda)}{\partial\boldsymbol{z}} = (-\boldsymbol{v} - \rho_1(\boldsymbol{\theta}-\boldsymbol{z}))$, $c_{\boldsymbol{z}} \in \mathbb{R}$ is the step-size, $\text{prox}_{\phi,\lambda c_{\boldsymbol{z}}}$ is a proximal operator dealing with the non-smooth function (here $\phi = ||.||_1$) and initially proposed in [12] and $\lambda c_{\boldsymbol{z}}$ denotes the shrinking threshold. Besides, as the proximal operator defined in equation (13) relies mainly on a gradient-descent scheme, the gradient learning step is a crucial parameter to be accounted for. According to [10], a wise choice of such parameter is $c_{\boldsymbol{z}} > L_{\boldsymbol{z}}(\boldsymbol{z})$ where $L_{\boldsymbol{z}}$ is the Lipschitz modulus verifying [10]:

$$\begin{aligned}||\nabla_{\boldsymbol{z}}\mathcal{L}(\boldsymbol{x},\boldsymbol{z}_{i-1},\boldsymbol{\theta},\boldsymbol{v},\boldsymbol{g},\lambda) - \nabla_{\boldsymbol{z}}\mathcal{L}(\boldsymbol{x},\boldsymbol{z}_i,\boldsymbol{\theta},\boldsymbol{v},\boldsymbol{g},\lambda)||_2 \leq \\ L_{\boldsymbol{z}}||\boldsymbol{z}_{i-1} - \boldsymbol{z}_i||_2\end{aligned} \tag{14}$$

where $\boldsymbol{z}_i$ is the estimate of the vector $\boldsymbol{z}$ at the $i$-th iteration. By substituting the expression of $\nabla_{\boldsymbol{z}}\mathcal{L}(\boldsymbol{x},\boldsymbol{z}_{i-1},\boldsymbol{\theta},\boldsymbol{v},\boldsymbol{g},\lambda)$ in the above inequality, we get $L_{\boldsymbol{z}} \geq \rho_1$. This condition leads to define a lower bound on the value of the gradient learning step $c_{\boldsymbol{z}}$. More precisely, as suggested in [10], a good behavior of the PALM algorithm is guaranteed when the gradient learning step verifies $c_{\boldsymbol{z}} = \gamma_{\boldsymbol{z}}L_{\boldsymbol{z}}$ with $\gamma_{\boldsymbol{z}} > 1$. Thus, a lower bound on the gradient learning step is obtained by combining the obtained condition on the Lipschitz modulus with the given expression on $c_{\boldsymbol{z}}$. This leads to $c_{\boldsymbol{z}} \geq \gamma_{\boldsymbol{z}}\rho_1$. In the current study the equal part of the latter inequality is considered and then the parameter $\gamma_{\boldsymbol{z}}$ is tuned, while fixing the parameter $\rho_1$ to one, in such a way good estimation results are obtained. As far as the regularization parameter $\lambda$ is concerned, it is optimally computed, at each iteration, by means of the discrepancy principle. In fact, the latter principle states that the regularization parameter is laying in the set $\{\boldsymbol{x} : ||\boldsymbol{x}-\boldsymbol{y}||_2^2 \leq c\}$ where $c \in \mathbb{R}$ is a coefficient related to the noise variance [13] and can be obtained through the equivalent degree of freedom method [14] [15]. Then, by considering the equality part of the latter condition together with equation (11), the update rule of $\lambda$ can be written as follows:

$$\lambda = \frac{||\rho_2(\boldsymbol{y}-\boldsymbol{D}_1\boldsymbol{\theta}) - \boldsymbol{g}||_2}{\sqrt{c}} - \rho_2 \tag{15}$$

At each iteration, equations (10), (11), (12), (13) and (15) are called alternatively where each variable is updated by fixing the other ones to their last estimate. The optimization process stops either when the relative estimation error on the parameter $\boldsymbol{\theta}$ exhibits a value that is smaller than (or equal to) a predefined threshold determined empirically, or when the maximum number of iterations is reached.

## III. DATASET

The evaluation of the proposed approach is performed on both simulated and real iEEG signals.

### A. Simulated iEEG signals

A 3-channel nonlinear model generating iEEG-like signals [16] is considered and defined hereafter:

$$\begin{aligned}y_1(k) &= 3.4y_1(k-1)(1-y_1^2(k-1))e^{-y_1^2(k-1)} + w_1(k)\\ y_2(k) &= 3.4y_2(k-1)(1-y_2^2(k-1))e^{-y_2^2(k-1)} - 0.5y_1^2(k-1)\\ &\quad + 0.25\sqrt{2}y_2(k-1) - 0.5y_3(k-3) + w_2(k)\\ y_3(k) &= 3.4y_3(k-1)(1-y_3^2(k-1))e^{-y_3^2(k-1)} - 0.5y_1^2(k-2)\\ &\quad - 0.5y_2(k-2) - 0.25\sqrt{2}y_3(k-2) + w_3(k)\end{aligned} \tag{16}$$

where $w_m \sim \mathcal{N}(0,1), 1 \leq m \leq 3$. The interest in such model is that it covers a variety of non-linearity types which is, to a large extent, in accordance with the nonlinear characteristic of the interactions between brain regions. In this study, the initial dictionary, denoted by $\boldsymbol{D}$, is defined as the collection of sixty candidates defined as follows:

- $\{f_i^{(m)}(\boldsymbol{y}_m^{\tau_m})\}_{\substack{1\leq i\leq 3\\ 1\leq m\leq 3}}, \forall\tau_m \in \{1,2,3\}$ is the set of their related time lags with $f_i^{(m)}(\boldsymbol{y}_m^{\tau_m}) = (\boldsymbol{y}_m^{\tau_m})^{\odot i}$.
- $\{f_i^{(m)}(e^{-\boldsymbol{y}_m^{\tau_m}})\}_{\substack{1\leq i\leq 3\\ 1\leq m\leq 3}}, \forall\tau_m \in \{1,2,3\}$.
- $\{f_{i_1}^{(m)}(\boldsymbol{y}_m^1)\}_{\substack{i_1\in\{1,3\}\\ 1\leq m\leq 3}} \times \{f_2^{(m)}(e^{-\boldsymbol{y}_m^1})\}_{\substack{1\leq i_2\leq 3\\ 1\leq m\leq 3}}$.

where a time period of four seconds of iEEG signals sampled at 256 Hz (*i.e.*, 1024 time samples) is simulated.

### B. Real iEEG signals

Real iEEG signals were recorded in Rennes Hospital Epilepsy Unit in one female patient aged 35. In this patient who suffered from temporal lobe epilepsy, twelve intracerebral electrodes (10-15 contacts) were implanted in the left temporal, insular, inferior frontal and inferior parietal regions. From these recordings, a 64s-epoch, sampled at 256 Hz, was considered. Based on the clinician's expertise and according to preliminary clinical and electrophysiological examinations, we only kept the most interesting bipolar channels leading to a set of 12 channels. The objective is to classify these channels into three groups. The 'Onset' group ($O$) is a group where rapid discharges were observed by the clinician and therefore considered as the main regions responsible for the initiation of the seizure. The 'Propagation Sink' group ($P_S$) consists of channels that are majorly triggered by the Onset group, and considered as less involved in the triggering of the seizure. Finally, the 'Propagation Internal' group ($P_I$) consists of regions that can be triggered by other regions in the $O$ group. Besides, this $P_I$ group can be slightly involved in the seizure setting up through delayed electrical discharges with lower intensity compared to the ones of the $O$ group. Consequently, this $P_I$ group refers to less epileptogenic brain regions, and therefore considered as the one linking the most epileptogenic zones to those who are the less epileptogenic. According to the neuroscience expert, the most interesting time period to be considered corresponds to the onset of the ictal phase, *i.e.*, between the 18th and 22th seconds in the recording.

## IV. Results

### A. Simulated model

To assess the performance of the proposed approach on the estimation of the coefficients associated to the retained candidates, a mean squared error (MSE) criterion averaged over $K = 1000$ Monte-Carlo (MC) trials was computed for each simulated signal. The MSE related to the $m$-th channel is given by:

$$MSE^{(m)} = \frac{1}{K}\sum_{k=1}^{K} ||\boldsymbol{y}^{(m)} - \hat{\boldsymbol{y}}_k^{(m)}||_2^2 \tag{17}$$

$\forall m \in \{1, \cdots, M\}$ where $\hat{\boldsymbol{y}}_k^{(m)}$ is the estimate of $\boldsymbol{y}^{(m)}$ at the $k$-th trial. Obtained MSE results for both the original ERR-based method and the proposed rERR-based one are given in Table I. A higher performance of the proposed rERR-based method over the ERR-based one can be clearly noticed from this table.

More precisely, we can state from Table I that the proposed rERR-based solution provides around 18%, 11% and 40% improvement in the nonlinear identification quality of the simulated iEEG-like signals, $y_1, y_2$ and $y_3$ (16), respectively. Furthermore, the improvement in the obtained MSE standard

TABLE I
MSE±STD Computed Over $K = 1000$ MC Trials. Case of Simulated iEEG-Like Signals.

| | *ERR-based method* | *rERR-based method* |
|---|---|---|
| $y_1$ | $3.39 \pm 0.22$ | $\mathbf{2.84} \pm 0.18$ |
| $y_2$ | $6.51 \pm 0.72$ | $\mathbf{5.81} \pm 0.37$ |
| $y_3$ | $11.50 \pm 2.34$ | $\mathbf{7.70} \pm 0.54$ |

deviation shows that the proposed rERR-based approach provides statistically more consistent system identification results. This fact is also confirmed through Figure 1 where a clear gap in the estimation quality between the two considered methods is to be stated in favor of the proposed rERR-based solution.

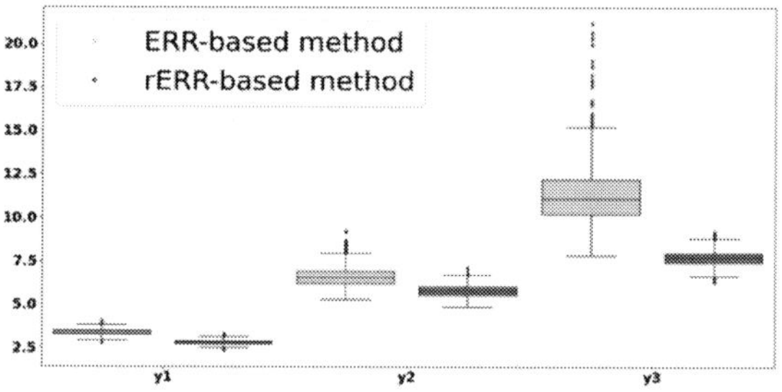


Fig. 1. MSE box-plots for the three simulated signals described in (16).

### B. Real iEEG signals

In this study, each real iEEG signal, $\boldsymbol{y}_m, 1 \leq m \leq M$ (where $M = 12$) is assigned to either the $O$, $P_I$ or $P_S$ group using a defined threshold $\phi_{th}$:

$$\phi_{th} = \frac{1}{4M}\sum_{m=1}^{M} |\phi_m| \tag{18}$$

where $\phi_m$ is defined as follows:

$$\phi_m = \frac{OD_m - ID_m}{OD_m + ID_m} \tag{19}$$

with $OD_m$ and $ID_m$ stand respectively for the outward and the inward degrees of the $m$-th signal (node) in the estimated brain network. More precisely, let $\boldsymbol{\Theta} = [\boldsymbol{\theta}_1, \cdots, \boldsymbol{\theta}_M] \in \mathbb{R}^{M \times M}$ be the adjacency matrix associated to the directed graph associated to the estimated brain network. Then, we have [17]:

$$OD_m = \sum_{i=1}^{M} \Theta_{m,i} \quad , \quad ID_m = \sum_{i=1}^{M} \Theta_{i,m} \tag{20}$$

where $\Theta_{m,i}$ denotes the $(m, i)$-th entry of $\boldsymbol{\Theta}$. It is noteworthy that the adjacency matrix associated to a directed graph is a square asymmetric matrix (*i.e.*, $\Theta_{i,j} \neq \Theta_{j,i}$). Thus, the classification rule for a given signal $\boldsymbol{y}_m$ is defined by:

$$\boldsymbol{y}_m \in \begin{cases} O, & \text{if } \phi \geq \phi_{th} \\ P_I, & \text{if } -\phi_{th} \leq \phi_m \leq \phi_{th} \\ P_S, & \text{if } \phi_m \leq -\phi_{th} \end{cases} \tag{21}$$

Table II shows the expert's classification of the 12 iEEG channels. In addition, obtained classification results using both the original ERR-based method and the proposed rERR-based one are reported in Table III and Table IV respectively. Note that the two considered methods were tested on the seizure collected from the epileptic patient on the $[18s; 22s]$ time interval.

TABLE II
EXPERT'S CLASSIFICATION OF THE IEEG CHANNELS.

| Expert | *Classification* | Expert | *Classification* |
|---|---|---|---|
| $Bp1$-$Bp2$ | $O$ | $Cp4$-$Cp5$ | $P_I$ |
| $Cp1$-$Cp2$ | $O$ | $Ap6$-$Ap7$ | $P_I$ |
| $Ap2$-$Ap3$ | $O$ | $Bp6$-$Bp7$ | $P_I$ |
| $Pp1$-$Pp2$ | $O$ | $Fp1$-$Fp2$ | $P_S$ |
| $Pp4$-$Pp5$ | $O$ | $Dp1$-$Dp2$ | $P_S$ |
| $Pp8$-$Pp9$ | $O$ | $Tp1$-$Tp2$ | $P_S$ |

TABLE III
CLASSIFICATION OF REAL EPILEPTIC IEEG SIGNALS USING THE ORIGINAL ERR-BASED METHOD.

| ERR-based method | *Classification* | ERR-based method | *Classification* |
|---|---|---|---|
| $Bp1$-$Bp2$ | $P_S$ | $Cp4$-$Cp5$ | $P_S$ |
| $Cp1$-$Cp2$ | $P_I$ | $Ap6$-$Ap7$ | $O$ |
| $Ap2$-$Ap3$ | $O$ | $Bp6$-$Bp7$ | $O$ |
| $Pp1$-$Pp2$ | $P_I$ | $Fp1$-$Fp2$ | $P_S$ |
| $Pp4$-$Pp5$ | $O$ | $Dp1$-$Dp2$ | $P_S$ |
| $Pp8$-$Pp9$ | $P_I$ | $Tp1$-$Tp2$ | $P_S$ |

TABLE IV
CLASSIFICATION OF REAL EPILEPTIC IEEG SIGNALS USING THE RERR-BASED METHOD.

| rERR-based method | *Classification* | rERR-based method | *Classification* |
|---|---|---|---|
| $Bp1$-$Bp2$ | $P_S$ | $Cp4$-$Cp5$ | $P_S$ |
| $Cp1$-$Cp2$ | $O$ | $Ap6$-$Ap7$ | $O$ |
| $Ap2$-$Ap3$ | $O$ | $Bp6$-$Bp7$ | $O$ |
| $Pp1$-$Pp2$ | $O$ | $Fp1$-$Fp2$ | $P_S$ |
| $Pp4$-$Pp5$ | $O$ | $Dp1$-$Dp2$ | $P_S$ |
| $Pp8$-$Pp9$ | $P_S$ | $Tp1$-$Tp2$ | $P_S$ |

From Tables III and IV, we observe that both methods were able to correctly classify $Ap2$-$Ap3$ and $Pp4$-$Pp5$ in the $O$ group. Besides, ERR and rERR were able to group properly all the $P_S$ channels. Moreover, according to the expert, $Pp8-Pp9$ showed a delayed discharge, which can explain that it was classified in the $P_I$ / $P_S$ groups using both algorithms. As for $Ap6$-$Ap7$, it showed a rapid discharge at the onset of the seizure, which may explain its classification by the two algorithms. Now, the proposed rERR-based method outperforms the original one in the classification of $Cp1$-$Cp2$ and $Pp1$-$Pp2$ channels, in accordance with the expert's opinion. To conclude, following the expert's classification, the rERR-based approach appears attractive and more reliable in the identification of brain regions involved in the seizure onset, which is a crucial point from a therapeutic point of view.

## V. CONCLUSION

In this paper, a refined ERR-based solution for nonlinear system identification problem was proposed with application to epilepsy. More precisely, the proposed solution handles the issue of the overestimation of the number of candidates required to decompose the signal at hand, which is a commonly encountered issue in the original ERR-based approach. The proposed solution relies on the assumption of a sparse representation of the model coefficient vector that the ERR-based approach provides. The defined optimization problem was solved in the proximal optimization framework using the well-known PALM algorithm combined with an optimal computation of the regularization parameter at each iteration. Numerical experiments on simulated iEEG-like and real epileptic iEEG signals showed clearly a higher system identification quality of the proposed approach compared to the original ERR-based one.

## REFERENCES


[1] S. L. Moshé, E. Perucca, P. Ryvlin, and T. Tomson, "Epilepsy: new advances," *The Lancet*, vol. 385, no. 9971, pp. 884–898, 2015.

[2] K. Friston, "Functional and effective connectivity: A review," *Brain connectivity*, vol. 1, pp. 13–36, 01 2011.

[3] A. N. Almeida, V. Martinez, and W. Feindel, "The first case of invasive EEG monitoring for the surgical treatment of epilepsy: historical significance and context," *Epilepsia*, vol. 46, no. 7, pp. 1082–1085, 2005.

[4] W. Penfield and T. C. Erickson, *Epilepsy and cerebral localization*. Charles C. Thomas, 1941.

[5] S. Chen, S. A. Billings, and W. Luo, "Orthogonal least squares methods and their applications to non-linear system identification," Tech. Rep. 2-30, Sheffield University, 1989.

[6] S. A. Billings, M. J. Korenberg, and S. Chen, "Identification of nonlinear output-affine systems using an orthogonal least squares algorithm," Tech. Rep. 1-11, Sheffield University, 1987.

[7] Y. Zhao, S. A. Billings, H. Wei, and P. G. Sarrigiannis, "Tracking time-varying causality and directionality of information flow using an error reduction ratio test with applications to electroencephalography data," *Physical Review E*, vol. 86, no. 5, pp. 1–11, 2012.

[8] P. G. Sarrigiannis *et al.*, "Quantitative eeg analysis using error reduction ratio-causality test; validation on simulated and real eeg data," *Clinical Neurophysiology*, vol. 125, pp. 32–46, 2014.

[9] Y. Zhao *et al.*, "Imaging of nonlinear and dynamic functional brain connectivity based on eeg recordings with the application on the diagnosis of alzheimer's disease," *IEEE Transactions on Medical Imaging*, vol. 39, pp. 1571–1581, 2020.

[10] J. Bolte, S. Sabach, and M. Teboulle, "Proximal alternating linearized minimization for nonconvex and nonsmooth problems," *Mathematical Programming*, vol. 146, pp. 459–494, 2014.

[11] R. Shefi and M. Teboulle, "On the rate of convergence of the proximal alternating linearized minimization algorithm for convex problems," *EURO Journal on Computational Optimization*, vol. 4, no. 1, pp. 27–46, 2016.

[12] L. Ding, "Reconstructing cortical current density by exploring sparseness in the transform domain," *Physics in Medicine and Biology*, vol. 54, pp. 2683 – 2697, 2009.

[13] K. El Houari *et al.*, "Investigating transmembrane current source formulation for solving the ecg inverse problem," in *2018 IEEE 10th Sensor Array and Multichannel Signal Processing Workshop (SAM)*, pp. 371–375, 2018.

[14] N. Galatsanos and A. Katsaggelos, "Methods for choosing the regularization parameter and estimating the noise variance in image restoration and their relation," *IEEE Transactions on Image Processing*, vol. 1, no. 3, pp. 322–336, 1992.

[15] C. He, C. Hu, W. Zhang, and B. Shi, "A fast adaptive parameter estimation for total variation image restoration," *IEEE Transactions on Image Processing*, vol. 23, no. 12, pp. 4954–4967, 2014.

[16] C. Mahjoub, J. Bellanger, A. Kachouri, and R. Le Bouquin Jeannès, "On the performance of temporal Granger causality measurements on time series: a comparative study," *Springer Nature*, vol. 14, no. 3, pp. 1–9, 2020.

[17] N. Biggs, E. K. Lloyd, and R. J. Wilson, *Graph Theory, 1736-1936*. Oxford University Press, 1986.

# Divergence-Based Regularization for End-to-End Sensing Matrix Optimization in Compressive Sampling Systems

Roman Jacome
*Department of Physics*
*Universidad Industrial de Santander*
Bucaramanga,Colombia
roman2162474@correo.uis.edu.co

Henry Arguello
*Department of Computer Science*
*Universidad Industrial de Santander*
Bucaramanga,Colombia
henarfu@uis.edu.co

Alejandra Hernandez-Rojas
*Department of Physics*
*Universidad Industrial de Santander*
Bucaramanga,Colombia
maria.hernandez26@correo.uis.edu.co

Paul Goyes-Peñafiel
*Department of Computer Science*
*Universidad Industrial de Santander*
Bucaramanga,Colombia
ypgoype@correo.uis.edu.co

***Abstract*—Sensing Matrix Optimization (SMO) in Compressed Sensing (CS) systems allows improved performance in the underlying signal decoding. Data-driven methods based on deep learning algorithms have opened a new horizon for SMO. The matrix is designed jointly with a decoder network that performs compressed learning tasks. This design paradigm, named End-to-End (E2E) optimization, comprises two parts: the sensing layer that models the acquisition system and the computational decoder. However, SMO in the E2E network has two main issues: i) it suffers from the vanishing of the gradient since the sensing matrix is the first layer of the network, and ii) there is no interpretability in the SMO, resulting in poorly compressed acquisition. To address these issues, we proposed a regularization function that gives some interpretability to the designed matrix and adds an inductive bias in the SMO. The regularization function is based on the Kullback-Leiber Divergence (KLD), which aims to approximate the distribution of the compressed measurements to a prior distribution. Thus, the sensing matrix can concentrate or spread the distribution of the compressed measurements according to the chosen prior distribution. We obtained optimal performance by concentrating the distribution in the recovery task, while in the classification task, the improvement was obtained by increasing the variance of the distribution. We validate the proposed regularized E2E method in general CS scenarios, such as in the Coded Aperture (CA) design for the Single-Pixel Camera (SPC) and Compressive Seismic Acquisition (CSA) geometry design.**

***Index Terms*—Sensing Matrix Optimization; End-to-End optimization; Compressive Sensing; Compressive Imaging; Compressive Seismic Acquisition.**

## I. INTRODUCTION

Compressive Sensing (CS) [1] states that a signal $\mathbf{x} \in \mathbb{R}^n$ can be recovered from a small set of observations $\mathbf{y} \in \mathbb{R}^m$ such that $m \ll n$ as $\mathbf{y} = \mathbf{H}_\phi \mathbf{x} + \mathbf{w}$, where $\mathbf{H}_\phi \in \mathbb{R}^{m \times n}$ is the measurement matrix, $\phi$ denotes the free-parameters of the system, and $\mathbf{w} \in \mathbb{R}^m$ is additive noise in the acquisition. Decoding the measurements to obtain the underlying signal $\mathbf{x}$ requires additional knowledge to solve this ill-posed problem. While a plethora of decoding algorithms have been proposed, such as those based on sparsity-promoting solution [2] [3], dictionary learning [4], low-rank priors [5], or recent data-driven methods based on deep learning [6] [7]. Complementary to algorithm development, Sensing Matrix Optimization (SMO) has remarkably improved decoding performance [8]. Traditional design methods are based on improving the mutual coherence of the sensing matrix as well as the the representation basis [9], for block-sparse signals [10], joint dictionary and sensing optimization [11] or the restricted isometry property [12]. These designs are mostly based on sparse representations of the desired signal $\mathbf{x}$, which in practice might not be sufficient to describe the signal [13]. Thus, recent data-driven methods have enabled SMO based on data priors, i.e., the SMO is performed depending on the training dataset. The End-to-End (E2E) learning of the sensing matrix and the decoding process by a Deep Neural Network (DNN) has significantly improved the decoding performance. Here, the free parameters of the sensing matrix $\phi$ are trainable variables jointly optimized with the parameters of DNN that perform the decoding task. This E2E optimization has been successfully applied in CS [14]–[16], computational imaging where the free-parameters are optical coding elements such as Coded Aperture (CA) [17]–[19], diffractive optical elements [20]–[22] or in compressive seismic acquisition geometries, where the design is performed over the receivers or sensors [23]. However, the SMO in the E2E method has the following issues. i) Vanishing of the gradient: Since the sensing is performed in the first layer of the network, the gradient in that layer is smaller than the decoding network. Thus, the performance relies more on the decoder network parameters than the trained sensing matrix. ii) Lack of interpretability: traditional SMO results in interpretable optimization in terms of the mutual incoherence [24] or the eigenvalues concentration [25]. However, the resulting sensing matrix in the E2E methods does not have an interpretation other than the one adapted to the training data.

In this work, we propose to address these issues by including a regularization in the loss function of the E2E network. Here, we propose a regularization based on the Kullback-Leiber Divergence (KLD) over the distribution of the compressed measurements. The KLD is employed to measure the difference between two probability distributions. Here, we employed the KLD to approximate the distribution of the measurements to a chosen prior distribution. This function has been widely used in DNN to regularize latent representation distribution of the data, as in variational autoencoders [26] or in generative models [27]. One of the reasons for the wide use of this function in DNN regularization is the closed-form solution of the divergence for Gaussian distributions [26] and Laplacian distributions [28], which depends on the mean and variance of the data and prior distribution. We study the effect of the prior distribution for two computational tasks, recovery and classification. We found that smaller variance, i.e., the sensing matrix represents the data in a concentrated distribution, gives better reconstruction performance. While higher variance produces more accurate classification predictions. Thus, the regularizer can be set to obtain optimal performance in different computational tasks. The main interpretation for the recovery case comes from contractive autoencoders [29], which states that the original data is better represented in an invariant low-dimensional manifold. The intuition of the second behavior is that more separated measurements allow better identification of the classes by the decoding network. Preliminary results on this regularizer applied to compressive imaging were presented in [30].

We evaluate the proposed regularized E2E method in three cases. In a general CS setting where $\mathbf{H}_\phi$ is a dense matrix, and $\phi$ are all the entries of the sensing matrix. The second case is the Single-Pixel Camera (SPC) [31], which is one of the most common CS systems of imaging applications. Here the sensing matrix entries are binary values representing a CA. The last setting is a Compressive Seismic Acquisition (CSA) model, where the sensing matrix is a diagonal matrix in which entries are binary values denoting the removed receivers.

The rest of the paper is organized as follows. In section II the E2E model is established, III presents the proposed divergence-based regularizers for the E2E training. Section IV shows the mathematical models of the CS systems used to validate the proposed method. Section V contains the numerical simulations of the proposed method and comparisons with non-regularized models. Finally, in section VI the conclusions of this work are presented.

## II. End-to-End Optimization

With new developments in data-driven algorithms and deep learning, a method called End-to-End optimization (E2E) has been developed to optimize the sensing procedure and the decoding process jointly. In this approach, the sensing model $\mathbf{H}_\phi$ is cast into a differentiable neural network layer, where the free parameters $\phi$ are the weights of this layer, named Sensing Layer (SL). The SL is coupled to a neural network that receives as input the compressive measurements and performs the decoding operator, which is called Computational Decoder (CD), denoted by the operator $\mathcal{N}_\theta$ where $\theta$ are the trainable parameters of the network. Considering the dataset $\{\mathbf{x}_k, \mathbf{d}_k\}_{k=1}^K$ where $\mathbf{d}_k$ is the ground-truth, e.g., in the recovery case $\mathbf{d}_k$ is the same input image $\mathbf{x}_k$ and in classification $\mathbf{d}_k$ is the image label. Then, the E2E optimization problem is the following

$$\{\widehat{\phi}, \widehat{\theta}\} = \underset{\phi,\theta}{\arg\min} \frac{1}{K} \sum_{k=1}^{K} \mathcal{L}(\mathcal{N}_\theta(\mathbf{H}_\phi \mathbf{x}_k), \mathbf{d}_k), \tag{1}$$

where $\mathcal{L}$ is the loss function of the computational task. The main goal is to update the sensing matrix and the decoder parameters according to the loss function task. Particularly, following the chain rule, the gradient of the loss function with respect to the SL trainable parameters is

$$\frac{\partial \mathcal{L}}{\partial \phi} = \frac{1}{K} \sum_{k=1}^{K} \frac{\partial \mathcal{L}}{\partial \theta} \frac{\partial \mathcal{N}_\theta}{\partial \mathbf{y}_k} \frac{\partial \mathbf{y}_k}{\partial \phi}, \tag{2}$$

where $\mathbf{y}_k = \mathbf{H}_\phi \mathbf{x}_k$. While the network is training, the gradient of the loss function with respect to the CD parameters $\frac{\partial \mathcal{L}}{\partial \theta}$ is reduced due to the gradient descent optimizer of the network. Consequently, the gradient of the SL parameters decreases even more; thus, the optimization relies more on the CD than on the SL.

## III. Proposed Regularization Function

We propose a regularization function for E2E optimization based on KLD to approximate the distribution of the measurements to a prior distribution. First, define the matrices $\mathbf{X} \in \mathbb{R}^{K\times N}$ and $\mathbf{Y} \in \mathbb{R}^{K\times M}$ containing the set of the high-dimensional signal and compressed measurements, respectively, i.e., $\mathbf{X} = [\mathbf{x}_1^T, \ldots, \mathbf{x}_K^T]^T$ and $\mathbf{Y} = [\mathbf{y}_1^T, \ldots, \mathbf{y}_K^T]^T$. The regularized optimization problem is given by

$$\{\theta^\star, \phi^\star\} = \underset{\theta,\phi}{\arg\min} \frac{1}{K} \sum_{k=1}^{K} \mathcal{L}\left(\mathcal{N}_\theta(\mathbf{H}_\phi \mathbf{x}_k), \mathbf{d}_k\right) + R(\mathbf{Y}). \tag{3}$$

This type of regularization function is based on the idea behind variational auto-encoders [26]. Particularly, this regularization aims to approximate the probability distribution of the measurements set denoted by the posterior distribution $q_\phi(\mathbf{Y}|\mathbf{X})$, to a prior distribution $p_\beta(\mathbf{Y})$ where $\beta$ is the set of parameters defining the distribution. This regularizer is defined as

$$R_D(\mathbf{Y}) = \mathcal{D}\left(q_\phi(\mathbf{Y}|\mathbf{X}) \| p_\beta(\mathbf{Y})\right), \tag{4}$$

where $\mathcal{D}$ denotes the divergence function. Several divergences have been used as loss functions in neural network training. The most common is the Kullback-Leiber Divergence (KLD), employed in variational-autoencoders [26], generative adversarial networks [27], self-supervised learning [32] among others. Particularly, the KLD is defined as follows, given two probability distributions $P(x)$ and $Q(x)$, we have $\mathcal{D}_{KL}(P||Q) = \int P(x)\log\left(\frac{P(x)}{Q(x)}\right)dx$. One of the main reasons the KLD is widely used is that it has a closed-form solution when $P(x)$ and $Q(x)$ are Gaussian or Laplacian distributions [26] [28]. In these cases, the parameters for the prior distribution $p_\beta(\mathbf{Y})$ are $\beta = \{\mu_p, \sigma_p\}$, where $\mu_p$ is the mean value and $\sigma_p$ is the variance of the distribution. For the distribution of the measurements $q_\phi(\mathbf{Y}||\mathbf{X})$ we compute statistics of the measurements, where the mean $\boldsymbol{\mu}_\mathbf{Y} \in \mathbb{R}^m$ and variance $\boldsymbol{\sigma}_\mathbf{Y} \in \mathbb{R}^m_+$ are computed pixel-wise across the measurements training batch. For the Gaussian case, the KLD-based regularizer is defined as

$$R_{KL-G}(\mathbf{Y}) = \log\left(\frac{\boldsymbol{\sigma}_\mathbf{Y}}{\sigma_p}\right) - \frac{\boldsymbol{\sigma}^2_\mathbf{Y} + (\boldsymbol{\mu}_\mathbf{Y} - \mu_p)^2}{2\sigma_p^2} + \frac{1}{2}, \quad (5)$$

and for the Laplacian assumption, the KLD-based regularizer is given by

$$R_{KL-L}(\mathbf{Y}) = \log\left(\frac{\boldsymbol{\sigma}_\mathbf{Y}}{\sigma_p}\right) - \frac{\sigma_p + e^{\left(\frac{-|\mu_p - \boldsymbol{\mu}_\mathbf{Y}|}{\sigma_p}\right)} + |\mu_p - \boldsymbol{\mu}_\mathbf{Y}|}{\sigma_p} - 1. \quad (6)$$

The mean and variance of the prior distribution are hyperparameters that control the effect of the regularizers. Therefore, those hyperparameters must be tuned to obtain the desired goal. The computational complexity of employing these regularization functions in the E2E optimization relies only on computing element-wise logarithm and its corresponding derivative; thus, they do not increase the computational complexity significantly with respect to the baseline E2E

## IV. Compressive Sensing System Models

In this section, we present the compressive sensing system models to validate the proposed coding design in the E2E framework.

### A. Single Pixel Camera

The SPC uses a set of CA $\boldsymbol{\phi} = \{\boldsymbol{\phi}_p\}_{p=1}^P$ that spatially modulate all the information of the scene, where the index $p$ denotes each captured snapshot. In particular, it is a binary pattern in which we employ values $\{-1, 1\}$ as suggested in [33]. Mathematically, the sensing matrix is built as the concatenation of the vectorized CA of each shot $\mathbf{H}_\phi = [\boldsymbol{\phi}_1^T, \dots, \boldsymbol{\phi}_P^T]^T$ where $P$ denotes the total number of snapshots. Then, the sensing model is given by

$$\mathbf{y} = \mathbf{H}_\phi \mathbf{x} + \mathbf{w}, \quad (7)$$

where $\mathbf{y} \in \mathbb{R}^P$ is the compressed SPC measurements. An important factor in the SPC is the compression ratio $\gamma$ defined as $\gamma = \frac{P}{N}$. Here, the optimized parameters are the CA. Since its entries are binary-valued, we add the regularization term proposed in [17] in the optimization problem in (3), which promotes this physical constraint. The E2E optimization for this case is the following

$$\{\theta^\star, \phi^\star\} = \underset{\theta,\phi}{\arg\min} \frac{1}{K}\sum_{k=1}^{K} \mathcal{L}\left(\mathcal{N}_\theta(\mathbf{H}_\phi \mathbf{x}_k), \mathbf{d}_k\right) + R(\mathbf{Y}) + \rho R_i(\boldsymbol{\phi}), \quad (8)$$

where $\rho$ is a regularization parameter and the regularization $R_i(\boldsymbol{\phi}) = \sum_{ij}(1-\phi_{ij})^2(1+\phi_{ij})^2$.

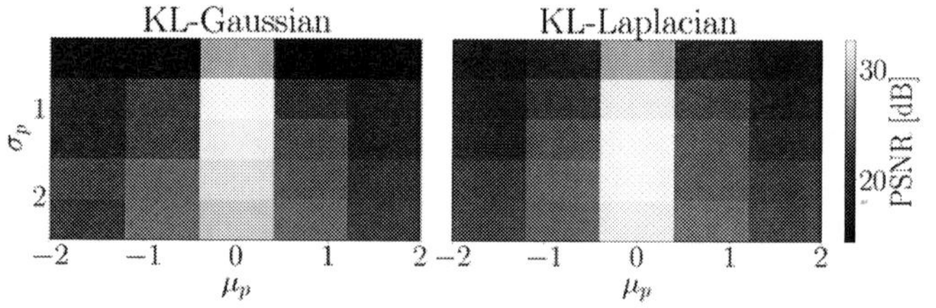


Fig. 1. Recovery performance for the general CS scenario employing the KLD regularizers with the Gaussian (left) and Laplacian (right) cases.

### B. Compressive seismic acquisition

The cross-spread is a fundamental seismic acquisition geometry involving one linear arrangement of shot points and receivers perpendicular to each other [34] [35]. To mathematically represent the seismic data acquired by a cross-spread, let $\mathcal{X} \in \mathbb{R}^{I_1 \times I_2 \times I_3}$ be a data cube where each dimension represents $I_1$ time samples, $I_2$ receivers, and $I_3$ number of shots. However, due to different reasons, such as economic limitations and environmental constraints, the observed seismic field data is irregular and incomplete along the receiver dimension, leading to a recovery task. To simulate the undersampled data, let $\boldsymbol{\phi} \in \{0,1\}^{I_2}$ be a sampling vector with dimensions equal to the number of receivers. The entries of $\boldsymbol{\phi}$, denoted as $\phi_i$, define whether the information is acquired. If $\phi_i = 0$, the receiver is removed; otherwise, $\phi_i = 1$, and it is acquired. The diagonalization of the sampling vector derives the diagonal sampling matrix as $\mathbf{H}_\phi = \text{diag}(\boldsymbol{\phi})$. Once $\mathbf{H}_\phi$ is built, the undersampled measurements are obtained via $n$-mode product($\times_n$) defined in [36]

$$\mathcal{Y} = \mathcal{X} \times_2 \mathbf{H}_\phi, \quad (9)$$

where Eq. 9 represents the 2-mode product between the full data $\mathcal{X}$ and $\mathbf{H}_\phi$. The undersampled measurements $\mathcal{Y} \in \mathbb{R}^{I_1 \times I_2 \times I_3}$ contains the removed receivers as columns in zero for each shot.

A conventional relation that determines the number of acquired receivers by the sensing matrix is the transmittance, calculated as

$$\delta_\phi = \sum_{i=1}^{M} \frac{\phi_i}{I_2}. \quad (10)$$

For instance, when $\delta_\phi = 0.7$, the 70% of the total receivers are acquired. The E2E optimization is mathematically expressed as

$$\{\hat{\phi}, \hat{\theta}\} = \arg\min_{\phi,\theta} \mathcal{L}\left(\mathcal{N}_\theta\left(\mathcal{X} \times_2 \mathbf{H}_\phi\right), \mathcal{X}\right) + \rho R(\phi), \quad (11)$$

where the regularization $R(\phi) = (\delta_0 - \delta_\phi)^2$ controls the transmittance to converge to a desired value $\delta_0$, and $\rho$ represents a weight parameter.

## V. Simulations and Results

The implementation of the method was performed on Tensorflow and Keras libraries [37]. We trained the E2E network for 100 epochs for all the experiments, halving the learning rate every 40 epochs. The Adam optimizer [38] was employed, setting its hyperparameter with the default values. The input of each network was the transpose operation of the sensing matrix to the measurements, i.e., $\mathbf{H}_\phi^T \mathbf{y}_k$. To evaluate the performance on the classification task, we employ the accuracy metric defined as

$$A = \frac{1}{C} \sum_{c=1}^{C} \frac{\text{TP}_c}{\text{Total}_c},$$

where $C$ is the number of the classes and TP are the True Positive. For the recovery task, we employ the Peak-Signal-to-Noise-Ratio (PSNR) defined as

$$\text{PSNR} = 10 \log_{10} \left( \frac{\max(\mathbf{x})}{\text{MSE}(\mathbf{x}, \hat{\mathbf{x}})} \right),$$

where max returns the maximum value of $\mathbf{x}$ and $\text{MSE}(\cdot, \cdot)$ is the mean squared error.

### A. General compressive sensing case

In the first experiment to validate the performance of the proposed regularized E2E network, we study a general compressive imaging scenario, not imposing any physical and structural meaning on the sensing matrix $\mathbf{H}_\phi$. Here we use a compression ratio of 10%. The MNIST dataset of handwritten digits was employed. This dataset contains 60000 training examples and 10000 for testing. We upscale the image to $32 \times 32$. For the CD model, we employed a fully connected layer.

We analyze the effect of the prior distribution's mean and variance ($\mu_p, \sigma_p$) on the network performance. Here, we vary $\mu_p$ from -2 to 2, and $\sigma_p$ was changed from 0.1 to 2.0, taking five equispaced values. The results of this experiment are shown in Figure 1 where the test set reconstruction PSNR is plotted in terms of $\mu_p$ and $\sigma_p$. The optimal reconstruction PSNR values are obtained at variances close to 1.0 and for means close to 0. These results suggest better reconstruction performance is obtained by concentrating on the measurement distribution. The main interpretation is that reducing the representation space can improve the CD performance since the variability of the data is reduced. Some visual results of the reconstructions test set examples are shown in Figure 2 employing the best models for each regularization function, where an improvement is presented in regularized models compared with the non-regularized ones.

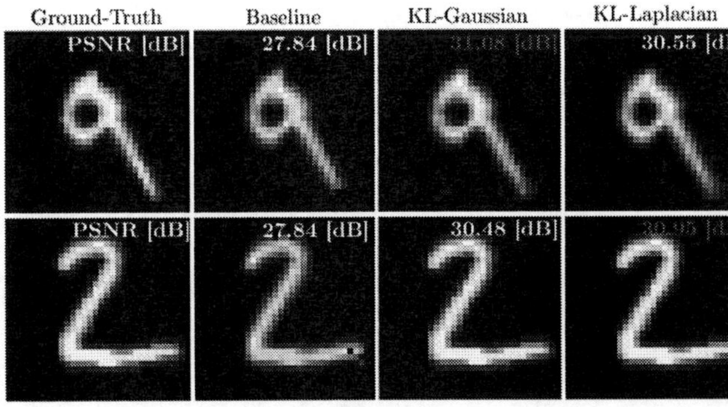


Fig. 2. Visual results of two reconstructed MNIST test images for the non-regularized model and the models trained with the KL-Gaussian and KL-Laplacian regularizers.

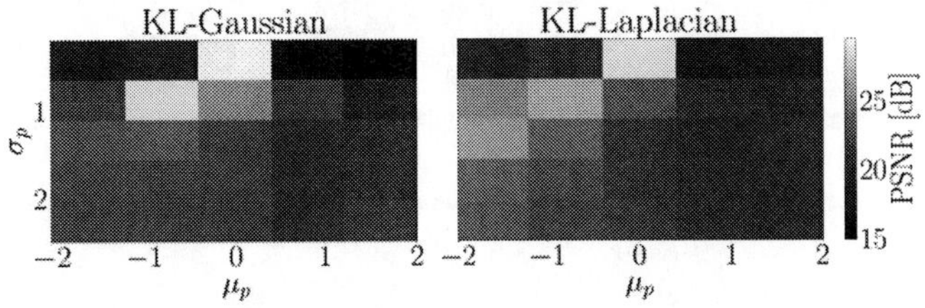


Fig. 3. Recovery performance for the SPC system the KLD regularizers with the Gaussian (left) and Laplacian (right) cases.

### B. Single Pixel Camera Setting

For the SPC, we performed experiments on classification and recovery tasks. The classification is performed directly from the compressed measurements without reconstructing the underlying scene. During the training of the E2E network, the parameter of the physical constraint regularizer $\rho$ was dynamically updated during training as suggested in [17], which in the first epochs the $\rho$ is very low, thus not constraining the training of the SL and it is increased to obtain a binary CA. For both the recovery and classification tasks, we employed the Fashion MNIST dataset with 60000 images for training and 10000 for testing. All images were resized to $32 \times 32$.

**Recovery experiments:** For this experiment, we vary the values of $\mu_p$ from -2 to 2, and $\sigma_p$ was changed from 0.1 to 2.0, taking five equispaced values. The CD in this experiment is a UNET [39] with five downsampling and five upsampling blocks. The results of this experiment are shown in Figure 3. Here, the performance obtained is similar to that obtained in the CS case, where lower variance yields better reconstruction performance. Also, similar to the results in Figure 1, the optimal performance is obtained in $\mu_p = 0$, following the concept of batch normalization where the centered output distribution yields more stable training and better performance [40]. Figure 4 presents visual results of two reconstructed test images where the regularized models outperform the baseline model.

**Classification experiments:** Here, we evaluate the proposed regularization functions on the classification high-level task. The CD is a Mobilnet-V2 [41], which is a lightweight classification network. The same values in the experiment of Figure

TABLE I. OVERALL TEST PERFORMANCE FOR EVERY SETTING. IN BOLD AND UNDERLINED ARE SHOWN THE BEST RESULTS OF EACH EXPERIMENT.

| System | Dataset | Task | Metric | Model | | |
|---|---|---|---|---|---|---|
| | | | | No Regularized | KL-Gaussian | KL-Laplacian |
| General Compressive Sensing | MNIST | Recovery | PSNR | 31.87 | **32.56** | 32.42 |
| SPC | Fashion MNIST | Recovery | PSNR | 28.35 | **29.49** | 28.60 |
| | Fashion MNIST | Classification | Accuracy | 0.866 | **0.886** | 0.881 |
| CSA | SEAM Phase II | Recovery | PSNR | 34.27 | 37.38 | **41.22** |

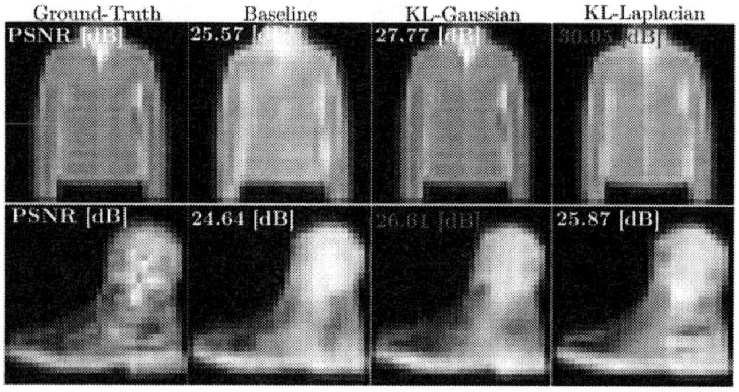


Fig. 4. Visual results of the reconstructed image of the Fashion MNIST dataset in SPC setting for the non-regularized model and the models trained with the KL-Gaussian and KL-Laplacian regularizers.

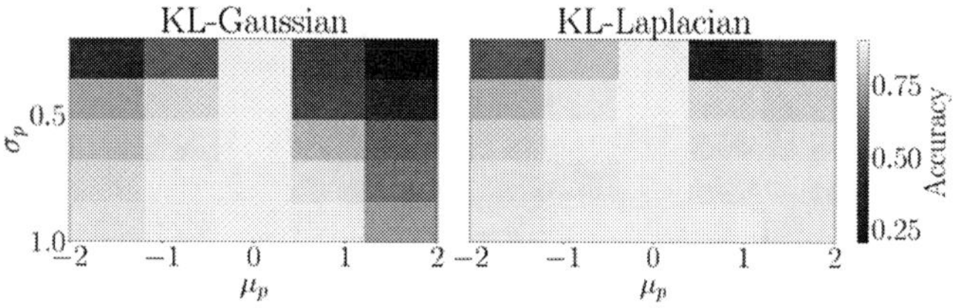


Fig. 5. Classification performance for the SPC system the KLD regularizers with the Gaussian (left) and Laplacian (right) cases.

3 of $\mu_p$ and $\sigma_p$ were used in this scenario. The results are shown in Figure 5, where an opposite performance is obtained compared to the recovery case. Higher variance gives better classification performance.

### C. Compressive seismic acquisition setting

For the compressive seismic acquisition, we employed the synthetic dataset SEAM Phase II built by the SEG Advanced Modeling Program (SEAM) during its second project, named "SEAM Phase II–Land Seismic Challenges". The Foothills model is focused on mountainous regions with sharp topography at the surface and high geological complexity at depth, which makes this data set a challenge for seismic data reconstruction [42]. The seismic survey covers a rectangular patch of $1.5 \times 1.2$ km with a total sampled depth of 4100 ms. The training and testing datasets comprise 381 images of $128\times128$. The transmittance value was set to $\delta_0 = 0.6$. The CD network is a convolutional neural network with 5 convolutional layers with 128 filters each. Here we set for both regularizers $\mu_p = 0.5$ and $\sigma_p = 1.6$. Figure 6 shows the reconstruction of two seismic test data, where the best results are obtained by the KL-Laplacian regularization. Nevertheless, the KL-Guassian model outperforms the non-

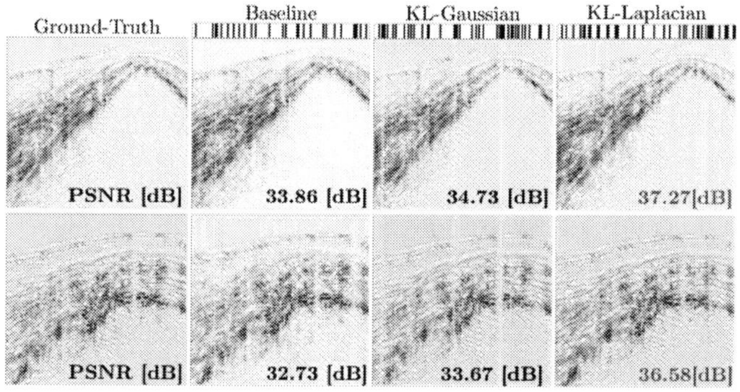


Fig. 6. Visual results of the reconstructed seismic data for the non-regularized model and the models trained with the KL-Gaussian and KL-Laplacian regularizers.

regularized model. Also, it is shown the subsampling vector for each model.

Finally, summarizing the performance of the aforementioned experiments, for the general CS scenario, the SPC and the CSA, Table I presents the test set performance for every experiment. In the CS case, the KL-Gaussian performs better at obtaining almost 1 dB than the non-regularized training. Both regularizers improve the baseline model for the SPC in the recovery task. Similarly, in classification, the optimal performance was obtained by the KL-Gaussian, gaining up to 2% respect to the base E2E model. Finally, in CSA, the KL-Lapacian significantly improved up to 7 [dB] in recovery performance.

## VI. CONCLUSION AND FUTURE WORK

We proposed two regularizations based on the KLD end-to-end joint sensing matrix optimization and decoding. The proposed regularizations approximate the distribution of the measurements set to a prior distribution. We show that the low-variance and zero-mean prior distributions yield optimal recovery since they concentrate the training data in the low-dimensional space, thus easing the decoding process. While for the classification task, high-variance and zero-mean priors provide improved classification performance since spreading the distribution allows easier class identification by the decoding network. We validate the performance of the proposed design in a general compressed-sensing case (unconstrained and unstructured sensing matrix), in the single-pixel camera, obtaining up to 1 [dB] and 2% gain in recovery and classification, and for compressive seismic acquisition showing improvements of up to 7 [dB].

## Acknowledgment

This work was supported by project 110287780575 through the agreement 785-2019 between the Agencia Nacional de Hidrocarburos and the Ministerio de Ciencia, Tecnología e Innovacion and Fondo Nacional de Financiamiento para la Ciencia, la Tecnología y la Innovacion Francisco José de Caldas.

## References

[1] E. J. Candes and M. B. Wakin, "An introduction to compressive sampling," *IEEE Signal Processing Magazine*, vol. 25, no. 2, pp. 21–30, 2008.

[2] T. Blumensath and M. E. Davies, "Iterative hard thresholding for compressed sensing," *Applied and computational harmonic analysis*, vol. 27, no. 3, pp. 265–274, 2009.

[3] J. M. Bioucas-Dias and M. A. Figueiredo, "A new twist: Two-step iterative shrinkage/thresholding algorithms for image restoration," *IEEE Transactions on Image processing*, vol. 16, no. 12, pp. 2992–3004, 2007.

[4] G. Chen and D. Needell, "Compressed sensing and dictionary learning," *Finite Frame Theory: A Complete Introduction to Overcompleteness*, vol. 73, p. 201, 2016.

[5] W. Dong, G. Shi, X. Li, Y. Ma, and F. Huang, "Compressive sensing via nonlocal low-rank regularization," *IEEE transactions on image processing*, vol. 23, no. 8, pp. 3618–3632, 2014.

[6] J. Zhang, B. Chen, R. Xiong, and Y. Zhang, "Physics-inspired compressive sensing: Beyond deep unrolling," *IEEE Signal Processing Magazine*, vol. 40, no. 1, pp. 58–72, 2023.

[7] Y. Wu, M. Rosca, and T. Lillicrap, "Deep compressed sensing," in *International Conference on Machine Learning*, pp. 6850–6860, PMLR, 2019.

[8] V. Abolghasemi, S. Ferdowsi, B. Makkiabadi, and S. Sanei, "On optimization of the measurement matrix for compressive sensing," in *2010 18th European Signal Processing Conference*, pp. 427–431, IEEE, 2010.

[9] G. Li, Z. Zhu, D. Yang, L. Chang, and H. Bai, "On projection matrix optimization for compressive sensing systems," *IEEE Transactions on Signal Processing*, vol. 61, no. 11, pp. 2887–2898, 2013.

[10] L. Zelnik-Manor, K. Rosenblum, and Y. C. Eldar, "Sensing matrix optimization for block-sparse decoding," *IEEE Transactions on Signal Processing*, vol. 59, no. 9, pp. 4300–4312, 2011.

[11] J. M. Duarte-Carvajalino and G. Sapiro, "Learning to sense sparse signals: Simultaneous sensing matrix and sparsifying dictionary optimization," *IEEE Transactions on Image Processing*, vol. 18, no. 7, pp. 1395–1408, 2009.

[12] C. F. Gaumond and G. F. Edelmann, "Sparse array design using statistical restricted isometry property," *The Journal of the Acoustical Society of America*, vol. 134, no. 2, pp. EL191–EL197, 2013.

[13] M. Grasmair and V. Naumova, "Conditions on optimal support recovery in unmixing problems by means of multi-penalty regularization," *Inverse Problems*, vol. 32, no. 10, p. 104007, 2016.

[14] L. Baldassarre, Y.-H. Li, J. Scarlett, B. Gözcü, I. Bogunovic, and V. Cevher, "Learning-based compressive subsampling," *IEEE Journal of Selected Topics in Signal Processing*, vol. 10, no. 4, pp. 809–822, 2016.

[15] S. Wu, A. Dimakis, S. Sanghavi, F. Yu, D. Holtmann-Rice, D. Storcheus, A. Rostamizadeh, and S. Kumar, "Learning a compressed sensing measurement matrix via gradient unrolling," in *International Conference on Machine Learning*, pp. 6828–6839, PMLR, 2019.

[16] A. Adler, M. Elad, and M. Zibulevsky, "Compressed learning: A deep neural network approach," *arXiv preprint arXiv:1610.09615*, 2016.

[17] J. Bacca, T. Gelvez-Barrera, and H. Arguello, "Deep coded aperture design: An end-to-end approach for computational imaging tasks," *IEEE Transactions on Computational Imaging*, vol. 7, pp. 1148–1160, 2021.

[18] R. Jacome, J. Bacca, and H. Arguello, "D 2 uf: Deep coded aperture design and unrolling algorithm for compressive spectral image fusion," *IEEE Journal of Selected Topics in Signal Processing*, pp. 1–11, 2022.

[19] E. Vargas, J. N. Martel, G. Wetzstein, and H. Arguello, "Time-multiplexed coded aperture imaging: Learned coded aperture and pixel exposures for compressive imaging systems," in *Proceedings of the IEEE/CVF International Conference on Computer Vision*, pp. 2692–2702, 2021.

[20] H. Arguello, J. Bacca, H. Kariyawasam, E. Vargas, M. Marquez, R. Hettiarachchi, H. Garcia, K. Herath, U. Haputhanthri, B. Singh Ahluwalia, *et al.*, "Deep optical coding design in computational imaging," *arXiv e-prints*, pp. arXiv–2207, 2022.

[21] V. Sitzmann, S. Diamond, Y. Peng, X. Dun, S. Boyd, W. Heidrich, F. Heide, and G. Wetzstein, "End-to-end optimization of optics and image processing for achromatic extended depth of field and super-resolution imaging," *ACM Transactions on Graphics (TOG)*, vol. 37, no. 4, pp. 1–13, 2018.

[22] H. Arguello, S. Pinilla, Y. Peng, H. Ikoma, J. Bacca, and G. Wetzstein, "Shift-variant color-coded diffractive spectral imaging system," *Optica*, vol. 8, no. 11, pp. 1424–1434, 2021.

[23] A. Hernandez-Rojas and H. Arguello, "3d geometry design via end-to-end optimization for land seismic acquisition," in *2022 IEEE International Conference on Image Processing (ICIP)*, pp. 4053–4057, IEEE, 2022.

[24] J. Xu, Y. Pi, and Z. Cao, "Optimized projection matrix for compressive sensing," *EURASIP Journal on Advances in Signal Processing*, vol. 2010, pp. 1–8, 2010.

[25] Y. Mejia and H. Arguello, "Binary codification design for compressive imaging by uniform sensing," *IEEE Transactions on Image Processing*, vol. 27, no. 12, pp. 5775–5786, 2018.

[26] D. P. Kingma and M. Welling, "Auto-encoding variational bayes," *arXiv preprint arXiv:1312.6114*, 2013.

[27] T. Nguyen, T. Le, H. Vu, and D. Phung, "Dual discriminator generative adversarial nets," *Advances in neural information processing systems*, vol. 30, 2017.

[28] C. A. Metzler, H. Ikoma, Y. Peng, and G. Wetzstein, "Deep optics for single-shot high-dynamic-range imaging," in *Proceedings of the IEEE/CVF Conference on Computer Vision and Pattern Recognition*, pp. 1375–1385, 2020.

[29] S. Rifai, G. Mesnil, P. Vincent, X. Muller, Y. Bengio, Y. Dauphin, and X. Glorot, "Higher order contractive auto-encoder," in *Joint European conference on machine learning and knowledge discovery in databases*, pp. 645–660, Springer, 2011.

[30] R. Jacome, A. Hernandez-Rojas, and H. Arguello, "Probabilistic regularization for end-to-end optimization in compressive imaging," in *Computational Optical Sensing and Imaging*, pp. CW1B–1, Optica Publishing Group, 2022.

[31] M. F. Duarte, M. A. Davenport, D. Takhar, J. N. Laska, T. Sun, K. F. Kelly, and R. G. Baraniuk, "Single-pixel imaging via compressive sampling," *IEEE signal processing magazine*, vol. 25, no. 2, pp. 83–91, 2008.

[32] W.-C. Hung, V. Jampani, S. Liu, P. Molchanov, M.-H. Yang, and J. Kautz, "Scops: Self-supervised co-part segmentation," in *Proceedings of the IEEE/CVF Conference on Computer Vision and Pattern Recognition*, pp. 869–878, 2019.

[33] J. Bacca, L. Galvis, and H. Arguello, "Coupled deep learning coded aperture design for compressive image classification," *Optics express*, vol. 28, no. 6, pp. 8528–8540, 2020.

[34] O. Yilmaz, *Seismic Data Analysis: Processing, Inversion, and Interpretation of Seismic Data*, vol. 1. Society of Exploration Geophysicists, 2008.

[35] C. L. Liner, *Elements of 3D Seismology*. Society of Exploration Geophysicists, jan 2016.

[36] L. D. Lathauwer, B. D. Moor, and J. Vandewalle, "A multilinear singular value decomposition," *SIAM Journal on Matrix Analysis and Applications*, vol. 21, pp. 1253–1278, 1 2000.

[37] F. Chollet *et al.*, "Keras: The python deep learning library," *ascl*, pp. ascl–1806, 2018.

[38] D. P. Kingma and J. Ba, "Adam: A method for stochastic optimization," *arXiv preprint arXiv:1412.6980*, 2014.

[39] O. Ronneberger, P. Fischer, and T. Brox, "U-net: Convolutional networks for biomedical image segmentation," in *Medical Image Computing and Computer-Assisted Intervention–MICCAI 2015: 18th International Conference, Munich, Germany, October 5-9, 2015, Proceedings, Part III 18*, pp. 234–241, Springer, 2015.

[40] S. Santurkar, D. Tsipras, A. Ilyas, and A. Madry, "How does batch normalization help optimization?," *Advances in neural information processing systems*, vol. 31, pp. 2488–2498, 2018.

[41] M. Sandler, A. Howard, M. Zhu, A. Zhmoginov, and L.-C. Chen, "Mobilenetv2: Inverted residuals and linear bottlenecks," in *Proceedings of the IEEE conference on computer vision and pattern recognition*, pp. 4510–4520, 2018.

[42] C. Regone, J. Stefani, P. Wang, C. Gerea, G. Gonzalez, and M. Oristaglio, "Geologic model building in seam phase ii — land seismic challenges," *The Leading Edge*, vol. 36, pp. 738–749, 9 2017.